BIOENERGY
DEVELOPMENT

AGRICULTURE AND RURAL DEVELOPMENT

Seventy-five percent of the world's poor live in rural areas, and most of them are involved in agriculture. In the 21st century, agriculture remains fundamental to economic growth, poverty alleviation, and environmental sustainability. The World Bank's Agriculture and Rural Development publication series presents recent analyses of issues that affect the role of agriculture, including livestock, fisheries, and forestry, as a source of economic development, rural livelihoods, and environmental services. The series is intended for practical application, and we hope that it will serve to inform public discussion, policy formulation, and development planning.

Titles in this series:

Agribusiness and Innovation Systems in Africa

Agricultural Land Redistribution: Toward Greater Consensus

Agriculture Investment Sourcebook

Bioenergy Development: Issues and Impacts for Poverty and Natural Resource Management

Building Competitiveness in Africa's Agriculture: A Guide to Value Chain Concepts and Applications

Changing the Face of the Waters: The Promise and Challenge of Sustainable Aquaculture

Enhancing Agricultural Innovation: How to Go Beyond the Strengthening of Research Systems

Forests Sourcebook: Practical Guidance for Sustaining Forests in Development Cooperation

Gender and Governance in Rural Services: Insights from India, Ghana, and Ethiopia

Gender in Agriculture Sourcebook

Organization and Performance of Cotton Sectors in Africa: Learning from Reform Experience

Reforming Agricultural Trade for Developing Countries, Volume 1: Key Issues for a Pro-Development Outcome of the Doha Round

Reforming Agricultural Trade for Developing Countries, Volume 2: Quantifying the Impact of Multilateral Trade Reform

Shaping the Future of Water for Agriculture: A Sourcebook for Investment in Agricultural Water Management

The Sunken Billions: The Economic Justification for Fisheries Reform

Sustainable Land Management: Challenges, Opportunities, and Trade-Offs

Sustainable Land Management Sourcebook

Sustaining Forests: A Development Strategy

BIOENERGY
DEVELOPMENT

Issues and Impacts for Poverty and Natural
Resource Management

Elizabeth Cushion, Adrian Whiteman, and Gerhard Dieterle

THE WORLD BANK
Washington, D.C.

ISBN: 978-0-8213-7629-4
eISBN: 978-0-8213-8129-8
DOI: 10.1596/978-0-8213-7629-4

Library of Congress Cataloging-in-Publication Data
Cushion, Elizabeth.
  Bioenergy development : issues and impacts for poverty and natural resource management / Elizabeth Cushion, Adrian Whiteman, and Gerhard Dieterle.
    p. cm.
  Includes bibliographical references and index.
  ISBN 978-0-8213-7629-4 — ISBN 978-0-8213-8129-8 (electronic)
  1. Biomass energy. 2. Biomass energy—Environmental aspects. I. Whiteman, Adrian. II. Dieterle, Gerhard. III. Title.
  HD9502.5.B542C87 2009
  333.95'39—dc22
                                                                                    2009048128

Cover photos: © istock.com/Sheriar Irani; © World Bank/Curt Carnemark

Cover design: Patricia Hord Graphik Design

CONTENTS

BOXES, FIGURES, AND TABLES

Boxes

Figures

Tables

ACKNOWLEDGMENTS

The authors would like to thank the following people for their input and comments: Maxim Lobovikov (FAO); Michel Francoeur and Teresa Malyshev (International Energy Agency); LMC International; Bob Perlack (Oak Ridge National Laboratory); Augusta Molnar and Andy White (Rights and Resources Initiative); David Cleary and Joseph Fargione (The Nature Conservancy); Kenneth Skog (USDA Forest Service); Cerese Muratore (consultant); and World Bank colleagues Garo Batmanian (LCSEN), Marjory-Anne Bromhead (ARD), Derek Byerlee (DECRG), Mark Cackler (ARD), Diji Chandrasekharan Behr (ARD), Anne Davis Gillet (ARD), Chris Delgado (ARD), Cristina Dengel (ARD), Fionna Douglas (ARD), Barbara Farinelli (LCSEG), Erick Fernandes (ARD), Gabriel Goodliffe (ARD), Todd Johnson (LCSEG), Kieran Kelleher (ARD), Masami Kojima (COPCO), Renate Kloeppinger-Todd (ARD), Mark Lundell (LCSSD), Sonia Madhvani (ARD), Grant Milne (SASDA), Donald Mitchell (AFTAR), Adriana Moreira (LCSEN), Elizabeth Petheo (ARD), Klas Sander (ENV), Jimmy Smith (ARD), and Juergen Voegele (ARD).

ABOUT THE AUTHORS

Elizabeth Cushion is a member of the forest team at the World Bank. She holds BS degrees in environmental resource management and ecology from the Pennsylvania State University and a Masters of Environmental Management degree from Duke University. Her work at the World Bank has focused on bioenergy, building forest partnerships, and the role of forests in adapting to climate change.

Adrian Whiteman is an economist in the Forestry Department of the Food and Agriculture Organization (FAO). He holds a BA in economics from the University of Leicester and a PhD in economics from the University of Edinburgh. His work at the FAO focuses on analysis of fiscal policies in the forestry sector, supply and demand forecasting, valuation of nonwood goods and services, and investment appraisal.

Gerhard Dieterle is the forestry advisor for the World Bank. He is a German national and has 24 years of experience in national and international forest and environmental policies, development policies, and projects relating to sustainable forest management for forest conservation. He has also served as a member of the European Commission Forest Certification Advisory Group, Haze Emergency Coordinator for GTZ for Indonesia, as a lecturer for sustainable forest management at the Freiburg Forest Faculty, and as a civil servant in the German Ministry for Food and Agriculture and Forestry.

ABBREVIATIONS

ARD	Agriculture and Rural Development
CIFOR	Center for International Forestry Research
CO_2	carbon dioxide
CO_2e	carbon dioxide equivalent
E10	fuel mixture of 10 percent ethanol and 90 percent gasoline
E85	fuel mixture of 85 percent ethanol and 15 percent gasoline
EIA	Energy Information Administration
FAO	Food and Agriculture Organization
FTE	full-time equivalent
GJ	gigajoule
IEA	International Energy Agency
KTOE	thousand tonnes oil equivalent
kWh	kilowatt hour
l	liter
LPG	liquified petroleum gas
m^3	cubic meter
MJ	megajoule
MT	metric tonne
MTOE	million tonnes of oil equivalent
MW	megawatt
N_2O	nitrous oxide

NEB	net energy balance
NGO	nongovernmental organization
TOE	tonnes of oil equivalent
TPES	total primary energy supply
UNCTAD	United Nations Conference on Trade and Development
WHO	World Health Organization

(All dollars figures are U.S. dollars.)

Executive Summary

This report overviews recent developments in the consumption and production of bioenergy. It examines the main issues and possible economic implications of these developments and assesses their potential impact on land use and the environment, especially with respect to forests. The report examines both solid biomass and liquid biofuels, identifying opportunities and challenges at the regional and country levels. The report does not claim to be definitive, especially with respect to the controversial interplay of issues such as the impact of bioenergy on food prices. Instead, it identifies the tradeoffs that need to be examined in considering bioenergy policies.

The past 5–10 years have seen a strong resurgence of interest in bioenergy, along with the gradual development of more modern and efficient bioenergy production systems. This resurgence has been driven by several factors, including higher oil prices, instability in oil-producing regions, the shift of financial investments into commodities and oil in 2007–08, extreme weather events, and surging energy demand from developing countries. Other drivers behind biofuel production include domestic agricultural support programs, demand for self-supply of energy commodities, mitigation of climate change, and the belief that biofuels are less expensive than fossil fuels.

Bioenergy systems present opportunities for countries with land resources suitable for energy crop cultivation to develop a national source of renewable energy (and possibly provide additional export revenues). Most countries encouraging bioenergy development have at least one of the following policy objectives: to increase energy security, stimulate rural development, reduce the impact of energy use on climate change, or improve the environment more generally.

The development of bioenergy presents both opportunities and challenges for economic development and the environment. It is likely to have significant impacts on the forest sector, directly, through the use of wood for energy production, and indirectly, as a result of changes in land use. The impact of bioenergy on poverty alleviation in developing countries will depend on the opportunities for agricultural development, including income and employment generation, the potential to increase poor peoples' access to improved types of bioenergy; and the effects on energy and food prices.

Bioenergy can create opportunities for income and employment generation, and it can increase poor people's access to improved types of energy. But significant concerns remain about its effect on combating climate change and the environment; on agriculture, food security, and sustainable forest management; and on people, particularly the poor people in developing countries who will be affected by the changes in land use, land tenure, and land rights it will bring about.

GENERAL FINDINGS

Five main messages emerge from this report:

- *Solid biomass will continue to be a principal source of energy. It should not be overlooked.* Globally, primary solid biomass (both traditional and modern uses for heat and energy production) accounted for more than 95 percent of total primary energy supply (TPES) from bioenergy in 2005. Traditional biomass use is expected to decline slightly by 2030 (from almost 80 percent of TPES to about 55 percent), but it will still be a significant source of energy in developing countries. At the same time, modern uses for heat and energy production are projected to increase significantly (from about 18 percent of TPES to almost 35 percent).
- *Developments in bioenergy will have major implications for land use.* One of the greatest environmental concerns related to biofuel expansion is the deforestation and land clearing that comes with increasing capacity and expansion. The increase in area used for bioenergy feedstock cultivation will come from a variety of other land uses, principally agricultural production, natural ecosystems (forests), and marginal lands.
- *Tradeoffs, including those related to poverty, equity, and the environment, must be evaluated when choosing a bioenergy system.* Policy makers should identify the expected outcomes of a system, choose a system based on the stated program goals for a particular location, and attempt to reduce negative impacts. Cost considerations are likely to play a role in making these decisions.

- *There is considerable potential for making greater use of forestry and timber waste as a bioenergy feedstock.* Processing facilities can be developed that serve more than one purpose. Some timber and biofuel operations are already energy self-sufficient as a result of co-firing. Logging and milling wastes from traditional timber operations provide additional opportunities for heat and power generation, particularly in developing countries, where waste products are not fully utilized.
- *The climate benefits of bioenergy development are uncertain and highly location and feedstock specific.* Greenhouse gas reductions from liquid biofuels and solid biomass versus fossil fuels range widely, depending on which crop is used and where it is planted. Most estimates do not take into account emissions from land conversions, nitrous oxide emissions from degradation of crop residues during biological nitrogen fixation, or emissions from nitrogen fertilizer. When these emissions are accounted for, the true value of emissions reductions is often significantly lower for many feedstocks—and can even generate higher emissions than fossil fuels.

REGIONAL FINDINGS

The choice of a feedstock and the siting of a biofuel production facility are important decisions that should be based on the goals a country is hoping to achieve from bioenergy production. These goals will vary across as well as within regions. This report identifies specific issues that policy makers in different regions should consider.

Africa

Given the high level of interest and investment in acquiring land on which to develop both liquid biofuel and solid biomass fuels, it is important for countries in Africa to evaluate the potential impacts in detail and plan appropriate responses. Once investments are made, they need to be managed in ways that reduce both the potential for land conflicts and negative effects on the poor.

Another important consideration in Africa is the continued dependence on traditional woodfuel as a source of energy. Much work has been done on the topic of energy accessibility in this region, through use of enhanced stoves and fuelwood plantations (including in the forest poor regions of the Sahel). There are opportunities to follow up on some of these programs.

Water is scarce in Africa. Care should be taken to select bioenergy systems that will not create conflicts over water use.

East Asia and Pacific

A major concern in East Asia and Pacific is the effect of converting forests into biofuel plantations. Policy makers need to identify opportunities to increase biofuel production without clearing peatland or felling natural forests, both of which increase carbon emissions. Given the significant potential for land-use conflicts in some countries in this region, local participation in bioenergy production and development will also be critical. Opportunities to use biomass wastes as an energy source appear to be significant and should be investigated.

Europe and Central Asia

Bioenergy production is minimal in Europe and Central Asia and is not expected to grow significantly. There may be some opportunities to export wood pellets (especially those made from waste products) to the European Union.

Latin America and the Caribbean

Latin America is poised to become one of the principal global net exporters of liquid biofuels and biofuel feedstocks, including both ethanol from sugarcane and oil feedstocks such as palm and soy oil. Expansion of production, however, depends on high premiums above crop prices paid by countries with biofuel mandates: uncertainty is currently too great for developers to invest in oil seed production based on external markets and politically determined price premiums.

Sustainability criteria could help ensure that production of biofuels in Latin America and the Caribbean does not come at the expense of forests or other land uses that would cancel out the greenhouse gas benefits of biofuels. It will also be important to explore opportunities to more fully incorporate smallholders into bioenergy production.

Middle East and North Africa

Given the dry conditions and surplus of oil resources in this region, bioenergy is unlikely to play a large role. There may be some opportunities for small-scale production of biofuels as a part of a broader rural development plans that use crops adapted for dry land conditions (which may also help combat desertification).

South Asia

Bioenergy expansion in South Asia often targets degraded land that is already being used, potentially leading to land-use conflicts. Land-use assessment is critical to determining where bioenergy development is best suited.

Bioenergy production in this region should be balanced in the use of water resources. Crops that are planted on drylands should not undergo irrigation to increase yields, as irrigating such crops could further deplete resources and has the potential to create conflicts with other water users.

POLICY IMPLICATIONS

The local, national, regional, and global implications of biofuels are vast. For this reason, policy makers in both consumer and producer countries need to carefully weigh their decisions.

Implications for Consumer Countries

Countries that consume biofuels should consider the upstream impacts of their bioenergy mandates and targets, including the social and environmental effects. The European Union has already begun discussions regarding the potential environmental implications their standards will have in producer countries and what those implications may mean for EU targets. Consumer countries can help drive the development of biofuel production standards (through forums such as the roundtable on sustainable biofuels). They can also purchase biodiesel only from producers that already meet previously established standards (such as those agreed to at the roundtables on sustainable soy and sustainable palm oil).

Implications for Producer Countries

Producer countries should balance production targets with environmental and social concerns, including concerns about food security. They need to weigh the tradeoffs associated with bioenergy production in determining the appropriate feedstock for a particular location. Some regional criteria may also need to be applied, because the environmental risks associated with expanding biofuel production may be very low in some areas and very high in others. Investors and development organizations can help drive investments into feedstocks that meet best practices for environmental, social, and climate change considerations.

The use of wood pellets and liquid biofuels is expected to increase in developed and some developing countries. This growth in demand will not be met without imports, including from the tropics. Production of bioenergy could increase pressures on land and local populations if sustainable production schemes are not adopted.

The production of conventional bioenergy development (at both large and small scales) may provide employment and income opportunities for the poor. Other options should also be studied, including the production of biochar. Increased production of black liquor (a by-product of the pulping process) and adoption of modern stoves may also help to improve the lives of the poor.

Economies of scale could drive bioenergy toward large production schemes. Opportunities to incorporate small-scale producers into bioenergy production systems need to be investigated in order to maximize social benefits.

The Uncertain Future

Much about the future of bioenergy development remains unclear. Food crops may continue to be the primary feedstock for bioenergy in the future. Alternatively, new technologies may promote grasses, trees, and residues (lignocelluloses) as the principal feedstocks, muting fears that the increased use of biofuels will raise food prices. Developments are moving forward at a rapid pace, with substantial investment by both governments and private companies. But despite such investment, producing biofuels from nonfood crops is not expected to be commercially viable for another 5–10 years.

Recent studies suggest that soot released from burning woodfuels, industry, farming, and transportation may contribute more to climate change than originally thought. Further analysis is needed to understand this potentially important source of global warming.

As a result of various initiatives being developed to reduce carbon emissions and environmental degradation—including payments for environmental services, carbon markets, and bioenergy developments—new demands are being placed on environmental goods and services, and lands (including forests) are being assigned monetary value. These initiatives may provide new opportunities for income generation and job creation. They are also likely to attract investors. To prevent investment under these initiatives from undermining the rights of the poor—by reducing their access to land and their ability to secure products, for example—new initiatives should ensure the participation and protect the land rights of the people already living in targeted areas.

From a climate change perspective, a sustainably produced bioenergy supply may provide a promising substitute for nonrenewable energy sources. Given this, as well as the continued importance of traditional bioenergy in developing countries, long-term sustainable use and management of bioenergy resources should receive appropriate attention in a future climate change regime.

Given the potential changes in land use identified in this report and the impact bioenergy may have on natural and agricultural lands, it is crucial that land-use analyses be conducted for countries that plan to implement large-scale bioenergy production. It would also be useful to identify which countries have the greatest opportunity to use wood residues as a source of energy and to analyze the full potential of wood residues for energy generation.

CHAPTER ONE

Overview

The past 5–10 years have seen a strong resurgence of interest in bioenergy, along with the gradual development of more modern and efficient bioenergy production systems. The change has been driven by several factors, including biofuel mandates, higher oil prices and instability in oil-producing regions, the shift of investment toward commodities and oil in 2007–08, extreme weather events, and surging energy demand from developing countries. Other drivers behind biofuel production include domestic agricultural support programs, demand for self-supply of energy commodities, and the belief that such fuels are less expensive than fossil fuels. In response to these factors, many countries have begun to explore bioenergy alternatives. Although traditional fuels remain important in most developing countries, some developing countries also have ambitions to increase renewable energy production, including bioenergy.

Most countries encouraging bioenergy development have at least one of the following policy objectives: to increase energy security, stimulate rural development, reduce the impact of energy use on climate change, and improve the environment more generally. Recently, attention has been given predominantly to the production of liquid biofuels that substitute for oil-derived transport fuels, but there has also been increased interest in modern systems for heat and energy production using solid biomass in regions such as Europe. Some of the larger developing countries are also interested in using liquid biofuels to reduce imports of oil-derived fuels or to export them to developed countries.

Bioenergy developments present both opportunities and challenges for economic development and the environment. They also have potential impacts on forests and the rural poor who depend on forests for their livelihoods. Bioenergy can create opportunities for income and employment generation, and it can increase poor people's access to improved types of energy. But growing bioenergy consumption is likely to result in increased competition for land, which could reduce the overall quality of the environment and restrict poor people's access to resources.

The technology for first-generation biofuels (cereal and oil crops) is well established; major breakthroughs in this area are unlikely. In contrast, the development of second-generation technology is moving forward at a rapid pace, funded by both governments and private companies. Although this technology is not expected to be commercially viable for another 5–10 years, demonstration-scale plants are already operating (principally in developed countries). Major breakthroughs in technology could mean that these fuels become economically feasible much earlier than expected. Once developed, such technology could shift the focus away from food feedstocks (the supplier of first-generation fuels) toward cellulosic sources, including grasses and wood (likely to be produced at an industrial scale on agricultural lands or from forestry processing wastes). Such a shift would have major implications for the forestry sector.

This chapter is organized as follows. The first section describes the main types of bioenergy. The following sections examine the contribution of bioenergy to total primary energy supply; the outlook for bioenergy consumption; the forces affecting bioenergy development; concerns about bioenergy development; and policies, targets, and instruments. The last section describes the organization, data sources, and methodology and approach of the rest of the report.

MAIN TYPES OF BIOENERGY

The Food and Agriculture Organization (FAO) defines bioenergy as all energy derived from biofuels, which are fuels derived from biomass (that is, matter of biological origin) (FAO 2004). The FAO definition of biofuels subdivides them by type (solid, liquid, and gas) and by origin (forest, agriculture, and municipal waste). It notes that biofuels from forests and agriculture (woodfuel and agrofuel) can come from a wide range of sources, including forests, farms, specially grown energy crops, and waste after harvesting or processing of wood or food crops.

The main source of global energy statistics is the International Energy Agency (IEA). Its statistics do not fully capture FAO's level of detail and are defined slightly differently. Biofuels in energy statistics comprise primary solid biomass, biogas, liquid biofuels, and some municipal waste (figure 1.1).

Total primary energy supply (TPES) is the total amount of primary energy consumed by a country to meet its energy needs.[1] It is the basic measure of energy consumption used by policy makers. It is usually measured in million tonne of oil equivalent (MTOE). For each of the main types of primary energy,

Figure 1.1   Biofuels in International Energy Statistics

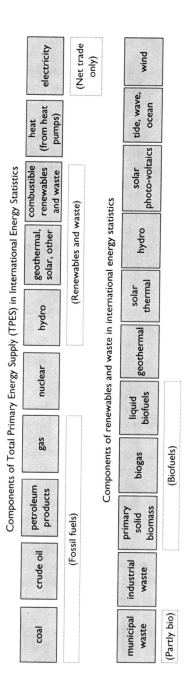

Components of Total Primary Energy Supply (TPES) in International Energy Statistics

coal	crude oil	petroleum products	gas	nuclear	hydro	geothermal, solar, other	combustible renewables and waste	heat (from heat pumps)	electricity

(Fossil fuels)   (Renewables and waste)   (Net trade only)

Components of renewables and waste in international energy statistics

municipal waste	industrial waste	primary solid biomass	biogas	liquid biofuels	geothermal	solar thermal	solar photo-voltaics	hydro	tide, wave, ocean	wind

(Partly bio)   (Biofuels)

Main types and subcategories of biofuels included in this study

Primary solid biomass		Liquid biofuels	
Traditional uses (mostly residential) • fuelwood (firewood) • charcoal • dung • crop residues (straw, rice husks)	Modern uses (mostly industrial) • black liquor • commerical heat and power generation • wood pellet heating systems	First generation • ethanol from sugars and starches • biodiesel from oil seeds	Second and third generations • cellulosic ethanol • pyrolosis oil • higher alcohols and other diesels from various thermomechanical processes • biofuel from algae

Source: Authors, based on FAO and IEA definitions.

TPES is calculated as production plus imports and stock changes less exports and transfers to international marine bunkers (UN 1987). At the country level, it also includes net trade in electricity between countries.

TPES comprises the four main types of fossil fuel (coal, crude oil, petroleum products, and gas); nuclear fuel; renewables and waste; power generated from heat pumps; and net electricity trade (if applicable). Biofuels are a subcategory of renewables and waste.

Renewables and waste are divided into 11 subcategories, including 6 types of energy from natural forces (geothermal, solar thermal, hydropower, solar photovoltaics, tidal/wave/ocean, and wind) and 5 main types of fuel called combustible renewables and waste. IEA defines combustible renewables and waste as municipal waste, industrial waste, primary solid biomass, biogas, and liquid biofuels.[2]

- *Municipal waste:* Waste produced by households, industry, hospitals, and the tertiary sector that is collected by local authorities and incinerated at specific installations. Municipal waste is subdivided into renewable and nonrenewable waste, depending upon whether the material is biodegradable.[3] The quantity of fuel used should be reported on a net calorific value basis.
- *Industrial waste:* Waste of industrial nonrenewable origin (solids or liquids) combusted directly for the production of electricity or heat. Renewable industrial waste should be reported in the solid biomass, biogas, or liquid biofuels categories. The quantity of fuel used should be reported on a net calorific value basis.
- *Primary solid biomass:* Organic, nonfossil material of biological origin that may be used as fuel for heat production or electricity generation. It comprises charcoal and wood, wood waste, and other solid waste. Charcoal covers the solid residue of the destructive distillation and pyrolysis of wood and other vegetal material. Wood, wood waste, and other solid waste covers purposegrown energy crops (poplar, willow, and other crops); a multitude of woody materials generated by industrial processes (in the wood/paper industry in particular) or provided directly by forestry and agriculture (firewood, wood chips, bark, sawdust, shavings, chips, black liquor, and so forth); and waste such as bagasse, straw, rice husks, nut shells, poultry litter, and crushed grape dregs. Combustion is the preferred technology for this solid waste. The quantity of fuel used should be reported on a net calorific value basis.
- *Biogas:* Gas composed principally of methane and carbon dioxide (CO_2) produced by anaerobic digestion of biomass. It includes landfill gas, sewage sludge gas, and other biogas. Landfill gas is formed by the digestion of waste in landfills. Sewage sludge gas is produced from the anaerobic fermentation of sewage sludge. Other biogas includes gas produced from the anaerobic fermentation of animal slurries and of waste in abattoirs, breweries and other agrofood industries. The quantity of these fuels used should be reported on a net calorific value basis.

- *Liquid biofuels:* Biogasoline, biodiesel, and other liquid biofuels. Biogasoline includes bioethanol (ethanol produced from biomass or the biodegradable fraction of waste), biomethanol (methanol produced from biomass and/or the biodegradable fraction of waste), bioETBE (ethyl-tertio-butyl-ether produced on the basis of bioethanol), and bioMTBE (methyl-tertio-butyl-ether produced on the basis of biomethanol).[4] Biodiesels include biodiesel (a methyl-ester produced from vegetable or animal oil of diesel quality), biodimethylether (dimethylether produced from biomass), Fischer-Tropsch (a catalytic conversion process used to make biofuels) produced from biomass, cold-pressed bio-oil (oil produced from oil seed through mechanical processing only), and all other liquid biofuels that are added to, blended with, or used straight as transport diesel. Other liquid biofuels includes liquid biofuels used directly as fuel that are not biogasoline or biodiesels. The reported quantities of liquid biofuels should relate to the quantities of biofuel and not to the total volume of liquids into which the biofuels may be blended.

Waste of biological origin is excluded from industrial waste (waste from the forestry and agricultural processing sectors is included as primary solid biomass). Therefore, biofuels in energy statistics comprise (part of) municipal waste, primary solid biomass, biogas, and liquid biofuels.

THIS REPORT

This report focuses on both the direct and indirect impacts of primary solid biomass (that is, wood potential) and the indirect impacts of liquid biofuels on the forestry sector. Because the biomass components of municipal waste and biogas are produced largely from wastes, they do not currently have a significant impact on the forestry sector (and the statistics on municipal waste are generally not detailed enough to identify the biomass component).

The bottom part of figure 1.1 lists the main types of primary solid biomass and liquid biofuels covered in this report. Some of the items listed there cannot be defined precisely, because they cover a wide range of technological options for energy production that are currently under consideration or development.

Organization

The rest of the report is organized as follows. Chapter 2 examines solid biomass, chapter 3 looks at liquid biofuels, and chapter 4 identifies opportunities and challenges at the regional and country level. Appendixes A–B provide additional information on the issues and impacts associated with production of various feedstocks. Appendix C briefly overviews future generations of bioenergy.

Data Sources

The statistics used in this report were obtained from a variety of national and international sources. For primary solid biomass and biogas, the main databases used were the FAOSTAT Database (for woodfuel and charcoal statistics) and the IEA Energy Statistics Database (for total primary solid biomass and biogas). These databases can be accessed on the FAO and IEA Web sites (www .fao.org and www.iea.org).

For liquid biofuels, the IEA Energy Statistics Database was used as a starting point. A number of other sources were also used, including the following:

- Brazil: Ministry of Mining and Energy (http://www.anp.gov.br) and Ministry of Agriculture, Livestock and Food Supply (Bressan and Contini 2007)
- Europe: FO Licht (World Ethanol and Biofuels Reports) and the European Biodiesel Board (http://www.ebb-eu.org)
- United States: The Renewable Fuels Association (http://www.ethanolrfa.org) and the National Biodiesel Board (http://www.biodiesel.org)
- Other countries: FO Licht (World Ethanol and Biofuels Reports) and USDA Foreign Agricultural Service biofuels reports (available at: http://www.fas .usda.gov).

Where possible, figures were checked and updated with recent industry data supplied by LMC International Ltd. (http://www.lmc.co.uk).

TOTAL BIOENERGY SUPPLY AND CONTRIBUTION TO TPES

The long-term trend in total bioenergy supply is driven largely by primary solid biomass; biogas and liquid biofuels (bioethanol and biodiesel) are currently insignificant in comparison. At the global level in 2005, primary solid biomass accounted for 95 percent of TPES from bioenergy. In contrast, biogas and bioethanol accounted for about 2 percent each, and biodiesel accounted for just 1 percent. At the regional level, biogas and liquid biofuels account for 15 percent of TPES in North America, 10 percent in the European Union, and 5 percent in Latin America and the Caribbean. They represent a negligible share of bioenergy elsewhere.

Bioenergy represented only about 10 percent of global TPES in 2005, down from about 15 percent in 1970. Bioenergy still makes a remarkable contribution to TPES in Africa (almost 65 percent), although its contribution there declined slightly between 1970 and 2005 (figure 1.2). The contribution of bioenergy to TPES fell much more rapidly in Asia: by 2005 bioenergy contributed just 15 percent of TPES in East Asia and Pacific and just over 30 percent in South Asia. In Latin America and the Caribbean bioenergy accounted for slightly more than 15 percent in 2005. In all other regions (including the three developed regions), bioenergy accounts for less than 5 percent of TPES.

Figure 1.2 Contribution of Bioenergy to TPES, by Region, 1970–2005

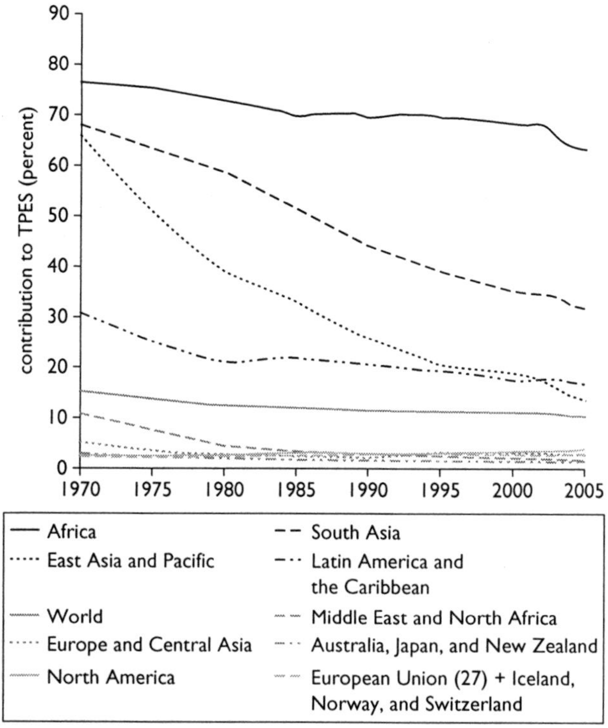
contribution to TPES (percent)
90
80
70
60
50
40
30
20
10
0
1970
1975
1980
1985
1990
1995
2000
2005
Africa
East Asia and Pacific
World
Europe and Central Asia
North America
South Asia
Latin America and the Caribbean
Middle East and North Africa
Australia, Japan, and New Zealand
European Union (27) + Iceland, Norway, and Switzerland

Source: Authors, based on Broadhead, Bahdon, and Whiteman 2001; IEA 2006b; and FAO 2008.

OUTLOOK FOR BIOENERGY CONSUMPTION

The outlook presented below is based on the reference scenario in the IEA *World Energy Outlook 2006* (IEA 2006b), which has been updated to reflect FAO projections for woodfuel and recent policy initiatives (such as higher blending mandates for liquid biofuels) that were not taken into account in that study. The basis for the projections for each type of bioenergy was as follows:

- *Traditional biomass use (forestry and agriculture):* Figures for 2005 derived from IEA and FAO databases and then projected using the growth rates in Broadhead, Bahdon, and Whiteman (2001) and IEA (2006b)
- *Internal use of biomass energy:* Figures for 2005 taken from the IEA database and projected using the IEA projections for combustible renewables and waste (IEA 2006b)
- *Biomass for heat and power:* Figures for 2005 taken from the IEA database and projected using the IEA projected growth rates for combustible

renewables and waste (IEA 2006b), then adjusted to reflect renewable energy targets (see table 1.1), the likely contribution of biomass to renewable energy in the future, and the projections for the other three components of primary solid biomass

- *Biogas:* Figures for 2005 taken from the IEA database and projected using the IEA projected growth rates for combustible renewables and waste (IEA 2006b)
- *Ethanol:* Projections based on IEA projections of petrol consumption (IEA 2006b) and gradual adoption of current and planned blending mandates and targets shown in table 1.2
- *Biodiesel:* Projections based on IEA projections of diesel consumption (IEA 2006b) and gradual adoption of current and planned blending mandates and targets shown in table 1.3.

Total bioenergy production is projected to increase from 1,171 MTOE in 2005 to 1,633 MTOE in 2030 (figure 1.3). Traditional use of biomass (wood and agricultural residues) is projected to decline slightly, but modern uses of primary solid biomass (co-firing,[5] heat and power installations, or pellets) are projected to increase significantly, driven largely by expected increases in

Figure 1.3   Projected Bioenergy Production, by Type, 2005–30

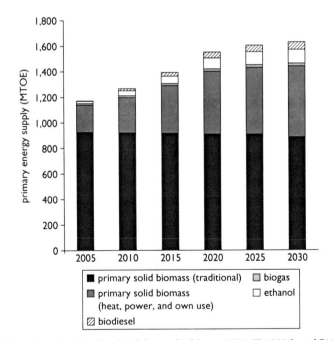

Source: Authors, based on Broadhead, Bahdon, and Whiteman 2001; IEA 2006b; and FAO 2008.

developed countries, especially members of the European Union. As a result, the share of primary solid biomass in total bioenergy production is likely to remain high, despite the significant projected increases in liquid biofuel consumption.

Traditional biomass energy is used primarily by the poor for heating and cooking. Wood biomass is also used at a larger scale for heat and power generation, although there are applications for small-scale use. The move away from traditional producers toward large producers is likely to require larger land area in order to produce the necessary quantities of feedstocks.

Major increases in ethanol production are projected in North America, and huge increase in sold biomass use for heat and power are projected in Europe (figure 1.4). East Asia and the Pacific, South Asia, and Latin America and the Caribbean are likely to move away from traditional forms of bioenergy to more advanced forms, such as energy production from modern solid biomass systems and liquid biofuels.

Figure 1.4 Contribution of Solid, Gas, and Liquid Biofuels to Bioenergy, by Region, 2005 and 2030

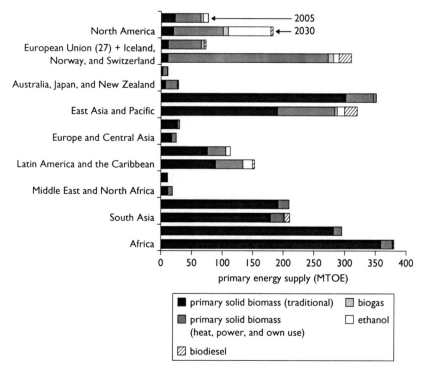

Source: Authors, based on Broadhead, Bahdon, and Whiteman 2001; IEA 2006b; and FAO 2008.

At the global level, the projected contribution of bioenergy to TPES is expected to remain at about 10 percent (figure 1.5). The contribution of bioenergy is expected to increase in developed countries (significantly so in the European Union) and to decline in all developing regions.

The increase in biofuel in developed regions largely reflects the renewable energy targets of the European Union. In developing regions, targets for liquid biofuels stimulate some increase in bioenergy production, but the lack of overall policies or targets for bioenergy means that total bioenergy production is not likely to expand as rapidly as TPES.

The declining importance of bioenergy production in developing countries can probably be attributed to the availability of coal and gas in significant energy consumers such as China, India, and the Russian Federation and to the (lack of) cost-competitiveness of bioenergy production compared with such alternatives. The one region that shows only a minor decline in the contribution of bioenergy to TPES is Latin America and the Caribbean, where biomass

Figure 1.5 Projected Contribution of Bioenergy to TPES, by Region, 2005–30

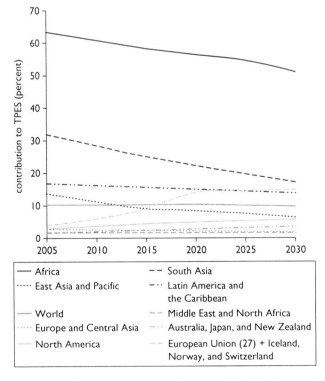

Source: Authors, based on Broadhead, Bahdon, and Whiteman 2001; IEA 2006b; and FAO 2008.

is relatively abundant and fossil fuels relatively scarce. Not all countries in Latin America and the Caribbean have significant policies and targets for overall renewable energy production (although many do have targets for liquid biofuels). Increased bioenergy production there is therefore probably driven by a combination of policies, incentives, and the competitiveness of bioenergy against fossil fuels. These projections show some significant structural shifts in bioenergy production, including an expansion in bioenergy consumption (of all types) in developed regions and Latin America and the Caribbean; a decline in consumption in South Asia and East Asia and Pacific, albeit with a shift toward more modern forms of bioenergy; and increased production of traditional bioenergy in Africa.

Bioenergy development presents a tradeoff between increased energy security and rural development on the one hand and food price volatility and natural resource impacts on the other. In developing countries, these changes could create opportunities for income and employment generation, and they have the potential to increase poor peoples' access to improved types of bioenergy. Set against this, consumption of bioenergy is likely to result in increased competition for land, which can negatively affect the poor through their effects on agriculture and forestry, changes in access to resources, and effects on overall environmental quality.

Many countries promoting bioenergy are giving preference to its domestic production. However, many of the potential impacts are likely to affect other countries, through global markets for food and forest products. In addition, the potential for international trade in biofuel and biomass will have a significant impact on rural economic development and the selection of the best options to meet the stated policy goals. This report does not address the international trade of biofuels in much detail. It does examine the comparative advantage of different regions with respect to bioenergy production.

FORCES AFFECTING BIOENERGY DEVELOPMENT

Several driving forces are stimulating the production and consumption of bioenergy. Each is briefly described below.

Economic Factors

The vast majority of the world's bioenergy is currently produced from traditional uses of primary solid biomass in developing countries. Consumption of biomass is driven by a variety of factors, including the lack of income to purchase more attractive fuels, surplus labor, lax enforcement of fuelwood collection, and user preferences, all of which make traditional uses of primary solid biomass an attractive source of energy.

Some industrial bioenergy production from primary solid biomass has been economically viable for decades. For example, the production of heat and power from pulping waste (black liquor) is economically viable because of the high value of the pulping chemicals recovered during the process and the high demand for heat and power in pulp and paper processing facilities (box 1.1). Heat production from the combustion of residues in sawmilling, plywood manufacturing, and sugar refining has also long been economically viable in many locations, because of the demand for heat in these manufacturing

Box 1.1 Black Liquor: An Economically Viable and Significant Source of Bioenergy

Black liquor is a by-product of the kraft (or sulfate) pulping process used to manufacture paper. In this process, wood is decomposed into cellulose fibers (from which paper is made), hemicellulose, and lignin fragments. Black liquor is an aqueous solution of lignin residues, hemicellulose, and the inorganic chemicals used in the process.

Early kraft pulp mills discharged black liquor into watercourses. The invention of the recovery boiler by G. H. Tomlinson in the early 1930s enabled pulp mills to recover and burn much of the black liquor, generating steam and recovering the chemicals (sodium hydroxide and sodium sulfide) used to separate lignin from the cellulose fibers needed to make paper. Today, most modern kraft pulp mills recover almost all black liquor (generally 97–98 percent and up to 99.5 percent), although some very small mills may still discharge black liquor into watercourses.

For every MT of kraft pulp produced, about 1.35–1.45 MT (dry solid content) of black liquor is produced. This material has an energy content of 14–16 gigajoules (GJ)/MT, or about 0.33–0.38 MT oil equivalent per MT of black liquor.

In most countries, black liquor is used to produce heat and electricity in Tomlinson boilers that supply the needs of the pulp mill; the product may also supply power to the national electricity grid. The pulp and paper industry in North America, for example, supplies about half of its energy needs from the combustion of black liquor and other materials. Many countries are now considering introducing gasification technology, either to improve the efficiency of energy production from black liquor or to produce other types of bioenergy, such as biogas or liquid biofuels.

During the 1990s, Raval Paper Mills, in India, a plant with an operating capacity of 25 MT/day, used black liquor in a demonstration project sponsored by the United Nations Industrial Development Organization (UNIDO). By using black liquor in processing, the plant was able to reduce steam requirements (at a savings of about $35 a day) as well as waste product disposal (at a savings of about $20 a day) for a total savings of about $20,000 a year.

Source: UNIDO n.d.

processes. The use of primary solid biomass for energy production is likely to be affected by underlying economic and demographic variables, such as the level of income and the degree of urbanization in countries, which strongly influence traditional uses; the size of the forestry and agricultural-processing industries; and energy prices.

The economic viability of biogas, liquid biofuels, and power generation from biomass depends on the costs of production, local energy prices, and, most important, the fiscal and regulatory policies governing bioenergy. As technologies improve, economies of scale are achieved in the supply of technology. If fossil fuel prices trend high, it is possible that some of these types of bioenergy may become economically feasible without subsidy in the future.

Energy Security

Rapid industrialization in some major developing countries has led to significant increases in global energy demand. In addition, in July 2008 oil prices hit record levels, before declining as a result of the global financial crisis. The high demand and prices led many countries to reconsider their views about future energy supplies and increased concerns about energy security. Most projections indicate that high energy prices are likely to remain a concern in the future unless there is a global shift to alternative fuels.

The impact of shifting prices has been felt mostly in the liquid fuel sector. Although almost 100 countries produce oil, 20 countries account for about 85 percent of global production. The same 20 countries account for almost 90 percent of global oil exports (OPEC 2009). Apart from concerns about this concentration of global oil supply in such a small number of countries, there are concerns about the political stability of many of the main oil exporters and the risks of future supply disruptions. These concerns have been a major force behind the sudden and rapid increase in interest in liquid biofuels. Concerns about the security of supply of other types of energy are less acute, but some countries see bioenergy as an opportunity to reduce their overall dependence on imported fuel.

Rural Development and Economic Opportunities

Bioenergy is being promoted in some countries as an opportunity to stimulate rural development. For example, the opportunity to diversify income and employment in rural areas of the European Union is listed as a benefit of biofuel development in the EU Strategy for Biofuels (CEC 2006a). Indeed, the wide range of incentives for bioenergy production in the European Union and other developed countries is just the latest development in a long history of support to agriculture and rural development in many of these countries.

Although only a few developing countries are currently promoting modern bioenergy systems and liquid biofuel production, many have a long history of interventions to support improvements in efficiency and technology in the traditional bioenergy sector. The development of improved charcoal production technology, more efficient biomass stoves, fuelwood plantations, and improvements in natural resource management have all been promoted for various objectives, with varying degrees of success.

Traditional biomass provides energy security and income opportunities (through collection and sale) for the poor and small producers in developing countries. This important aspect of woodfuels is not generally met by other sources of energy (with the exception of net coal- or oil-producing countries). Generating revenues on domestically produced energy sources contributes positively to the overall fiscal situations of poor counties and regions. Given the importance of woodfuel production in many developing countries, there is a scope for better incorporation into national energy strategies for developing countries, especially in regions that continue to rely heavily on solid biomass for energy. Most liquid biofuels are being produced at a commercial scale, although as with solid fuels, there are opportunities for small producers.

Policy makers have been focusing on advanced biomass technologies, especially where they see opportunities to adopt technologies still under development at the moment. With these new opportunities, there may be potential to incorporate smallholders into bioenergy production schemes, thereby supplementing incomes.

Environmental Benefits

Over the past century, global temperatures have risen 0.7°C (IPCC 2007). Continued warming of the atmosphere is expected to have severe consequences, including flooding and droughts, severe storms, and impacts to ecosystems, water resources, agriculture, and human health.

The use of fossil fuels is the major source of greenhouse gas emissions in most countries. Bioenergy produced from biomass waste or sustainably managed biomass resources may provide a substitute for fossil fuel use that produces less greenhouse gas.

Waste treatment is the main factor behind biogas production in many countries. Increasing urbanization and industrialization is likely to continue to increase the need for waste treatment facilities, which can also be used to produce bioenergy.

Developing countries have cited the benefits of soil protection, reversal of land degradation, and broader natural resource management benefits from the development and sustainable management of biomass resources as factors that have encouraged bioenergy development. Many national and international initiatives (such as the United Nations Convention to Combat Desertification) cite bioenergy development as a priority (although have few resources to support it). Given the extreme energy poverty in many developing countries, support for bioenergy development seems likely to remain important to achieving poverty reduction goals.

CONCERNS ABOUT BIOENERGY DEVELOPMENT

Significant concerns have been raised about the sustainability of bioenergy production. Major concerns include questions about the following:

- The efficiency of different bioenergy options to combat climate change
- The impact of bioenergy development on agriculture, food security, and sustainable forest management
- The social impact of bioenergy development, particularly with respect to changes in land use, land tenure, and land rights.

The strength of public support for bioenergy development is difficult to judge, because of the lack of comparable statistics and the presence of many vocal and active nongovernmental organizations (NGOs) and industry associations interested in these developments. However, some statistics collected in recent years (particularly in Europe) show how public opinion has developed (box 1.2).

Most of these concerns (examined in more detail throughout this report) have been raised with respect to the production of liquid biofuels, an area in

---

Box 1.2   Public Support for Bioenergy Development

Concerns about pollution from energy use have been recorded in Europe since the mid-1980s. A 1997 Eurobarometer poll lists reducing the risk of pollution from energy use as the most important concern of EU citizens in 1993 (51 percent of respondents) and 1996 (46 percent of respondents), ahead of energy prices and stability of supplies. However, a subsample that was also asked about cutting greenhouse gas emissions in 1996 rated this as a relatively minor concern (only 18 percent cited it as important). Questions about renewable energy were not asked in early surveys such as this (surveys focused more on reducing energy use and increasing energy efficiency as policy options), although the 1997 Eurobarometer results reveal that since the mid-1980s EU citizens have believed that renewable energy involves the lowest risk of pollution.

A 2000 Eurobarometer poll reports a similarly high level of concern about the environment (71 percent listed it as the first- or second-highest priority in the energy sector). It reports that EU citizens continue to believe that renewable energy is best for the environment (hydropower and other renewables were chosen as the best options, to the exclusion of almost all others). The poll also reveals that the public believes that renewable energy will become inexpensive in the future and strongly supports research and development in this area.

(continued)

Box 1.2 (Continued)

A more detailed opinion survey of energy issues in 2006 (Eurobarometer 2007) indicates that energy prices were of most interest at that time (33 percent of respondents), followed by renewable energy (14 percent). Environmental concerns were of relatively little interest, ranking 6th out of 16 (with only 7 percent listing such concerns as of most interest). Energy prices and supply were stated as the highest priorities for policy at that time, with less priority given to environmental protection and fighting global warming. These data were collected at a time of rapidly increasing oil prices, indicating that concerns about energy prices are very real when prices are increasing. However, the same survey also shows continuing support for the development of renewable energy. Given nine alternative sources of energy, EU citizens were most in favor of the five renewable options, followed by the three fossil fuels (gas, coal, oil) and finally nuclear power. Of the five renewable options, bioenergy was ranked fifth, with 55 percent in favor (only slightly above natural gas). Renewables were also expected to become much more important as a source of supply in the future (less so in the case of biofuels).

A 2008 survey of attitudes toward climate change (Eurobarometer 2008) reports that Europeans consider global warming and poverty the two most important global problems, with global warming slightly more important. This survey reports very strong support for the use of alternative fuels to reduce greenhouse gas emissions and shows strong European support for reducing emissions in Europe by 20 percent and increasing the use of renewable energy to 20 percent.

Several recent surveys in North America also show public support for the development and use of biofuels. A 2006 Harris Poll (Pavilion Technologies 2007) reports that 70 percent of car drivers in the United States believe that biofuels are better for the environment than fossil fuels. Among the 5 percent of the sample that was using biofuel users, 53 percent stated that reducing dependence on oil supplies was their reason for doing so; 40 percent cited concerns about the environment. This survey also highlights fuel costs and the ease of use as major issues affecting biofuel use.

Several other public opinion surveys (reviewed in Public Agenda 2008) show broad public support for the development of alternative fuels in North America; they also capture a high level of concern about fuel prices. A survey funded by the Canadian Renewable Fuels Association (2008) reports strong public support for biofuel blending mandates in Canada as well as a high level of concern about the environment.

The Climate Decision Makers Survey (GlobeScan 2008), supported by the World Bank and others, elicited the opinions of experts and decision makers around the world about how they thought climate change issues should be addressed. Two interesting and relevant findings emerged. First, respondents stated that overall sustainable development and protection of biodiversity are the two most important issues that should be considered in parallel with

(continued)

Box 1.2 (Continued)

measures to address climate change. Second, with respect to the potential of different energy technologies to reduce atmospheric CO_2 levels over the next 25 years, several renewable technologies are believed to have high potential. Of the renewable technologies, solar, wind, and tidal power were ranked highest; second-generation biofuels and the use of solid biomass were ranked lower (but with more respondents believing that they had high potential than those believing they do not). First-generation biofuels were ranked last, with a majority of respondents believing that they had a very low potential.

The results of opinion surveys reveal broad public support for renewable energy development, but they also suggest that this support may be fragile. They indicate that bioenergy is viewed as one of the least attractive renewable options (although it is still preferred to fossil fuels). However, this result may not be very reliable, because the public was unfamiliar with bioenergy development issues at the time these surveys were conducted.

Results from both Europe and North America confirm that energy prices are the most important consideration for consumers, suggesting that continued public subsidy for renewable energy (including bioenergy) will be required until economic factors change in their favor. Concerns about the environment in Europe, Canada, and, to a lesser extent, the United States are generally high and appear to support the continued use of subsidies. Given this linkage, it will be very important to demonstrate that renewable energy can be produced sustainably. This would appear to be particularly important for bioenergy, given weaker public support and the doubts about its suitability as a renewable energy option.

Information has not yet been collected about the level of public understanding of and opinions about the linkages between bioenergy development, food security, and broader social issues, the subject of intense debate during 2008. Gauging this concern will require attention as part of any future support for bioenergy development.

Source: Eurobarometer 1997, 2002, 2007, 2008; Pavilion Technologies 2007; GlobeScan 2008; Canadian Renewable Fuels Association 2008; and Public Agenda 2008.

which they could restrict the opportunities for bioenergy development in the future. In response, initiatives have been created to address some of these issues and challenges. These include multistakeholder initiatives to develop standards (principles and criteria) and governmental and multistakeholder initiatives to provide general policy support and analysis. Some of the most notable initiatives to develop production standards include the following:

- *Roundtable on Sustainable Biofuels.* International initiative bringing together farmers, companies, NGOs, experts, governments, and intergovernmental agencies concerned about ensuring the sustainability of biofuels production and processing. It is developing principles and criteria for sustainable biofuels production around four main topics: greenhouse gas lifecycle analysis, environmental impacts, social impacts, and implementation (http://cgse.epfl .ch/page65660.html).

- *Roundtable on Sustainable Palm Oil.* Association created by organizations carrying out their activities in and around the supply chain for palm oil to promote the growth and use of sustainable palm oil through cooperation within the supply chain and open dialogue with its stakeholders. In October 2007, the Roundtable on Sustainable Palm Oil published its principles and criteria for sustainable palm oil production (http://www.rspo.org), which cover both the management of existing plantations and the development of new ones.

- *Roundtable on Sustainable Soy.* Multistakeholder partnership focused on soy production in South America, with participation of industry and civil society organizations from around the world. The goal of the organization is to establish a multistakeholder and participatory process that promotes economically viable, socially equitable, and environmentally sustainable production, processing, and trading of soy. The Roundtable on Sustainable Soy is developing principles and criteria for responsible soy production, processing, and commerce (http://www.responsiblesoy.org).

- *Better Sugarcane Initiative.* Multistakeholder collaboration whose mission is to promote measurable improvements in the key environmental and social impacts of sugarcane production and primary processing. It is engaging stakeholders in a dialogue to define, develop, and encourage the adoption and implementation of practical and verifiable performance-based measures and baselines for sugarcane production and primary processing on a global scale (www.bettersugarcane.org). The guidelines will seek to minimize the effects of sugarcane cultivation and processing on the off-site environment; maintain the value and quality of resources used for production, such as soil, health, and water; and ensure that production is profitable and takes place in a socially equitable environment.

- *Green Gold Label.* Certification system for sustainable biomass energy production that includes the production, processing, transport, and final use of biomass for energy production. Developed by Essent (one of the major Dutch producers and suppliers of sustainable energy), the system is owned by the independent Green Gold Label Foundation. In order to become certified, biomass energy producers must meet defined standards along the entire production chain.

Some of the numerous other existing certification standards used in forestry and agriculture may also play a role in bioenergy development in the future.

Some of the prominent international initiatives to provide policy advice and support to sustainable bioenergy development include the following:

- IEA Task 40 on Sustainable International Bioenergy Trade (http://www.fairbiotrade.org)
- Global Bioenergy Partnership (http://www.globalbioenergy.org)
- International Bioenergy Platform (http://www.fao.org)
- Renewable Energy and Energy Efficiency Partnership (http://www.reeep.org)
- Renewable Energy Policy Network for the 21st Century (http://www.ren21.net)
- UNCTAD BioFuels Initiative (http://www.unctad.org)
- UN Energy (http://esa.un.org/un-energy).

At the national level, several European countries have developed or are considering developing national sustainability standards that would apply to all bioenergy producers.[6] Given that these standards are likely to be tied to incentives for bioenergy or the satisfaction of mandatory requirements, such developments will have a significant impact on bioenergy development.

Initiatives to support and promote the sustainable production of bioenergy are one of many different approaches, supported by different stakeholders to varying degrees and with different likely levels of influence on final outcomes. This is very similar to the situation experienced with respect to the certification of other goods with social and environmental characteristics, such as wood from sustainably managed forests. It remains to be seen what impact these initiatives will have in terms of cost and effectiveness. Although the outlook is unclear, it seems likely that some sort of certification of sustainability will be required in some of the major potential export markets for bioenergy, such as Europe.

POLICIES, TARGETS, AND INSTRUMENTS

Most of the driving forces affecting bioenergy production are related to the social and environmental benefits of bioenergy. They have been translated into action in the energy sector by various policies, targets, and instruments, implemented by national or subnational governments.

Renewable Energy Production

At the broadest level, many governments have policies and targets for renewable energy production (in terms of TPES, final consumption of energy, or sometimes heat and power production from renewables).[7] Almost all developed countries have targets for renewable energy production, even if these targets are not set at the national level (as is the case in

North America) (table 1.1). Twenty-three developing countries also have renewable energy targets that may include some development of bioenergy in the future (a few others have targets that focus on renewable energy from natural forces).

The impact of the targets shown in table 1.1 on future bioenergy production will depend on the viability of bioenergy to help countries meet their targets compared with the viability and availability of other renewable energy sources. In developed countries, other renewable energies (for example, wind and hydro) have largely been exploited. Many countries are now turning to bioenergy as the main remaining source of renewable energy production that can be expanded on a significant scale.

The amount of renewable energy production is still quite small (with the exception of hydropower) in most developing countries, so bioenergy must be competitive with other renewables. including wind (one of the least expensive forms of renewable energy) and solar (which is competitive for water heating and for electricity in off-grid applications). Bioenergy production may be a competitive source of renewable energy in countries with significant biomass resources. For example, the renewable target for China includes the installation of heat and power production from biomass of 30GW by 2020. This would translate into consumption of about 18.1 MTOE of biomass resources (equal to about 60 million MT of biomass).

Numerous countries also have policies and targets for future consumption or production of liquid biofuels.[8] These blending mandates often apply only to transport fuels (in Australia, the European Union, and New Zealand, they are formulated as a percentage of all transport fuels rather than as a blending mandate). Unless known otherwise, it is assumed here that targets apply to both ethanol and biodiesel.

Ethanol Consumption

Most developed countries have targets for ethanol consumption (table 1.2) All developed countries except Japan have policies that strongly favor domestic production of bioethanol. Many of these countries are importers of ethanol, however, and it seems likely that they will continue to import some ethanol in the future from developing countries. Brazil's ethanol exports increased 46 percent in 2009, and the country plans to triple exports over the next five years. In Africa companies are investing to supply the European market with ethanol.

In developing regions, 18 countries have (or are proposing) projects, policies, or targets for ethanol production or consumption. They will have the greatest impact in Brazil, China, and India.

Sugar cane and molasses are currently the main feedstocks for ethanol production in most countries (the main exception is China, which is considering a wide range of feedstocks). In some countries, officials are reconsidering

Table 1.1 Targets for Renewable Energy Production, by Region, 2008

Region/country	Renewable target Amount	Year	Renewable share in 2005	Comment
Africa				
Mali	15.0%	2020	n.a.	Target and current contribution is for TPES
Nigeria	7.0%	2025	33.6%	Target and current contribution is for electricity only
Senegal	15.0%	2025	40.0%	Target and current contribution is for TPES
South Africa	10TWh	2010	n.a.	Target is for additional electricity production from renewables
Uganda	61.0%	2017	n.a.	Target and current contribution is for TPES
Australia, Japan, and New Zealand				
Australia	9.5TWh	2010	18.8 TWh	Target and current contribution is for electricity only
Japan	1.6%	2014	0.4%	Target and current contribution is for electricity excluding hydro
New Zealand	90.0%	2025	65.0%	Target and current contribution is for electricity only
East Asia and Pacific				
China	15.0%	2020	2.1%	Target and current contribution is for TPES excluding traditional biomass (target includes plan for 30GW of heat and power from biomass by 2020)
Indonesia	15.0%	2025	32.1%	Target and current contribution is for TPES
Malaysia	5.0%	2005	6.5%	Target and current contribution is for electricity only
Philippines	4.7GW	2013	<1 MW	Target and current contribution is for electricity only
Republic of Korea	5.0%	2011	0.5%	Target and current contribution is for TPES
Thailand	8.0%	2011	0.5%	Target and current contribution is for TPES excluding traditional biomass

(continued)

Table 1.1 (Continued)

| Region/country | Renewable target | | Renewable share in 2005 | Comment |
	Amount	Year		
Europe and Central Asia				
Armenia	35.0%	2020	6.0%	Target and current contribution is for TPES
Croatia	400MW	2010	<1 MW	Target and current contribution is for electricity excluding large hydro
European Union (27) , Norway, and Switzerland				
European Union	20.0%	2020	1.4–28.4%	Target is for final consumption, current contribution is for TPES
Norway	7TWh	2010	0.8 TWh	Target and current contribution is for biomass and wind power
Switzerland	3.5TWh	2010	0.05 TWh	Target and current contribution is for electricity and heat
Latin America and the Caribbean				
Argentina	8.0%	2016	1.2%	Target and current contribution is for electricity excluding hydro
Brazil	3.3GW	2006	n.a.	Target is for additional electricity production from wind, biomass, and small hydro
Mexico	4GW	2014	n.a.	Target and current contribution is for new electricity capacity

Middle East and North Africa				
Egypt	14.0%	2020	4.2%	Target and current contribution is for TPES
Iran	500MW	2010	<1 MW	Target and current contribution is for electricity only
Israel	5.0%	2016	0.1%	Target and current contribution is for electricity only
Jordan	10.0%	2020	1.4%	Target and current contribution is for TPES
Morocco	10.0%	2010	1.0%	Target and current contribution is for TPES excluding traditional biomass, will mostly come from wind and solar power
North America				
Canada	No national target	n.a.	n.a.	Renewable policies and targets exist in 9 provinces
United States	No national target	n.a.	n.a.	Renewable policies and targets exist in 44 states (where they account for 5–30% of electricity production)
South Asia				
India	n.a.	n.a.	n.a.	Various targets, mostly focused on wind power at present
Pakistan	10.0%	2015	32.8%	Target and current contribution is for electricity only

Source: REN21 2008.

Note: n.a.= Not applicable.

Table 1.2 Targets for Fuel Ethanol Consumption, by Region, 2008

Region/country	Target for consumption	Feedstocks					Comments
		Beet	Cane	Grain	Cellulose	Other	
Africa							
Ethiopia	E5 from 2008		M				Blending program will be introduced gradually, starting with Addis Ababa. Implemented blending 1983–93.
Kenya	10% proposed		C				In place since 1982.
Malawi	15–22% in 2008		C				
Nigeria	Proposed					P	Initiative launched on ethanol from cassava in partnership with Brazil.
South Africa	E10 proposed		P, M	C			Will be supported by program to produce 155 million l/year.
Sudan	250 million liters proposed						Proposed for 2007 onward, to include 250 million liters of production.
Zimbabwe	13–18% by 2017		C			P	Implemented blending 1980–92; plans to restart using mainly Jatropha.
Australia, Japan, and New Zealand							
Australia	Various existing and proposed targets		M	C			Ethanol blends are already mandated in Queensland and New South Wales. National target is for 350 million liters of liquid biofuels by 2010 (about 1% of consumption).
Japan	500,000 kiloliters by 2010	M		C	P	C	The Japanese government plans to replace fossil fuels with 500,000 kiloliters of ethanol for the transportation sector by 2010. Japan began testing E3 and ETBE (ethyl tertiary butyl ether) in 2007.

	Target				
New Zealand	2.5% by 2012			P	Target of 3.4% of all liquid fuels and a 3% ethanol blend in gasoline is expected. Imports seem likely.
East Asia and Pacific					
China	E15 by 2020	C	C	P	E10 is currently mandated in 10 provinces; E15 nationwide is planned. Imports are expected to meet 50% of consumption.
Philippines	E10 by 2011	C		C	E5 from 2009; until capacity is established, imports will be required.
Thailand	E10 by 2011	C,M		C	Blending of ethanol in different grades of petrol (to replace MTBE) is planned over 2007–11, but implementation of policy has been delayed.
European Union (27), Iceland, Norway, and Switzerland					
	10% of all transport fuels by 2020	C,M	C	P	Individual member states have lower targets. Continued imports seem likely.
Latin America and the Caribbean					
Argentina	E5 by 2010	C,M	P		Exports are likely.
Brazil	E25 + E85 market (flex-fuel vehicles)	C		P	Brazil is world's largest exporter and likely to remain so.
Colombia	E10 in 2008	C,M	C	P	
Dominican Republic	E15 by 2015		C		
Peru	E7.8 by 2010		C	P	Peru has ambitions to become a major ethanol exporter.
Uruguay	E5 by 2014	P	P	C	
Venezuela, R.B. de	E7 planned		P	P	Some ethanol is currently used (imported from Brazil). Proposes to increase use to 7% and use domestically produced sugarcane.

(continued)

Table 1.2 (Continued)

Region/country	Target for consumption	Feedstocks					Comments
		Beet	Cane	Grain	Cellulose	Other	
North America							
Canada	E5–E7.5 by 2007–12 in four provinces			C	P	C	Four provinces already have ethanol blending mandates. and others are considering them. Federal E5 target supported by tax incentive by 2010.
United States	35 billion gallons by 2022			C	P	P	The current target is 35 billion gallons in 2022: 15 billion gallons from corn (capped from 2015), 16 billion gallons from cellulose, and 4 billion gallons from other advanced biofuels. Continued imports seem likely.
South Asia							
India	E10 eventually		C, M			C	E5 mandate in several states, E10 postponed, E20 in 2020.

Source: Berg 2004; REN21 2008; and USDA 2008b.

Note: C = current, P = planned/expected, M = molasses byproduct. The use of sugar beet and cane includes the use of molasses (sugar-rich residues from the production of sugar). In some countries (such as India and Thailand), molasses rather than raw sugar cane is used for ethanol production. Blending mandates are indicated by an "E" (for example, E10); other targets are indicated in percent. Some of these targets are general aims of policy (soft targets) and are subject to some uncertainty.

mandates because of supply concerns, environmental concerns, or increasing values of nonfuel uses of feedstocks. The blending mandates presented for ethanol and biodiesel may therefore change.

Although Africa has no notable fuel ethanol consumption, several countries have been blending ethanol with gasoline. Rather than using blending mandates, several of these countries have adopted supply-side incentives to encourage blending, resulting in variations in ethanol use from year to year. These projects have had mixed results, and some have been discontinued or suspended (Batidzirai 2007).

The planned expansion of ethanol production in China combined with the proposed updated blending mandates and expected growth in fuel use suggest that domestic production is likely to meet only about half of future requirements; the remaining demand is likely to be met by imports (Liu 2005). A few other countries, including the Philippines and República Bolivariana de Venezuela, will also rely heavily on imports while they develop domestic production capacity. Most developing countries plan to produce their own ethanol; some—including Brazil, Indonesia, Malaysia, and Peru—are planning to become significant exporters. If current trends continue and importer countries are willing to pay high prices for bioethanol (often above the prices of fossil fuels), the main ethanol trade flows will likely be from Latin America to Asia, North America, and Europe and from Africa and East Asia and Pacific to the European Union.

Biodiesel

Several countries have policies or targets for biodiesel production, and almost all developed countries have targets for biodiesel consumption (table 1.3). The main locally grown feedstocks used to produce biodiesel are soybeans (the United States), rapeseed (the European Union), and palm oil (Indonesia and Malaysia). Europe is likely to be the main importer of biodiesel, although some of these imports may occur as imports of oil or oilseeds rather than biodiesel.

Twenty-two developing countries have policies or targets for biodiesel consumption, and eight countries have targets or policies supporting production. As with bioethanol, the largest biodiesel consumers in the future are likely to be Brazil, Argentina, China, and India, but Indonesia and Malaysia also have potential to be significant producers and consumers. Malaysia already exports most of its palm oil biodiesel to Europe (particularly Germany); and together with Indonesia, is lobbying the United States to lift the ban on palm oil biodiesel to increase its export potential. There is a risk that some of the ambitious mandates for biodiesel consumption in food-deficient countries like China and India may be discontinued if feedstock prices rise significantly. Moreover, the uncompetitive nature of biodiesel versus conventional diesel fuels may work against its production.

Table 1.3 Targets for Biodiesel Production and Consumption, by Region, 2008

Region/country	Policies and targets		Feedstocks					Comments
	Consumption	Production	Soy	Rapeseed	Waste	Palms	Jatropha	
Africa								
Kenya	B20 eventually						P	Foreign direct investment in Jatropha plantations in Kenya and Mozambique, with plans to export to Asia
Mozambique							P	
Nigeria	B20 eventually					P	P	
South Africa	B2–B5 proposed		C					
Australia and New Zealand								
Australia	1% by 2010			C	C			National target is for 350 million liters of liquid biofuels by 2010 (about 1% of consumption).
New Zealand	4.5% by 2012			P	C			The New Zealand target is for 3.4% of all liquid fuels. A 4.5% biodiesel use is expected.
East Asia and Pacific								
China	B10 by 2020	2 million MT by 2010		C	C		P	Imports expected to meet 50% of consumption.
Indonesia	5% by 2025	6 million MT in 2008				C	P	Production for export is planned.
Malaysia	5% by 2008	6 million MT in 2008				C	P	Production for export is planned.
Republic of Korea	B3 by 2012							Mostly imports.

Country	Mandate/target					Comments
Thailand	B5 by 2011					
Philippines	B2 by 2011	C	C			Low level of production from coconut oil.
Europe and Central Asia						
Belarus	Encouraged		C			All of these countries except Croatia have plans to export biodiesel to the European Union.
Croatia	B5.75 by 2010					
Kazakhstan	Planned	P				
Macedonia, FYR	Encouraged		C			
Ukraine	600Kt by 2010		C			
Serbia	Encouraged		C			
European Union (27) + Iceland, Norway, and Switzerland	10% by 2020 + specific biodiesel mandates in some countries	C	C	C	C	Continued imports, including imports of soybeans and palm oil, seem likely.
Latin America and Caribbean						
Argentina	B5 by 2010	C	C			Argentina exports biodiesel.
Bolivia	B20 by 2015		C			
Brazil	B5 by 2012	C	C	P	P	Brazil has plans to export biodiesel.
Chile	B5 expected					
Colombia	B5 by 2008	C	C			
Dominican Republic	B2 by 2015	P				
Ecuador		C	C			Ecuador exports biodiesel.
Guatemala		C	C			Small USDA project for local consumption.

(continued)

35

Table 1.3 (Continued)

| Region/country | Policies and targets | | | Feedstocks | | | | | | Comments |
	Consumption	Production	Soy	Rapeseed	Waste	Palms	Jatropha			
Paraguay	B5 by 2009		C	C	C					
Peru	B5 by 2011		C			C	P			B2 mandate introduced in 2009 (extending to B5 in 2011).
Uruguay	B5 by 2012		C		C					
North America										
Canada	B2 by 2012			C	C					
United States	1 billion gallons by 2012		C		C					
South Asia										
Bangladesh						P				Bangladesh is planning production for export.
India	B10				C	C				
Nepal	B10 expected						P			
Pakistan	Encouraged						P			

Source: APEC 2008; REN21 2008; and USDA 2008b.

Note: C = current, P = planned/expected. Blending mandates are indicated by a "B"; other targets are indicated in percent. Some of these targets are general aims of policy (soft targets) and are subject to some uncertainty.

The main current or planned feedstocks for biodiesel production reflect the climatic and agricultural situation in different regions. Soybeans are the main feedstock in Latin America; rapeseed in Europe, Central Asia, and China; palm oil in Southeast Asia and, to a lesser extent, Latin America; and Jatropha in arid zones (Africa, South Asia, and parts of some other countries). China and the Republic of Korea are expected to import significant quantities of biodiesel; most other countries with consumption targets expect to produce their own requirements.

Argentina, Malaysia, and Indonesia are the main net exporters of biodiesel, although Brazil and several countries in Europe and Central Asia also expect or plan to export biodiesel in the future (mostly to the European Union). In Africa there are no specific production policies or targets, but investments in biodiesel production from Jatropha are planned in several countries, with the focus on exports to Europe and Asia.

Cost of Support Measures

The measures and incentives used to support bioenergy production and consumption are many and varied. Support for liquid biofuels can occur at several points along the four stages of production, including feedstock production, biofuel production, distribution, and end-use (table 1.4). The range of measures used

Table 1.4	Examples of Incentives Used to Promote Liquid Biofuels in Europe		
Stage	**Measure/incentive**	**Cost**	**Burden**
Feedstock	Support to agriculture	Up to €0.50/GJ ($0.03/l)	Government
Production	Research, development, and demonstration	Low	Government
	Loans/subsidies for production facilities	Up to €0.50/GJ ($0.03/l)	Government
	Incentives for producers	Up to €10/GJ ($0.60/l)	Government
	Authorized quota system	Low	Government
Distribution	Fuel standards	Low	Government, industry
	Incentives for distributors	Up to €17/GJ ($1/l)	Government
	Mandates for fuel distributors	Up to €10/GJ ($0.60/l)	Consumers, distributors
	Loans and subsidies for filling stations	Low	Government
Market	Funding of demonstrations	Low	Government, industry
	Procurement policies	Low	Consumers
	Other user incentives	Low	Government

Source: PREMIA 2006.

Table 1.5 Subsidies for Ethanol and Biodiesel in Selected Locations, 2007 ($/net liter of fossil fuel displaced)

Country/region	Ethanol		Biodiesel	
	Low	High	Low	High
United States	1.03	1.40	0.66	0.90
European Union	1.64	4.98	0.77	1.53
Australia	0.69	1.77	0.38	0.76
Switzerland	0.66	1.33	0.71	1.54

Source: Doornbosch and Steenblik 2007.

in European countries includes subsidies and tax reductions; direct government expenditure (for example, investment in research and development and green procurement policies); and regulatory instruments, such as blending mandates and trade restrictions. The burden of these measures is borne by governments, biofuel producers, vehicle manufacturers, and consumers, depending on the type of instruments used. Similarly complicated and numerous incentives for liquid biofuel production are available in most developed countries (OECD 2008).

Little information is available about the total cost of support measures for bioenergy, but the amount is likely to be significant. The European Environment Agency estimates the total cost of government subsidies for renewable energy in the European Union in 2001 as 5.3 billion out of total support to energy of 29.2 billion (about €35/TOE of renewable energy production) (EEA 2004). The report does not specify how much support was given to bioenergy, but assuming that it was provided proportionally to the share of bioenergy in renewables, the figure would be about €7.50/MT of biomass used for energy.

In the United States, the federal appropriation for energy efficiency and renewable energy amounted to $1.2 billion in 2006, $91 million of which was allocated to bioenergy (equivalent to about $1.50/TOE of bioenergy production or about $0.40/MT of biomass). This does not include the cost of tax incentives and state level support, both of which are likely to be significant.[9]

Another indication of the scale of support for bioenergy is the level of government research and development expenditure on bioenergy, which totaled $4.4 billion between 1974 and 2003 (equivalent to about $1.20/TOE of bioenergy production, or about $0.30/MT of biomass) (IEA 2006a). This is only a tiny fraction of all support given to bioenergy.

Analysis by the Global Subsidies Initiative shows that the cost of replacing fossil fuels with ethanol and biodiesel in OECD countries ranges from $0.38/l to $4.98/l (table 1.5) (Doornbosch and Steenblik 2007). Based on these figures, the level of production in 2005 would suggest total subsidies for liquid biofuel production of about $11.5 billion. Most subsidies target national fuel production, but some have targeted imports (such as Indonesian palm oil).

NOTES

1. TPES is actually a measure of consumption rather than production. Final energy consumption is equal to TPES less transformation losses (the loss of energy content when one type of energy is converted to another) and distribution losses.
2. This definition is derived from IEA's 2008 Web site (http://www.iea.org/Textbase/stats/defs/sources/renew.htm) and notes to the annual IEA questionnaire on renewable energy.
3. Renewable municipal waste is another form of bioenergy, but this subdivision into renewable and nonrenewable waste is not generally available, so it is not included in this analysis.
4. By volume, about 47 percent of bioETBE is biofuel. The percentage of bioMTBE that is calculated as biofuel is 36 percent (IEA 2006b).
5. Co-firing is the use of forestry residues and bagasse.
6. Examples include the Netherlands' Climate Neutral Gaseous and Liquid Energy Carriers (GAVE) program and the United Kingdom's Renewable Transport Fuel Obligation (RTFO). For a comprehensive review of bioenergy certification standards, see Van Dam and others (2006).
7. Targets for renewable energy production are slightly different, depending on whether they are measured in terms of TPES or final energy consumption. A target measured in terms of final energy consumption (as in the European Union) would generally be equivalent to a slightly lower target measured in terms of TPES, because renewable energy produced from natural forces (for example, hydro, wind, and solar) does not result in conversion losses. However, if most of the renewable energy production comes from combustible renewables or waste (including bioenergy), the two could be the same or the TPES share could even be higher, because these forms of renewable energy do result in conversion losses.
8. In many cases, these targets are expressed in terms of blending mandates (E10, for example, is a blend of 10 percent of ethanol by volume in gasoline sales). The notable exception is the United States, whose targets are expressed in gallons.
9. The Database of State and Federal Incentives for Renewable Energy (DSIRE 2008) lists 13 federal incentives for renewable energy production and 562 state measures.

CHAPTER TWO

Solid Biomass

Key Messages

- Traditional uses of biomass are expected to decline at the global level, partially driven by a shift to other fuel sources in East Asia and Pacific. At the same time, modern uses of primary solid biomass are expected to significantly increase, partially driven by growth in East Asia and Pacific. Overall, global use of biomass for energy is expected to remain roughly constant.
- Developments in bioenergy are expected to have generally positive impacts on income and employment generation.
- Increased demand for biomass could result in forest conversion, deforestation, and forest degradation, particularly where biomass waste is not readily available as an option and there is little degraded land available for planting (as is the case where population density is high).
- Incentives are needed to encourage the widespread use of modern biomass, because, except in specific circumstances, it is not currently economically attractive for energy producers to substitute it for coal.

Solid biomass includes organic nonfossil material of biological origin that may be used as fuel to produce heat or generate electricity. Unlike most other renewable fuel options, which create expenses for governments (through subsidies), solid biomass can provide revenues (through fees and licenses). It also provides employment (for the cultivation or collection of wood and its conversion into fuel). Biomass fuels may directly affect natural forests, as a result of the conversion to plantations, the harvesting of existing resources, and the collection of residue.

This report highlights three uses of biomass for energy:

- Traditional uses include firewood/charcoal, dung, and crop residues. These uses account for the vast majority of bioenergy production in developing countries. They are directly relevant to poverty and natural resource management. A vast body of literature and experience is available on this sector.
- Modern and industrial uses include co-firing (burning biomass in existing power plants by mixing it with coal), heat and power installations fitted to processing facilities in forestry and agriculture, and stand-alone biomass heat and power plants. This report pays particular attention to the scope for the development of small-scale modern facilities in rural areas and developing-country situations.
- Biomass pellets are a concentrated form of solid biofuel, which may be economical to transport over long distances. Energy systems based on biomass pellets have distinct advantages for small-scale operation (in domestic and commercial heating applications, for example).

Traditional biomass energy for cooking and heating is supplied from forests and trees outside forests, dung, and crop residues. Traditional uses of biomass for energy account for only about one-quarter to one-third of all TPES from primary solid biomass in developed regions.[1] Developing regions account for the majority of global TPES from primary solid biomass, most of which is accounted for by traditional uses.

The International Energy Agency (IEA) estimates that more than 2.5 billion people—more than half the population of developing countries—depend on biomass as their primary source of fuel. Of this total, almost 1.4 billion live in China, India, and Indonesia. The highest proportion of the population relying on biomass is in Africa (76 percent). Heavy dependence on biomass is concentrated in, but not confined to, rural areas. In Africa, well over half of all urban households rely on fuelwood, charcoal, or wood waste to meet their cooking needs. More than a third of urban households in some Asian countries also rely on these fuels (IEA 2006b).

In many countries, fuelwood collection is the only affordable energy option. It is a source of income for the poor and energy for the poor and rural populations. Often the only (nonsocial) costs of using fuelwood are the opportunity costs associated with collecting it (which can be high).

Statistics on the TPES derived from primary solid biomass were taken from the IEA and the Food and Agriculture Organization (FAO). The IEA collects statistics on the following:

- Traditional use of wood for energy
- Traditional use of agricultural residues for energy

- Generation of heat and power from biomass
- Internal use of biomass energy in the forestry and agricultural processing industries.

Its statistics indicate the share of biomass for heat and power generation in the total and provide an indication of internal use of biomass energy in the forestry and agricultural processing industries. FAO's woodfuel statistics cover only wood harvested from trees and forests; these statistics are an approximation of traditional uses of wood for energy in most countries.[2] Therefore, it is possible to derive all four components of TPES from the two datasets.

TPES from primary solid biomass comes from traditional uses (of wood and agricultural residues) and modern uses (heat, power, and internal use) (figure 2.1). In developed regions, traditional wood energy is supplied largely from thinning forests, from harvesting residues, and from harvesting trees outside forests; biomass for heat, power, and internal use is supplied mostly from industry waste and recovered wood products. Biomass plantations are used as a source of energy supply in a few places (for example, the southern United States), but crops gown specifically for energy supply are not common.

Figure 2.1   TPES from Primary Solid Biomass, by Region and Type, 2005

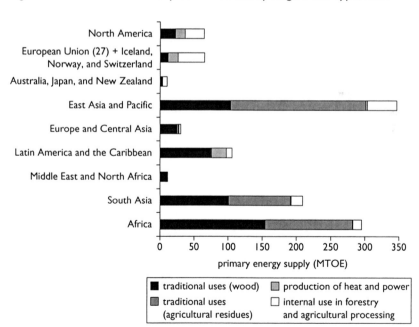

Source: Authors, based on data from IEA and FAO.

In developing regions, the vast majority of traditional biomass energy is supplied from forests and trees outside forests, from dung, and from crop residues. Much of this production is for subsistence use or informal trade; there are no reliable statistics on the importance of different supply sources. Biomass for heat, power, and internal use is probably supplied mostly from processing industry residues, but these uses of biomass are less important in these countries in terms of their contribution to total TPES from primary solid biomass.

LONG-TERM TREND AND OUTLOOK FOR PRIMARY SOLID BIOMASS

TPES from primary solid biomass increased by about 40 percent between 1970 and 2005, from about 800 MTOE to 1,150 MTOE (figure 2.2). As significant amounts of biomass used for energy are not traded across international borders, TPES is a reasonable approximation of both production and consumption of energy from solid biomass in each region.[3]

TPES from primary solid biomass has been declining in Europe and Central Asia and East Asia and Pacific. In both regions, traditional uses of biomass for energy have declined as a result of rising incomes and urbanization, and modern biomass energy production has not increased rapidly enough to counteract the decline. The opposite is true in the three developed regions, where traditional uses of biomass for energy have declined over the past 35 years but the production of heat and power for sale and internal use by processing industries has increased by more than the decline.

In Africa the TPES from primary solid biomass—almost all of which comes from traditional uses of biomass for energy—has more than doubled since 1970. Although rising incomes and urbanization have reduced per capita consumption in most African countries, these reductions have been outweighed by population growth and the gradual switching of woodfuel use from firewood to charcoal (which has a higher primary energy use because of energy losses during charcoal manufacturing). TPES from primary solid biomass in South Asia and in Latin America and the Caribbean has increased. This growth reflects both increased traditional uses of biomass for energy in highly populated countries and, to a lesser extent, increased production of heat, power, and internal energy use in countries with more developed forestry and agricultural processing industries.

Total production of bioenergy from primary solid biomass is expected to increase from 1,150 MTOE in 2005 to about 1,450 MTOE in 2030, an increase of 25 percent (figure 2.3). As in the past, the expected growth in bioenergy production from primary solid biomass in each region depends on the combination of changes in traditional use (which is generally expected to decline, except in Africa and in Latin America and the Caribbean, where population growth is

Figure 2.2   TPES from Primary Solid Biomass, by Region, 1970–2005

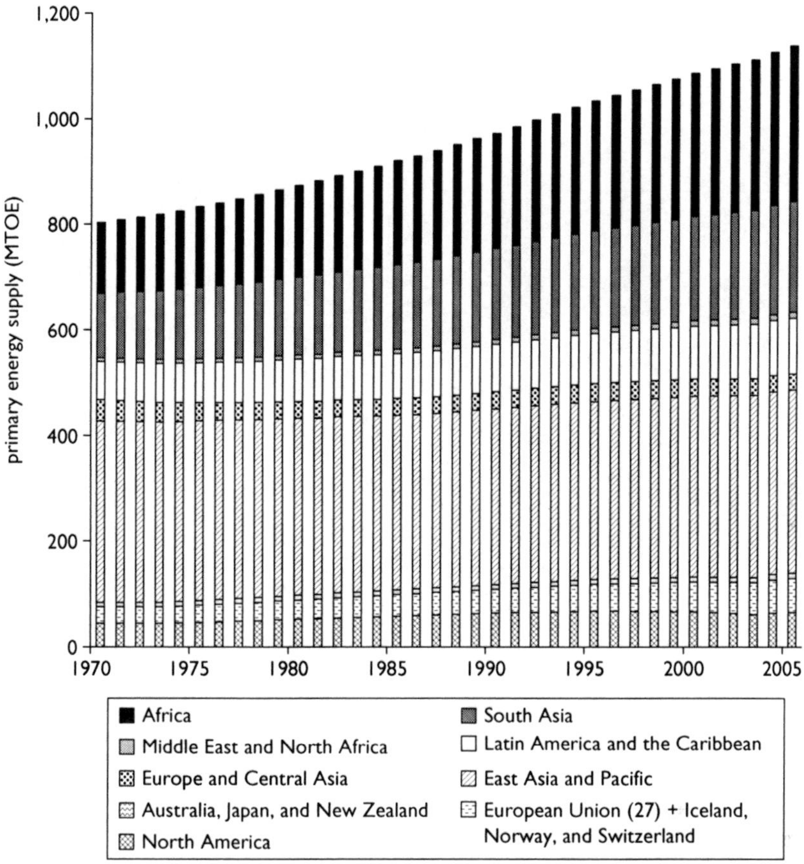

Source: Authors, based on data from IEA and FAO.

expected to drive increases in use) and the development of modern bioenergy production systems.

Bioenergy production is projected to increase in the European Union, which has set a target of deriving 20 percent of energy consumption from renewable energy by 2020. This growth accounts for most of the increase in global bioenergy production to 2020 and the reduced growth thereafter. Other regions with significant projected growth are Africa, Latin America and the Caribbean, and, to a lesser extent, other developed countries.

The composition of bioenergy production from primary solid biomass is projected to change by 2030 (figure 2.4). The change reflects the expected growth in modern uses of primary solid biomass for bioenergy production in

Figure 2.3   Projected TPES from Primary Solid Biomass, by Region, 2005–30

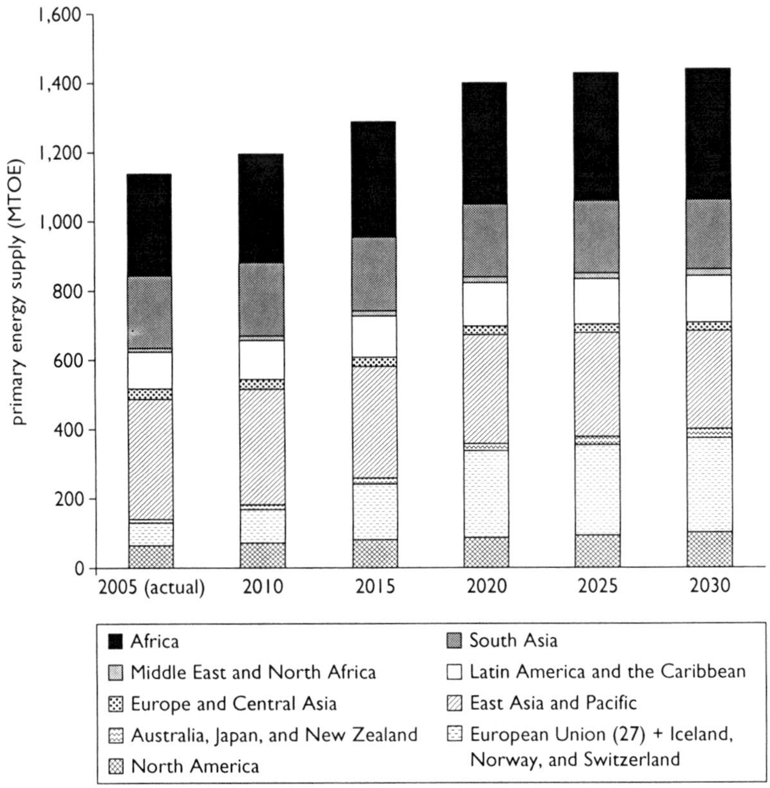

Source: Authors, based on Broadhead, Bahdon, and Whiteman 2001 and IEA 2006b.

developed countries and in East Asia and Pacific (caused largely by expected growth in China).

BIOENERGY PRODUCTION FROM SOLID BIOMASS

Different types of solid biomass can be used in various bioenergy production systems. To examine the impacts and issues of each bioenergy production system, this section reviews the main characteristics of the various biomass sources. The following sections examine traditional and modern uses of solid biomass for energy.

Economic Viability

The economic viability of biomass production varies greatly, depending on the cost of basic inputs (land, labor, and capital); supply sources and yields; overall

Figure 2.4   Projected TPES from Primary Solid Biomass, by Region and Type, 2005 and 2030

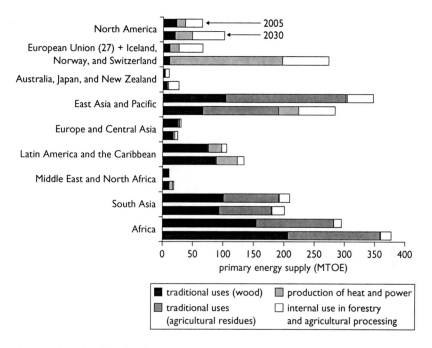

Source: Authors, based on data from Broadhead, Bahdon, and Whiteman 2001 and IEA 2006b.

supply and demand; and the fiscal arrangements that affect production. Because biomass has to compete with other forms of primary energy at the point of end-use, the delivered cost of biomass is the relevant variable that determines the economic viability of biomass production for energy use. This can be split into three main components:

- The cost at source of growing the biomass (or the cost of purchasing biomass waste)
- The cost of harvesting (and processing, if applicable)
- The cost of transporting the biomass to the end-user.

For managed biomass crops (as opposed to informal collection), the cost of growing depends on the inputs used, the yields, and any subsidies that may be available to support production. In many cases, the cost (or opportunity cost) of land is likely to be the largest input. The main factor affecting prices is likely to be the value of any alternative uses of the biomass (for example, the use of wood residues and waste in the forest-processing industry), which can be significant in developed countries. In contrast, in developing countries, the value of biomass waste may be much lower. In addition, biomass waste presents a disposal problem in some situations (where disposal in landfill is costly, for example), and producers may be willing to pay to have this material removed.

Much research and development has been conducted on low-cost techniques for biomass harvesting and processing in developed countries; these efforts continue to reduce the cost of harvesting and processing. The harvesting systems used in biomass production are usually mechanized and often based on modifications to standard agricultural or forest harvesters. Processing of biomass is also usually required (even for some types of waste) to produce biomass that can be transported more easily, resulting in a product with homogenous characteristics and desirable properties (for example, low moisture content).

Transport cost may account for half or more of the total cost of biomass. The distance from the production site to the end-user is thus a crucial variable in the economics of biomass production. Depending on the level of demand, it is usually economically feasible to transport biomass up to 50 kilometers, although longer distances may be feasible (and are often necessary) if the production capacity of the end-user is very high.

The cost of delivered biomass varies across countries, depending on local market conditions and average transport distances (table 2.1). Notwithstanding these differences, the least expensive sources of biomass are recovered wood (postconsumer waste) and forest-processing waste (residues from timber mill or timber processing),[4] followed by agricultural and forest residues (residues left over from logging operations). Crops specifically managed for biomass production (for example, energy crops such as switchgrass, miscanthus, and short-rotation coppice) are generally more expensive than these wastes, as are forest thinnings produced using traditional forest harvesting systems.[5]

These figures suggest that there are opportunities for the private sector (and organizations that invest in private sector development) to develop processing facilities serving more than one purpose. Some timber and biofuel operations are already energy self-sufficient, as a result of co-firing (using forestry residues and bagasse); the availability of logging and milling wastes (particularly in developing countries where waste products are not fully utilized) from traditional timber operations provide additional opportunities for heat and power generation.

Delivered biomass costs in developed countries range from $20/MT to $90/MT (figure 2.5) Using biomass as an alternative to coal does not involve significant incremental costs other than the lower energy content of biomass compared with coal. The energy content of biomass with a low moisture content is about two-thirds that of coal (per MT), so at typical delivered coal costs of $35–$50/MT, the price that consumers can pay for biomass is $21–$30/MT.

At the current delivered price of biomass, it is not economically attractive for energy producers to use biomass as a substitute for coal, except in

Table 2.1 Estimated Cost of Various Forms of Delivered Biomass

| Type of biomass | Reference | Location | Cost/MT | | | |
			At source	Harvest and processing	Transport	Total
Agricultural residues	Zhang, Habibi, and MacLean (2007)	Ontario	9–23	13–16	17	41–53
	PPRP (2006)	United States	—	—	—	40
	Scion (2007)	New Zealand	—	15–16	—	—
Agricultural residues and switchgrass	Sokhansanj and Fenton (2006)	Canada	11	44–59	7–26	51–87
	DOE (2005)	United States	10	26–40	14–15	50–55
	EPA (2007)	United States	9–19	6–8	8–11	22–35
Bark	Bios Bioenergysysteme (2004)	Austria	—	—	—	19–30
Clearings (fire control)	Nichols and others (2006)	Alaska	7	13	15	35
Forest residues	Wegner (2007)	United States	—	—	—	44
	PPRP (2006)	United States	—	—	—	35
	Scion (2007)	New Zealand	—	—	—	18–68
Mill residues	Wegner (2007)	United States	—	—	—	34
	PPRP (2006)	United States	—	—	—	27
Poultry litter	DOE (2003)	United States	—	—	—	12
Recovered wood	Scion (2007)	New Zealand	—	—	—	38
	DOE (2004)	United States	—	10	—	30
	PPRP (2006)	United States	—	—	—	17
Residues (fire control)	Loeffler, Calltin, and Silverstein (2006)	United States	–18	—	—	–3–19
Sawdust	Bios Bioenergysysteme (2004)	Austria	—	—	—	30–43

(continued)

49

Table 2.1 (Continued)

			Cost/MT		
Type of biomass	Reference	Location	At source	Harvest and processing	Transport	Total
Switchgrass	Kumar and Sokhansanj (2007)	Canada	30–36	—	37–48	67–84
	PPRP (2006)	United States	—	—	—	47
	Kszos, McLaughlin, and Walsh (2001)	United States	23–26	—	—	—
Short-rotation coppice	Scion (2007)	New Zealand	—	—	—	53–68
	Luger (2002)	Europe	—	—	—	50–110
	Buchholz and Volk (2007)	Uganda	—	—	—	22
Thinnings	Wegner (2007)	U.S. West	—	—	—	90
	Wegner (2007)	U.S. South	40	—	—	—
Wood (mixed)	Bios Bioenergysysteme (2004)	Denmark	—	—	—	45
Wood chips	Bios Bioenergysysteme (2004)	Austria	—	—	—	58–73
Wood pellets	Bios Bioenergysysteme (2004)	Austria	—	—	—	95–153

Source: Authors' compilation.

Note: Some figures are actual prices paid by consumers, some are general market prices of biomass suitable for bioenergy, and some are estimates constructed from cost models. — = Not available.

Figure 2.5   Delivered Costs of Coal and Various Forms of Biomass in Developed Countries

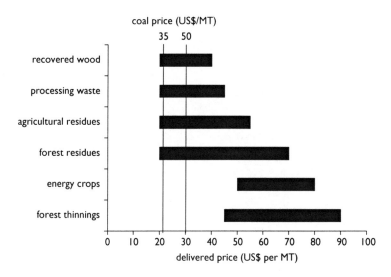

Source: Authors, based on data in table 2.1.

specific circumstances (for example, where the biomass resource is cheap and very close, there are disposal costs if it is not used, or it can be integrated into an existing processing operation in agriculture or forestry). The U.S. Department of Energy's biomass program aims to improve supply systems and logistics to bring the delivered cost of biomass down to $35/MT (DOE 2005).

The widespread use of biomass requires subsidies for biomass or bioenergy production or, alternatively, levies or restrictions on the use of coal that reflect its negative environmental externalities and raise its cost. Many developed countries already have such measures in place (to varying degrees), which explains why a significant amount of biomass is already used for bioenergy production.

The economic viability of using biomass to replace fuels other than coal is more promising, especially for small-scale applications. In small-scale heating applications, for example, where biomass (including wood pellets) is used to replace fuel oil, the delivered wood costs are economically viable in many cases. In developing countries it is often economically feasible to use small-scale bioenergy production facilities as an alternative to diesel generators used for rural electricity supply (Kartha, Leach, and Rajan 2005), especially if the delivered wood costs are lower than indicated above (as in Uganda, for example [see Buchholz and Volk 2007]).

Economic Impact

The economic impact of biomass production is difficult to measure. However, as solid biomass production does not generally compete with agriculture to a significant extent, expansion in production is likely to have few negative effects in terms of diverted or reduced agricultural production and higher food prices. Therefore, the main measurable economic impact of biomass production is likely to be the income and employment generated. Modern fuels provide formal employment opportunities; traditional fuels provide informal employment for the poorest members of the community.

Figures for employment in biomass production are not available; developing such data is complicated by the fact that a large proportion of biomass used for energy is produced in the informal sector. Total formal forestry employment figures give some sense of the potential employment opportunities in the sector (table 2.2).

In developed countries, about one to five full-time equivalent (FTE) employees are employed per KTOE of roundwood produced (in modern biomass energy production systems, employment per unit of output would likely be close to the bottom of this range). In developing countries, FTE employment is significantly higher, at about 20–40 employees per KTOE (employment in informal biomass collection is probably many times this figure).

Table 2.2 Estimated Employment in Roundwood Production, 2000

Region	Production (million m³)		Employment	
	Industrial	Total	Per KTOE	Total
Africa	67	568	10.26	179,363
Australia, Japan, and New Zealand	61	68	5.06	90,090
East Asia and Pacific	171	607	38.35	1,722,820
Europe and Central Asia	135	204	18.41	654,051
European Union (27), Iceland, Norway, and Switzerland	357	404	5.26	557,839
Latin America and the Caribbean	164	433	11.44	493,825
Middle East and North Africa	3	30	32.89	22,180
North America	604	678	1.05	186,983
South Asia	26	386	38.95	265,928
Developed countries	1,023	1,150	2.76	834,912
Developing countries	566	2,227	22.46	3,338,166
World	1,588	3,377	9.26	4,173,078

Source: Adapted from Lebedys 2004.
Note: Total employment figures represent formal employment only; employment per unit of output is thus measured for all production in developed countries and only for industrial roundwood production in developing countries.

Employment per hectare is much lower for biomass production than for agriculture. In terms of the energy produced, however, biomass production involves significantly more employment than other types of fuel, even with the introduction of highly mechanized and modern biomass production systems. Bonskowski (1999) reports U.S. coal production of 1.1 billion short tons in 1997 (equal to about 0.7 billion MT oil equivalent) and employment of 81,500, equivalent to just 0.12 workers per KTOE, an order of magnitude below the likely employment in biomass production. Similarly low levels of employment per unit of fuel production can be expected in almost all countries and probably for most other major types of fuel and energy. Therefore, biomass production would seem to perform well relative to other sources of energy in terms of developing livelihood opportunities.[6]

Social Impact

The monetary cost of informal production of traditional biomass is negligible, but it may have significant social costs. Collection may be hazardous, for example, or reduce the time available for other activities with long-term benefits, such as children's education. Traditional biomass collection may also have a negative impact on gender, because biomass is often collected by women and children.

The impact of biomass production on access to resources and the potential for smallholder participation depends on the scale of production. Small-scale production generally does not lead to major conflict over resources. Large-scale production increases the chance of conflict and the exclusion of the poor from development opportunities, although some countries have shown that it is possible to involve large numbers of smallholders in large-scale biomass production through innovative outgrower schemes (box 2.1).

Impact on Land and Other Resources

The impact of solid biomass production on land and other resources is determined by the demand for biomass and the efficiency of land use (that is, the energy yield/hectare). Once this is determined, the next most important question is whether the biomass crop can be grown on unused or degraded land or will take land out of agriculture or forestry (box 2.2). Another issue is whether bioenergy demand will compete with other uses of biomass or will be met by land-use change or use of wastes.

Estimates of forest plantation and energy crop yields for some of the main crops likely to be grown for biomass production around the world are available only for developed countries. Forest plantation yields for some of the more productive species are shown to give an indication of the yields that may be achieved (table 2.3).

Grasses grown for bioenergy production currently achieve yields of roughly 5–15 TOE/hectare in developed countries (less in high latitudes); short-rotation coppice yields are about 4–7 TOE/hectare. Species such as eucalyptus, acacia, pine, and poplar grown in forest plantations can achieve yields of 2–6 TOE/hectare in many parts of the world (for example, Africa, East Asia, Oceania, and South Asia). The best forest plantation yields occur in humid tropical zones, such as Southeast Asia and Latin America, where yields of 2–10 TOE/hectare are normal (yields in parts of Brazil are as high as 18 TOE/hectare). These forest plantation yields are likely to represent a lower bound for the biomass yield that might be achieved from crops managed specifically for biomass production in tropical and subtropical zones.

The theoretical yield of primary or on-site residues is related to the harvest index of crops (that is, the proportion of total biomass that is normally used). The realistic potential for residue recovery will be less than this, however, because of technical factors (for example, destruction and damage to residues during crop harvesting) and economic factors (for example, the economic viability of collection, the nutrient benefits of leaving residues on site, and competition for the resource). Secondary residues (waste after processing the main product) may be produced and possibly recovered. Primary and secondary residue yields for a variety of agricultural crops in Europe, North America,

Box 2.2 Use of Degraded and Marginal Lands for Bioenergy Production

The United Nations Environment Programme (UNEP) defines *degraded lands* as those that have experienced a long-term loss of ecosystem function and services, caused by disturbances from which the system cannot recover unaided. Land degradation will ultimately lead to a reduction of soil fertility and productivity. The reduced plant growth causes loss of protective soil cover and increased vulnerability of soil and vegetation to further degradation. *Marginal lands* are lands on which cost-effective production is not possible given site conditions, cultivation techniques, agriculture policies, and economic and legal conditions. Marginal land may supply food, feed, medical plants, fertilizer, or fuel to local people. It cannot support marketable production of crops.

Using degraded and marginal land for bioenergy production is not always a good idea. Such land may be extensively used by local people, creating tenure and rights issues if it is used for energy production. Some of these areas may also harbor high levels of biodiversity. Moreover, in some cases, these lands may not be capable of supporting bioenergy development, because they require fertilization or irrigation. Using these lands for energy production may drive the relocation of other projects to prime agricultural lands, greatly reducing the benefits.

In other cases, degraded lands offer good opportunities for bioenergy production and may be preferable to other options. In Indonesia, for example, some conservation groups have been advocating for palm oil development on the estimated 15–20 million hectares of degraded lands (previously cleared for timber or fiber), an option they view as superior to clearing rainforests. Producing bioenergy on marginal and degraded lands may thus provide opportunities, although it is not always the most sustainable option.

Source: El-Beltagy 2000; Schroers 2006; UNEP 2007; Wiegmann, Hennenberg, and Fritsche 2008.

and Southeast Asia are about 0.3–1.2 TOE/MT of crop production and 0.2–0.4 TOE/m³ of wood production (with secondary residues accounting for a major share of all residues in the case of wood) (table 2.4).

Combining this information with average crop yields for some major crops shows the likely technical availability of agricultural residues in different parts of the world (table 2.5). Globally, the residues from most grains fall in the range of 1–4 TOE/hectare (sugarcane can produce three times this amount). Residue potential in developing countries is higher than in developed countries in some cases, not because crop yields are higher but because harvesting indices are generally lower, as a result of the lower-quality crop varieties grown in many

Table 2.3 Productivity of Energy Crops and Planted Forests, by Region

Region/crop	Subregion	Average annual yield (MT/hectare for energy crops; m³/hectare for forests)		Average annual yield (converted to TOE/hectare)	
		Low	High	Low	High
Africa					
Acacia	South and East Africa	10.0	12.0	2.6	3.2
Eucalyptus	South and East Africa	18.0	28.0	4.7	7.4
Pine	South and East Africa	12.0	18.0	3.2	4.7
Australia, Japan, and New Zealand					
Eucalyptus	Oceania	15.6	25.0	4.1	6.6
Pine	Oceania	15.7	21.0	4.1	5.5
East Asia and Pacific					
Acacia	Southeast Asia	19.0	40.0	5.0	10.5
Chinese cedar	East Asia	2.5	13.5	0.7	3.5
Eucalyptus	East Asia	1.6	8.7	0.4	2.3
Eucalyptus	Southeast Asia	7.0	12.0	1.8	3.2
Poplar	East Asia	3.7	18.5	1.0	4.9
Teak	Southeast Asia	4.0	17.3	1.1	4.5
Europe and Central Asia					
Eucalyptus	West and Central Asia	4.0	10.0	1.1	2.6
Poplar	West and Central Asia	5.0	12.0	1.3	3.2

	Location			
European Union (27), Iceland, Norway, and Switzerland				
Miscanthus		15.0	6.1	12.2
Short-rotation coppice		10.0	4.1	6.1
Conifers (mixed)		3.5	0.9	5.8
Oak		3.0	0.8	2.4
Latin America and the Caribbean				
Eucalyptus		15.0	3.9	18.4
Pine		14.0	3.7	8.9
Middle East and North Africa				
Acacia	North Africa	15.0	3.9	5.3
Eucalyptus	North Africa	12.0	3.2	3.7
North America				
Pine	U.S. South	7.0	1.8	2.6
Switchgrass	U.S. South	16.0	6.5	14.6
Switchgrass	U.S. West	11.0	4.5	5.7
Switchgrass	U.S. North/Canada	2.0	0.8	4.5
Short-rotation coppice	U.S. South	10.0	4.1	6.5
South Asia				
Eucalyptus		7.0	1.8	3.2
Teak		4.0	1.1	4.5

Source: Figures for planted forests (acacia, Chinese cedar, conifers, eucalyptus, oak pine, poplar, and teak) are derived from Del Lungo, Ball, and Carle 2006; figures for energy crops (miscanthus, switchgrass, and short-rotation coppice) are from Kszos, McLaughlin, and Walsh 2001; Pimentel and Patzek 2005; Bucholz and Volk 2007; and Kumar and Sokhansanj 2007.

Note: Yields for planted forests are roundwood yield rather than total biomass yield; conversion factors used are 1 MT (dry) biomass (energy crops) = 0.4060 TOE, 1 m^3 wood (planted forests) = 0.2627 TOE.

Table 2.4 Residue Production per Unit of Output

Crop, location, source	Residues/unit of production[a]		Residues (converted to TOE)[b]	
	Primary	Secondary	Primary	Secondary
Agricultural production				
European Union				
(Perry and Rosillo-Calle 2006)				
Rape	1.00	0.60	0.41	0.24
Wheat	0.60	—	0.24	—
Southeast Asia (Koopmans and				
Koppejan 2007)				
Cassava	0.05		0.02	—
Coconut	—	0.49	—	0.20
Coffee	—	1.79	—	0.72
Corn	1.70	0.43	0.69	0.17
Cotton	2.42	—	0.98	—
Groundnut	1.96	0.44	0.79	0.18
Jute	1.70	—	0.69	—
Millet	1.49	—	0.60	—
Palm oil	0.90	0.26	0.37	0.11
Rice	1.53	0.24	0.62	0.10
Soybeans	2.98	—	1.21	—
Sugarcane	0.27	0.15	0.11	0.06
Tobacco	2.00	—	0.81	—
Wheat	1.49	—	0.60	—
United States (PPRP 2006)				
Barley	1.00	—	0.41	—
Corn	0.71	—	0.29	—
Sorghum	0.71	—	0.29	—
Wheat	1.20	—	0.49	—
Roundwood production				
Brazil (Enters 2001)	0.22	0.22	0.06	0.06
China (Enters 2001)	0.79	0.28	0.21	0.07
Finland (Hakkila 2004)	0.27	0.19	0.07	0.05
Indonesia (Enters 2001)	1.10	0.43	0.29	0.11
Malaysia (Enters 2001)	0.81	0.50	0.21	0.13
New Zealand (Scion 2007)	0.17	0.34	0.04	0.09
United States (McKeever 2004)	0.28	0.35	0.07	0.09

Source: Authors' compilation.

Note: — = Not available.

a. Agricultural residues are measured in MT (dry) per MT of production and the forest residues are m^3 per m^3 of production.

b. Conversion factors used are 1 MT of agricultural residues = 0.4060 TOE and 1 m^3 of wood residues = 0.2627 TOE.

Table 2.5 Estimated Agricultural Residue Production, 2006 (TOE/hectare)

Region	Corn	Oil palm fruit	Rapeseed	Soybeans	Sugarcane	Wheat
Africa	1.4	0.3	0.7	1.4	8.2	3.1
Australia, Japan, and New Zealand	1.7	n.a.	0.3	2.1	15.3	1.1
East Asia and Pacific	4.2	1.9	1.2	2.0	11.3	6.6
Europe and Central Asia	3.7	n.a.	1.3	1.5	n.a.	3.1
European Union (27), Iceland, Norway, and Switzerland	1.9	n.a.	1.9	3.0	10.2	3.1
Latin America and the Caribbean	2.9	1.5	1.2	2.9	12.3	3.8
Middle East and North Africa	4.5	n.a.	1.1	3.3	18.5	3.3
North America	2.7	n.a.	1.1	3.6	12.5	3.3
South Asia	1.9	n.a.	0.7	1.3	10.7	3.7
Developed countries	2.5	n.a.	1.4	3.6	14.0	2.8
Developing countries	3.0	1.3	1.0	2.5	11.5	3.9
World	2.9	1.3	1.2	2.9	11.6	3.6

Source: Authors, based on figures in table 2.4 and production statistics from FAO.
Note: n.a. = Not applicable.

countries and with less intensive management. These figures should be interpreted with some caution; the actual amount that could feasibly be collected is only a proportion of the amounts shown here.

Demand for solid biomass for bioenergy is likely to have a small impact on agriculture, except possibly in developed countries, where it may be encouraged by financial support for energy crop development. Increases in biomass supply are likely to be satisfied by an expansion of energy crop areas on forests, degraded land, or unused land. Alternatively, supply could come from increased harvesting of existing forest resources or greater residue recovery.

The use of waste is the most attractive option for securing increased supplies of biomass for energy (see figure 2.5). However, the development of energy crops may be viable in some developing countries. Because energy crops can grow on degraded land, there is potential to increase biomass supplies without diverting agricultural land. Key factors determining the suitability for degraded land for the production of energy crops are its proximity to bioenergy production facilities and whether it has additional uses (see box 2.2).

If biomass waste is not readily available and there is little degraded land, replacement of forests with energy crops or increased harvesting of forest resources ("mining" the resource) is likely to occur. Given the projected increasing demand for modern uses of biomass in developed countries (particularly the European Union, where demand is projected to reach about 185 MT/year in 2030 [see figure 2.3]), imports from timber-producing countries, including countries in the tropics, could dramatically increase, potentially involving millions of hectares of land. By adding to the value of wood resources, it is also possible that bioenergy developments could result in spontaneous tree planting by individuals or communities for additional income.

The impact of increased bioenergy demand on competition for other uses of biomass resources will depend very much on local circumstances. In Europe, for example, the growth of bioenergy has already led to considerable diversion of wood waste (from both consumers and industry) into bioenergy production. In developing countries, where the use of wood waste is often much lower, the development of bioenergy may have fewer negative effects. However, if waste collection includes the collection of residues on site, attention should be paid to the nutrients provided by biomass left on site and the level of residue collection that is consistent with maintaining soil productivity (see EEA 2007 for a discussion of this issue).

Environmental Impact

Potential environmental impacts related to the production of solid biomass for energy include their impacts on climate (carbon emissions from production and possibly, land conversion); water and soil resources; and biodiversity. Large-scale harvesting of biomass resources is likely to have more environmental implications than small-scale operations (because of construction of roads, soil compaction, and high water use). The impacts are difficult to quantify and are very site specific, but some general indications are described below.

Impact on Climate

The impact of solid biomass production on atmospheric pollution can be quantified using three variables:

- Energy intensity (fossil fuel input/unit of energy output)
- Carbon intensity (carbon dioxide emissions/unit of energy output)
- Cost/tCO_2e avoided (based on the carbon intensity and economic viability of each option).

The first two variables have been widely used in life-cycle assessments of biofuels and other materials; the third variable is examined in CEC (2006b) and elsewhere. Methods for quantifying impacts from land-use changes are still being developed. It is also possible to examine the impact of biofuels on emissions of other harmful pollutants (where they generally perform better than conventional fossil fuels). The three variables are normally assessed for the whole bioenergy production system (that is, including both the production of the feedstock and the conversion into the final energy product). They are therefore addressed in the section of this chapter on modern uses of biomass.

Recent studies suggest that soot (also known as black carbon) released from burning woodfuels, industry, farming, and transportation may contribute more to climate change than originally thought. Soot is reportedly the second-largest contributor to climate change (after carbon) and may be responsible for up to 18 percent of the planet's warming (CO_2 reportedly accounts for 40 percent) (Rosenthal 2009). Soot travels widely; when it is deposited on snow packs (in Antarctica or the Himalayas, for example), it lowers the albedo (reflectivity), which can raise temperatures by up to 1°C. This effect could be reduced by minimizing slash and burn agriculture or by replacing inefficient stoves with ones that capture soot (the change would also reduce respiratory diseases). Replacing the hundreds of millions of inefficient cook stoves worldwide is an enormous task, however, that faces many challenges, including high upfront costs and user preferences.

Several studies compare the emissions of greenhouse gases from bioenergy production and coal or gas.[7] Assuming that the biomass is produced sustainably (that is, the carbon stock of the growing biomass is replaced with new growth after harvesting), the main greenhouse gas emissions from biomass energy production are associated with the use of fossil fuel–derived inputs, such as fertilizer and emissions from machinery used in harvesting, transporting, and processing the biomass. If the biomass collection is unsustainable and leads to forest degradation (as is sometimes the case) net emissions will occur and can be higher than the fossil fuel alternatives. For fossil fuels, the largest source of emissions is the combustion of the fuel itself.

In general, the use of solid biomass for energy reduces greenhouse gas emissions by at least 50–60 percent and often by as much as 80–90 percent (depending on the inputs used for biomass production and transport distances).[8] Several studies report greenhouse gas emission reductions of more than 100 percent. This can occur when waste biomass is used that would have been sent to landfill, eventually causing methane emissions.

Greenhouse gas emissions from the use of biomass pellets are likely to be slightly higher than emissions from the use of other types of primary solid biomass for heat and power production, because the use of pellets introduces another processing stage (that is, pellet production). Pellets may be transported over longer distances, which could result in more emissions from transportation. The effect of these factors depends on the modes of transport used; it could be mitigated by the greater energy density of pellets. Imports from timber-producing countries, including countries in the tropics, are likely to increase dramatically. This could increase pressures on land and for local populations if sustainable production schemes are not adopted.

Soils contain about three times more carbon than vegetation and twice as much as the atmosphere. Most of the carbon found in soils is included in soil organic matter (57 percent by weight). However, agricultural activities (tilling, burning, and so forth); forest land conversion; and wind and water erosion have exposed soil organic matter to microbial action, causing a loss of organic matter through decomposition. Loss of soil carbon increases the amount of carbon in the atmosphere (causing global warming) and reduces soil productivity. Most agricultural soils have lost 30–40 MT of carbon/hectare; their current reserves of soil organic carbon are much lower than their potential capacity. Replenishing soil carbon reserves (sequestration) has been suggested as one step in helping reduce atmospheric carbon.

Biochar, a fine-grained, porous charcoal substance, has begun to draw attention as an interesting method for removing atmospheric carbon and replenishing soil carbon. The origins of biochar come from the pre-Columbian era, when rich *terra preta* (Portuguese for *dark earth*) soils were developed over many years in the central Amazonian basin by adding a mixture of bone, manure, and charcoal to the relatively infertile soils. The charcoal is believed to be the key ingredient in these fertile soils, which persist to this day.

Researchers have adapted this idea and are testing adding biochar to soils to remove greenhouse gases from the atmosphere, enrich the soil and increase soil fertility. Under controlled production conditions, the pyrolysis or gasification of biomass results in the production of biochar, a synthesis gas (syngas), bio-oil and heat. The carbon feedstock is converted almost entirely into these four products and the mixture of outputs can be varied, depending on the chosen technology and processes used (eg pressure, temperature and speed of combustion). Theoretically biochar production can amount to almost 50% of the feedstock used, with the remaining feedstock being converted into the other 3 products.

Some of the major concerns surrounding biochar are connected to large-scale development and application, which would require huge quantities of biomass inputs and could cause deforestation and land conversion for charcoal plantations, negating the positive impacts of adding carbon to the soil. There are also concerns over the amount of soot that could be released into the atmosphere if biochar is not completely incorporated into the soil. However, use at an individual or local level presents opportunities. Biochar stoves, for example, can be used to cook as well as capture biochar, which can then be added to agricultural lands. Doing so would have multiple benefits, including reducing deforestation by minimizing the amount of biomass necessary for heating and cooking, capturing atmospheric carbon, improving health (by releasing less smoke in the home), and improving soil fertility.

(continued)

Box 2.3   (Continued)

Biochar trials are still in their infancy, but early results are encouraging. It will be important to establish pilot programs that assess the benefits and potential social and environmental impacts of using biochar. Countries with large areas of degraded land or large stocks of waste biomass could be targeted for initial pilots. Biochar could be an interesting response to deal with issues such as food and energy while at the same time reducing carbon emissions.

Source: Sundermeier, Reeder, and Lal 2005; Flanagan and Joseph 2007; International Biochar Initiative 2009; Lal 2009.

Impact on Water Resources

In general, the demands of energy crops on water resources in temperate countries falls somewhere between the demands of forests and agricultural crops. In the United Kingdom, energy crops, which require about 500–650 millimeters of rain a year, use roughly 100 millimeters a year more water than food crops; their transpiration is similar to the upper boundary of transpiration recorded in broadleaved forests and at or below the typical range of transpiration in coniferous forests (Hall 2003; Nisbet 2005) (figure 2.6).

Comparable figures for water use in natural forests and agriculture are not readily available for tropical countries, but it is likely that biomass crops grown for energy production will have higher water demands than most agricultural crops. Transpiration of some common forest plantation species (the most likely candidates for biomass production) is relatively high. Some species, however, such as eucalyptus, are very efficient in water use and can therefore be grown in areas with relatively low rainfall.

Biomass crops are unlikely to be planted on prime agricultural land in tropical countries; consumption of water could be an issue if energy crops are grown on degraded land or marginal agricultural land. Whether this has a positive or negative impact depends on local circumstances. For example, although increased water use is generally thought of as having a negative effect, it can be beneficial in the reclamation of degraded land affected by salinity.

The impacts of changes in land use are even more complicated and site specific with respect to other impacts on water resources (such as water quality and flooding) (see, for example, Bonell and Bruijnzeel 2005; FAO 2005). They depend on the types of land used for biomass production, previous land uses, and the management regime used to grow and harvest the biomass.

Figure 2.6 Typical Range of Annual Transpiration for Forest, Agriculture, and Energy Crops

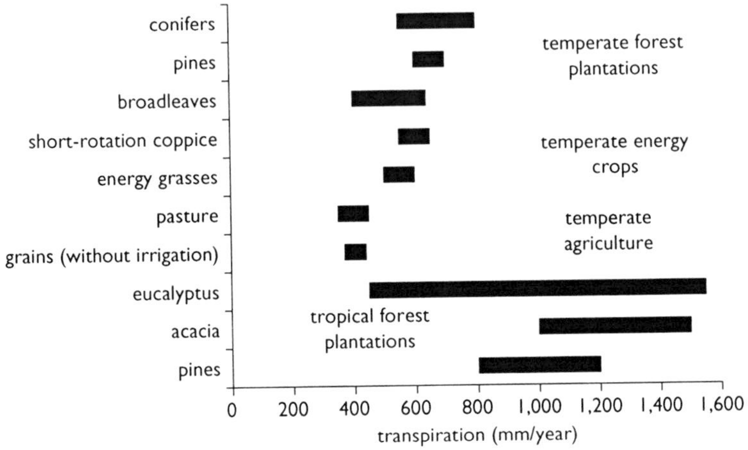

Source: Authors, based on Hall 2003 and Nisbet 2005.

Impact on Soil Resources

The impact of biomass production on soil resources is complex and variable. A few general observations are possible:

- Intensive production of energy crops (such as short-rotation coppice and energy grasses) is likely to require some use of artificial inputs on a regular basis if high growth rates are to be achieved. Tree crops managed on longer rotations and other crops that require less intensive management are also likely to require some inputs, albeit at a lower level.
- Large-scale biomass production can cause soil compaction if heavy equipment is used for harvesting.
- The collection of forest and agricultural residues should generally not attempt the complete removal of all residual biomass; an adequate amount should be left to maintain productive soil functions.
- With appropriate management, biomass crops generally have the potential to improve soil conditions in degraded areas and can be used to reclaim contaminated land. Nitrogen fixing, increased organic matter (from leaf litter), and improved soil structure are some of the benefits associated with planting biomass crops (Kartha and others 2005).

Impact on Biodiversity

The impact of biomass production on biodiversity depends on the crops used to produce biomass and the scale of production. Some energy crops are native species (switchgrass in the United States, poplars and willow in Europe); others are not (miscanthus in Europe, many tree species with high yields in tropical countries). Introduced species are often preferred for biomass production, because their yields are higher than native species. For this reason, the planting of energy crops is likely to have a negative impact on biodiversity.

Perhaps a more important factor is the likely scale of production. Large-scale production of energy crops is likely to result in biodiversity losses if it displaces natural vegetation. Production of biomass from unsustainable levels of forest harvesting or on-site residue collection is also likely to harm biodiversity. Planting energy crops on agricultural land (as may happen to some extent in temperate regions) will have less of an impact on biodiversity.

Small-scale planting of biomass crops could enhance biodiversity, even if introduced species are used. Biomass production systems that could increase biodiversity include small-scale plantations (along field boundaries, for example); biomass production in agroforestry systems; and planting of energy crops on some degraded lands.

As with the impacts of biomass production on soil and water resources, the impact on biodiversity could be positive or negative, major or minor, depending on local site conditions and the scale of production. It is not possible to generalize about whether biomass production will be good or bad for biodiversity. The potential to enhance or reduce biodiversity should be taken into consideration.

TRADITIONAL USES OF SOLID BIOMASS FOR ENERGY

The distinction between traditional uses of solid biomass for energy and modern and industrial uses is not clear. For the purpose of this study, traditional uses refer to the use of biomass for heating and cooking, mostly in domestic situations using open fires or simple, low-cost technology, such as stoves and enclosed fireplaces. The types of solid biomass used for energy are agricultural waste (dung and crop residues); firewood (including dead wood, roots, and branches); charcoal; and, in some cases, industrial wood waste. Traditional uses generally do not use more processed forms of solid biomass, such as wood pellets or wood chips.

Economic Viability

Traditional uses are characterized by very low investment costs in production, transformation, and utilization of the fuel. A significant proportion of production in developing countries occurs in the informal sector or is produced for subsistence use, using few tools and often with little or no management of the resource. As a result of increasing urban demand, much of the fuelwood produced in developing countries is converted into charcoal, often using very simple technology, such as earth kilns, with low conversion rates (see box 2.4).

Box 2.4 Charcoal Production in Tanzania

Charcoal is the main energy source for Tanzania's urban population. Across the country, only 10 percent of the population uses electricity as the primary energy source. As a result of limited cash flow and weak purchasing power, poorer households buy charcoal frequently and in small quantities, at a high unit price. The perceived low cost of charcoal and its widespread availability are the main reasons why it is used, according to a survey of 700 households in Dar es Salaam (CHAPOSA 2002). The majority of users buy charcoal several times a week, in small quantities from traders located only a few minutes from their homes.

As in many other Sub-Saharan countries, tens of thousands of rural and urban entrepreneurs in Tanzania earn income from charcoal production and trade. Production in the Tanzanian charcoal industry is estimated at about 1 MT/year.

The structure of the charcoal chain is complex, comprising many different actors with varying interests and stakes. Charcoal producers are often contracted by wholesalers or transporters, but they also work and sell their products individually. A small number of people consider charcoal production to be their main economic activity; the majority produce charcoal only occasionally, to generate income, particularly in times of financial stress.

Most charcoal is sold to transporters. Some large-scale transporters are also wholesalers, who pass the charcoal on to smaller-scale retailers and consumers.

Trade in charcoal is conducted by formal as well as informal actors. One commercialization chain begins with government-issued licenses for harvesting of wood to produce charcoal. The product is transported and traded by officially licensed transporters and traders, who pay the necessary duties and taxes. A second, and larger, commercialization chain is undertaken without official licensing. Charcoal produced through this informal chain is transported and traded clandestinely in an attempt to avoid authorities, taxation, and potential penalties. Nearly 80 percent of the charcoal arriving in Dar es Salaam is believed to follow this path (Malimbwi, Zahabu, and Mchombe 2007). With the value of Tanzania's charcoal business conservatively estimated at about $650 million, this represents unregulated trade of more than $500 million a year. The potential annual taxes and levies lost from this represent about 20 percent of the total value, or more than $100 million.

The complexity of the value chain of charcoal suggests that policy interventions should be targeted along the whole value chain, not only for specific projects, such as improved stoves or kilns or the promotion of reforestation. In addition, fiscal incentives should be introduced that make sustainable charcoal competitive with unsustainable charcoal.

Source: World Bank 2009.

At the point of end-use, low levels of technology are often used to produce the heat finally used for cooking or heating.

In developed countries, the technologies used in this sector are somewhat more advanced, but they are still relatively simple compared with other types of biomass production and energy consumption. Fuelwood producers are typically very small enterprises, serving local markets with minimal investment in harvesting technology.

The main economic factors driving traditional uses of biomass for energy are the low costs of production (or low purchase prices) and the low income of most consumers. In the case of subsistence production in developing countries, the cost of production is the opportunity cost of the time taken to collect fuelwood. Because the opportunity to earn paid income is very limited in many places, this cost is negligible. In developing country locations where biofuels must be purchased (for example, urban areas), most consumers have very little income; biofuels are chosen because they are the only affordable source of energy. Even in developed countries, in rural locations where forest cover is high, fuelwood is often less expensive than alternatives, such as heating oil or liquefied petroleum gas (LPG).[9]

The traditional use of solid biomass for energy is largely a private sector affair, driven by the price/cost competitiveness of this source of energy compared with alternatives. However, many governments have tried to intervene in this sector, for various reasons and with varying degrees of success. Some developing countries attempt to collect forest charges (for example, for fuelwood permits) as a source of funding for the government. Others have tried to restrict production (to protect forests) through regulation or, more often, have attempted to introduce local forest management regimes to ensure the sustainability of fuelwood supplies. Perhaps the most significant government interventions over the past few decades have been projects (often funded with the support of international donors) that have introduced new technologies (such as charcoal production or improved stoves) or encouraged the establishment of fuelwood plantations.

The results of these interventions have been mixed (Arnold and others 2003). Improved technologies have been adopted and sustained only where increased efficiency is economically justified. For example, improved stoves were introduced and are still used in urban areas where woodfuel is purchased, but they have generally not been adopted in rural locations. Fuelwood plantations have also had mixed results. Although many of these plantations have reached maturity, in most cases the wood has been harvested and sold into higher-value markets. Governments have generally not been able to monitor production and collect charges on more than a small fraction of total biofuel production (FAO 2001; Whiteman 2001). Government interventions have thus generally had little impact on the economics of traditional uses of solid biomass for energy and limited success in encouraging sustainability in this sector.

Health Impact

The World Health Organization recently produced the results of its investigation into the impact of solid biomass fuels on indoor air quality and health (WHO 2007). Its review of the literature reveals that exposure to indoor air pollution from biomass fuels is linked to many diseases, including acute and chronic respiratory diseases, tuberculosis, asthma, cardiovascular disease, and perinatal health outcomes.[10] Coal was included in this study, but its use was minor, suggesting that that most health impacts result from traditional biomass use. The report finds strong evidence for indoor air pollution as a cause of pneumonia and other acute lower respiratory infections among children under five and of chronic obstructive pulmonary disease (COPD) and lung cancer (related to coal use) among adults.

The WHO estimates that indoor air pollution was responsible for more than 1.5 million deaths and 2.7 percent of the global burden of disease in 2002.[11] In high-mortality developing countries, it had an even greater impact, accounting for 3.7 percent of the burden of disease, making it the most important risk factor after malnutrition, the HIV/AIDS epidemic, and lack of safe water and adequate sanitation. The study notes that indoor air pollution disproportionately affects women and children, who spend more time than men using solid fuels.

Impact on Land and Other Resources

Traditional biomass has less of an impact on natural forests than initially thought. Although woodfuel collection can contribute to severe deforestation (especially around urban areas), as much as two-thirds of fuelwood for cooking comes from roadside trees and trees on agricultural land rather than from natural forests. In contrast, charcoal is usually produced in an unsustainable manner from forest resources in response to urban demand (particularly in Africa), placing a strain on forest resources (IEA 2006b).

There is good evidence that woodfuel supply in developing countries can be sustainable even in densely populated areas, where government planting programs, community woodlots, and plantations are adequately managed. There is also evidence that woodfuel shortages or high prices can actually lead to afforestation in order to provide a source of energy (Matthews and others 2000).

Most of the impact of traditional biomass energy use on land and other resources occurs in the production of biomass. There is little or no additional impact from the transportation and utilization of biomass.

Environmental Impact

Most analyses of carbon emissions from modern uses of solid biomass for energy assume that the biomass is produced sustainably and that the stock of carbon in the biomass resource is constantly replenished through regrowth.

This assumption may not be valid. There may be emissions from the gradual degradation of soils and the biomass stock. In addition, traditional uses of biomass for energy sometimes include transportation over long distances (especially in the case of charcoal), which uses fossil fuels whose emissions should be taken into account.

Statistics for the energy intensity, carbon intensity, and cost of emission reductions from traditional uses of biomass for energy are not readily available, but it is possible to produce some estimates by comparing these uses with the most likely alternatives (for example, kerosene used for cooking).

Traditional biomass energy use has an energy intensity of zero when biomass is collected for local and subsistence uses (because no fossil fuels are used during collection). Where traditional biomass energy is transported, the energy intensity depends upon the transport distance, the size of the load, and the relative energy content and efficiencies of combustion of the alternative fuels. For example, 1 liter of kerosene contains about 40 MJ of energy; it would require about 2.7 kilograms of charcoal to produce the same amount of heat for cooking (taking into account the energy content of charcoal and the lower efficiency of charcoal cooking stoves–assumed to be half in this case). If the charcoal were transported in 10 MT loads with a round-trip distance of 300 kilometers (which is possible in some parts of Africa), the fossil fuel energy used to transport the charcoal would amount to roughly 0.3 MJ, or about 2 percent of the fossil fuel energy content of the original liter of kerosene.[12] If the charcoal were transported in smaller loads over shorter distances (for example, 200 kilograms with a round-trip distance of 60 kilometers), the energy intensity would increase to about 10 percent of the figure for kerosene. These examples are likely to represent the range of situations that are most common in charcoal transportation.

If the biomass used for energy is produced sustainably, the greenhouse gas emissions from traditional biomass energy use would be up to 10 percent of the emissions from a comparable amount of kerosene (CO_2 emissions/MJ of kerosene, gasoline, and diesel are roughly the same). However, if the biomass is not replaced by future plant growth, the emissions from traditional biomass use are potentially much higher. For example, CO_2 emissions from one liter of kerosene amount to roughly 2.9 kilograms, but the emissions from the 2.7 kilograms of charcoal required to produce the same amount of energy amount to about 11 kilograms CO_2. Therefore, the traditional use of charcoal only results in lower CO_2 emissions compared with kerosene if at least 75 percent of the biomass used to produce the charcoal is produced sustainably.

For the reasons indicated above, the cost of emissions reductions from the traditional use of biomass energy is also related to the sustainability of biomass production. For example, where biomass is the least expensive source of fuel and is produced sustainably, traditional biomass energy use results in much lower emissions than fossil fuel alternatives at no cost. In contrast, where the biomass is not produced sustainably and there are net emissions from the biomass combustion, the cost of emissions reductions depends on how this problem is addressed. Several options could be considered, including supporting the sustainable production of biomass for use as fuel (for example, fuelwood plantations); introducing improved technologies such as stoves and charcoal-making equipment to reduce emissions; and encouraging the adoption of other renewable energy technologies, such as solar cookers or the production and use of liquid biofuels. The cost and viability of different options to reduce emissions will vary greatly from place to place, so it is not possible to estimate what the cost of such interventions might be. However, given the magnitude of traditional biomass energy use, it seems likely that further investigation of this problem would be useful.

MODERN AND INDUSTRIAL USES OF SOLID BIOMASS FOR ENERGY

Modern and industrial uses of solid biomass for energy include co-firing in power stations (usually with coal); power stations that use only biomass; small to medium-scale facilities that provide power or heat in the forestry and agricultural processing industries; and small to medium-scale facilities that provide power or heat for other industries and commercial operations.

Statistics on the number of facilities producing power or heat from biomass are not readily available. However, the approximate number of large-scale power stations currently using biomass is known (table 2.6).[13]

The issues and impacts related to modern and industrial uses of solid biomass for energy vary greatly from case to case. Some general indications are presented below.

Economic Viability

The cost of heat and power production can be split into three main components: the capital cost of facilities and equipment, the operations and maintenance cost, and the cost of the fuel used. The capital cost of biomass power production has fallen in recent years, as new technology has been introduced and greater demand for such equipment has created economies of scale in production. Nevertheless, the cost of large-scale power production remains 10–20 percent higher than the capital cost of coal-fired power production. At smaller scales (for example, for industrial or commercial heating applications), the capital cost can be up to twice the cost of alternatives such as oil-fired heating. The capital cost of biomass power production per unit of capacity is likely to remain somewhat above the cost of alternatives because of the lower energy content of biomass, which requires a greater volume of material to be used to produce each unit of power output. In addition, more space is usually required to store biofuel supplies, and the equipment required for preparing biofuel for combustion is generally more expensive.

Table 2.6 Number of Large-Scale Power Stations Using Biomass, 2008

| Region | Number of power stations using biomass | | | Types of biomass used | | |
	Co-firing with coal	Pure biomass	Waste	Energy crops	Other	Not specified
Africa	0	0	0	0	0	0
Australia, Japan, and New Zealand	8	4	11	0	2	0
East Asia and Pacific	4	2	6	0	4	0
Europe and Central Asia	0	0	0	0	0	0
European Union (27), Iceland, Norway, and Switzerland	97	35	83	1	67	15
Latin America and the Caribbean	0	2	1	0	1	0
Middle East and North Africa	0	0	0	0	0	0
North America	40	33	51	4	18	7
South Asia	0	4	4	0	0	0
Developed countries	145	72	145	5	87	22
Developing countries	4	8	11	0	5	0
World	149	80	156	5	92	22

Source: Bergesen 2008; IEA 2008b.
Note: Types of biomass used add up to more than the number of power stations in each region because power stations use more than one type of biomass. Most co-firing power stations have capacity of more than 50MW; most of those using pure biomass are in the 5–50MW range.

Operations and maintenance costs are also higher for biofuels than for conventional fuel, partly because of the larger volumes of biofuel needed to produce each unit of power output. Other factors—including moisture content and biofuel variability (density, particle size, contaminants)—also increase these costs.

The cost of biomass is probably the most important factor affecting the economics of heat and power production from biomass compared with alternatives. The high production cost (in most cases) and the lower energy content of biomass make it more expensive than coal. Cost in per unit of energy content may be comparable to oil or gas, however.

Another factor affecting the fuel cost is the efficiency of energy production. The conversion efficiency of biomass is slightly lower than that of fossil fuels, but it has improved over the past few years and is now quite close to the levels achieved in coal-fired power production and oil-fired heating applications.

For power production, co-firing with coal is roughly $0.02–$0.03 more expensive/kWh than power production using only coal (table 2.7). Co-firing at

Table 2.7 Estimates of the Cost of Energy Production from Biomass

Country/reference	Energy production cost (cents/kWh)				Type of production
	Coal	Gas	Oil	Biomass	
Austria					
Bios Bioenergysysteme (2004)	—	—	—	13.2–17.3	Electricity from combined heat and power
Bios Bioenergysysteme (2004)	—	—	—	3.2–6.2	Heat from combined heat and power
Canada					
Kumar, Flynn, and Sokhansanj (2006)	—	—	—	6.8–7.4	Electricity (estimated cost)
Layzell, Stephen, and Wood (2006)	—	—	—	7.7–9.5	Electricity at 15 percent co-firing or 100 percent biomass (estimated cost)
Zhang, Habibi, and MacLean (2007)	2.7	—	—	+2.0–3.5[a]	Electricity at 10–15 percent co-firing (estimated cost)
Colombia					
Kartha, Leach, and Rajan (2005)	—	—	13.0	7.5	Small-scale electricity (compared with diesel with subsidy)
Denmark					
Bios Bioenergysysteme (2004)	—	—	—	13.1	Electricity from combined heat and power
Bios Bioenergysysteme (2004)	—	—	—	3.2	Heat from combined heat and power
Uganda					
Buchholz and Volk (2007)	—	—	25.0–33.0	22.0	Small-scale electricity (compared with diesel with/without subsidy)
United Kingdom					
Biomass Task Force (2005)	—	3.3–4.9	3.6–4.0	3.1–3.8	Heat

(continued)

Table 2.7 (Continued)

| Country/ reference | Energy production cost (cents/kWh) | | | | Type of production |
	Coal	Gas	Oil	Biomass	
United States					
Spath and Mann (2004)	2.0–3.0	4.0–5.0	—	8.0–9.0	Electricity, direct firing
				5.0–6.0	Electricity, gasification
Forest Products Laboratory (2004)	—	—	—	6.0–11.0	Electricity
Forest Products Laboratory (2004)	—	—	—	+2.0[a]	Electricity at 10–15 percent co-firing
Johnson (2006)	—	—	—	+2.6–3.0[a]	Electricity at 1–10 percent co-firing (excludes subsidy)

Source: Authors.

Note: In cases of co-firing, costs have been converted to an amount/kWh for the biomass component.

a. Incremental or additional cost of biomass energy production compared with the main fuel used (that is, coal). — = Not available.

modest levels (usually up to about 15 percent) does not require significant capital investments; the main cost factors are increased material handling and preparation costs and the cost of the fuel itself.

In the case of pure biomass power production, the best available technology (gasification rather than direct firing) can achieve costs as low as $0.05–$0.06/kWh, which is $0.02–$0.03 more expensive than coal and almost comparable to the cost of gas. In theory, this cost may be comparable to that of oil, but oil-fired power production is not common, except in countries in which oil is very cheap or has other advantages. Therefore, biomass is unlikely to be a realistic alternative to oil-fired power production in most cases. The one major exception is in small-scale power production in rural settings, where a few studies have shown that biomass power production is cheaper than using oil (Kartha, Leach, and Rajan 2005; Bucholz and Volk 2007).

The one other situation in which biomass energy is competitive with fossil-fuel alternatives is the production of heat. Pure heat production or heat from combined heat and power systems is comparable to the cost of using oil or gas (about $0.03–$0.06/kWh).

Economic Impact

The production of biomass for use as a fuel generates more income and employment than most other types of fuel. The production of heat and power from biomass may also result in more income and employment than generated by fossil fuels.

Recent announcements of new biomass power-generation facilities have indicated employment in the range of one employee per 0.8–1.6MW of generation capacity. This is roughly three to four times employment in coal-fired electricity production (Wright 1999 gives a figure of one employee per 3.7–5.3MW of installed coal-fired generation capacity in the United States). The higher employment generated by biomass heat and power production is caused by the relatively small size of production facilities and the larger volumes of material used to produce each unit of energy output. Similar levels of employment are reported for other types of renewable energy production, such as wind, geothermal, and hydro power production.

Impact on Land and Other Resources

Land and water requirements are similar to those of fossil fuels. The impact on land and other resources mostly occur in the production of biomass.

Environmental Impact

Biomass affects soil, water, and biodiversity resources. The environmental impact of biomass heat and power production can also be measured in terms of the fossil fuel energy intensity, carbon intensity, and cost of avoided emissions.

Various estimates of the environmental impact of heat and power production from solid biomass are available (table 2.8). Several studies have examined the emissions of greenhouse gases from bioenergy production compared with coal or gas.[14] Assuming that the biomass is produced sustainably (that is, the carbon stock of the growing biomass is replaced with new growth after harvesting), the main greenhouse gas emissions from biomass energy production are associated with the use of fossil fuel–derived inputs, such as fertilizer, and emissions from machinery used in harvesting, transporting, and processing the biomass. For fossil fuels, similar emissions are included (for example, for production and transportation of the fuel), but the largest source of emissions is the combustion of the fuel itself.

Land-Use Changes

Fossil fuel energy intensity is a measure similar to carbon intensity (because carbon or greenhouse gas emissions are closely linked to the use of fossil fuels). Several studies have measured the reduction in fossil fuel intensity

Table 2.8 Estimates of Environmental Impact of Biomass Energy Production

Study	Location	Environmental indicator	Percentage reduction
Mann and Spath (2001)	United States	Greenhouse gas reduction (coal)	108–121
Spath and Mann (2004)	United States	Greenhouse gas reduction (coal)	94–126
Spath and Mann (2004)	United States	Fossil fuel reduction (coal)	80–98
Woods and others (2006)	United Kingdom	Greenhouse gas reduction (coal)	75–217
WEC (2004)	Global estimate	Greenhouse gas reduction (coal)	73–98
Mann and Spath	United States	Fossil fuel reduction (coal)	70–83
Zhang, Habibi, and MacLean (2007)	Canada	Greenhouse gas reduction (coal)	70
Spath and Mann (2004)	United States	Fossil fuel reduction (gas)	54–66
Spath and Mann (2004)	United States	Greenhouse gas reduction (gas)	53–76
Khokhotva (2004)	Global estimate	Greenhouse gas reduction (coal)	50–60
Zhang, Habibi, and MacLean (2007)	Canada	$/tCO$_2$e	22–40
Spath and Mann (2004)	United States	$/tCO$_2$e	16–19
Katers and Kaurich (2007)	United States	Fossil fuel intensity (wood pellets)	9–13
Khokhotva (2004)	Global estimate	Fossil fuel intensity (wood)	7–13
Kumar and Sokhansanj (2007)	Canada	Fossil fuel intensity (switchgrass)	6–8
Nilsson (2007)	Sweden	Fossil fuel intensity (various)	3–17

Source: Authors' compilation.

where biofuels are substituted for fossil fuels or reported the fossil fuel intensity measured as the amount of fossil fuels used to produce each unit of biofuel, with both items measured in terms of energy content. Reported fossil fuel intensities in the production of solid biomass used for energy have been reported in the range of 3–17 percent, depending on the inputs used and transport distances. Other studies have suggested that if solid biomass is substituted for coal in heat and power production, the use of fossil fuels/unit of energy production can fall by 70 percent to almost 100 percent. However, where biomass substitutes for natural gas, the reduction is somewhat lower (54–66 percent), because of the higher transformation efficiency of heat and power production using natural gas.[15]

A few studies have reported the cost of emissions reductions from the use of solid biomass for heat and power production of $16–$40/tCO$_2$e. Given that CO$_2$ emissions from coal-fired power production are about 0.95 MT/MWh (DOE-EPA 2000) and the figures presented earlier suggested that using solid biomass to produce electricity costs about $0.02–$0.03/kWh more than coal, the reductions in fossil fuel intensity presented in table 2.8 would suggest a cost of emission reductions for CO$_2$ alone of about $25–$40/tCO$_2$, which is very similar to the range of costs presented in the literature.

ENERGY SYSTEMS BASED ON BIOMASS PELLETS

The production of energy from biomass pellets is a subcomponent of TPES from primary solid biomass. Energy production from biomass pellets is one of the modern uses of solid biomass for energy that has rapidly increased in importance in recent years (Peksa-Blanchard and others 2007). It is treated separately here, because biomass pellets have certain characteristics that are quite different from other types of primary solid biomass.

Pellets are made by compressing biomass and squeezing the compressed material through a die that has holes of the required size (usually 6 millimeters in diameter, but sometimes 8 millimeters or larger). The high pressure of the press causes the temperature of the biomass to increase; lignin in the biomass forms a natural glue that holds the pellet together as it cools. Pellets are usually made from wood, although it is also possible to manufacture pellets from other types of biomass. China, for example, plans to increase pellet production significantly from almost nothing to 50 million MT by 2020, mostly from the use of agricultural residues (Peksa-Blanchard and others 2007).

The quality of pellets produced is not affected by the type of biomass used. Sawdust is a preferred input, because the material is already broken down into small particle sizes and usually has low moisture content. However, to meet pellet industry standards, it is not generally possible to use recycled or treated wood for pellet manufacturing, because of concerns about noxious emissions and uncontrolled variations in the burning characteristics of the pellets.

Biomass pellets are extremely dense. They are usually produced with low humidity content (below 10 percent), allowing them to be burned with very high combustion efficiency. Their density reduces storage requirements and makes transportation over long distances economically feasible. Their regular shape and small size also reduces handling and transportation costs and allows automatic feeding into combustion equipment.

Pellets can be used in large-scale applications, such as power stations, but most are currently used in pellet stoves, central heating furnaces, and other small to medium-size heating appliances and the combustion efficiency of appliances has increased over the past decade to a level that is now comparable to oil-fired appliances.[16]

Most wood pellets are consumed in small to medium-size boilers to provide heat for residences, district heating, commercial buildings, and light industry. A few countries (for example, Belgium and the Netherlands) use wood pellets for large-scale electricity production, probably because of their need to meet renewable energy commitments and to import almost all of the biomass required to meet this demand.

The fact that it is economically feasible to transport pellets over long distances opens up opportunities for international trade in biomass between countries. Canada exported more than 1 million MT of pellets in 2006 (about half to Europe and half to the United States). Together, Brazil, Chile, and Argentina are believed to export about 50,000 MT of wood pellets a year. Several European countries also report significant levels of wood pellet exports (about 1 million MT in total from the Russian Federation, Poland, and the Baltic States) (Peksa-Blanchard and others 2007). Given the projected wood pellet increases in the European Union through 2030 (estimated at about 185 MT/year (see figure 2.4), imports are likely. As a result, imports from timber-producing countries are likely to increase dramatically, potentially increasing pressures on land and for local populations if sustainable production schemes are not adopted.

Wood pellets accounted for a growing share of heat and power supply from primary solid biomass between 1997 and 2006 (table 2.9). As a result of increases in fossil fuel prices and incentives, pellet production capacity and the installation of pellet heating appliances increased significantly, especially in Europe and North America, which together had 308 wood pellet manufacturing facilities in 2006 (figures 2.7 and 2.8).

Economic Viability

The main economic factors that affect the economics of heat and power production from biomass pellets are the same as those for other types of solid biomass. The capital cost of equipment and facilities and maintenance and operational costs are slightly higher than the same costs for facilities using fuel oil, natural gas, and propane (the main alternative fuels used in facilities that might switch to pellets). Larger facilities are required to handle the volumes of pellets required to produce a given amount of heat or power. However, as a result of the higher energy content of pellets (compared with other types of solid biomass) and the scope for mechanized handling of the material, the additional costs are likely to be small. The main factor affecting the economics of heat and power production is therefore the cost of the pellets.

Given that the combustion efficiency of appliances that use pellets is now comparable to that of appliances that use fuel oil, natural gas, or propane, the comparative cost of producing heat and power from pellets comes down to the cost of the potential energy contained within the pellets compared with

Table 2.9 Annual Wood Pellet Consumption in Selected Countries, 1997–2006

Country	1997	1998	1999	2000	2001	2002	2003	2004	2005	2006
Sweden	500	525	625	700	900	900	1,125	1,250	1,475	1,670
Netherlands	n.a.	n.a.	n.a.	n.a.	n.a.	n.a.	n.a.	n.a.	n.a.	1,400
Denmark	175	190	230	300	410	450	560	730	820	870
Germany	n.a.	n.a.	8	30	80	130	190	270	440	700
Belgium	n.a.	n.a.	n.a.	n.a.	n.a.	n.a.	n.a.	n.a.	400	675
Italy	n.a.	25	50	75	105	150	185	240	320	500
Austria	10	n.a.	n.a.	n.a.	n.a.	n.a.	n.a.	n.a.	59	400
Finland	n.a.	n.a.	n.a.	n.a.	n.a.	n.a.	5	5	30	100
France	n.a.	n.a.	n.a.	n.a.	n.a.	n.a.	n.a.	6	25	90
Poland	n.a.	n.a.	n.a.	n.a.	n.a.	n.a.	n.a.	17	21	35
Norway	n.a.	72	79	71	76	92	88	87	85	26
Canada	n.a.	n.a.	n.a.	n.a.	n.a.	n.a.	n.a.	n.a.	n.a.	120
United States	n.a.	618	602	569	654	727	761	816	945	1,024
Total	685	1,430	1,594	1,745	2,225	2,449	2,914	3,421	4,620	7,610
Total (MTOE)	0.28	0.59	0.66	0.72	0.92	1.01	1.20	1.41	1.91	3.14
Percent of total biomass heat and power	1	2	3	3	3	4	5	5	7	—

Source: Authors, based on data from Peksa-Blanchard and others 2007 and the IEA database.

Note: Most of the missing figures for European countries are likely to be zero or very small. — = Not available.

Figure 2.7 Number and Location of Wood Pellet Manufacturing Facilities in Europe, 2006

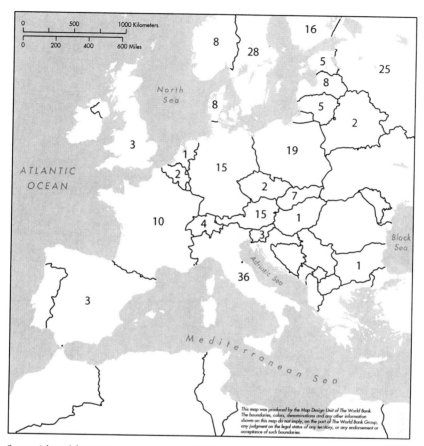

Source: Adapted from Bioenergy International 2005.

the same measure for other types of fuel. One MT of wood pellets contains roughly 19 GJ of energy, equivalent to 510 liters (135 gallons) of fuel oil or 760 liters (200 gallons) of propane. Dividing the cost of pellets by these figures yields the price at which the alternatives cost the same amount per unit of energy content.

Such a calculation is presented in figure 2.9, where the bold straight lines show the equivalent energy costs for wood pellets versus propane and heating oil at various prices. At a heating oil price of $1.50/gallon, for example, the equivalent wood pellet price would be $200/MT. If pellet prices fell below this amount, pellets would be a less expensive source of energy than heating oil.

Figure 2.8   Location of Wood Pellet Manufacturing Facilities in
North America, 2006

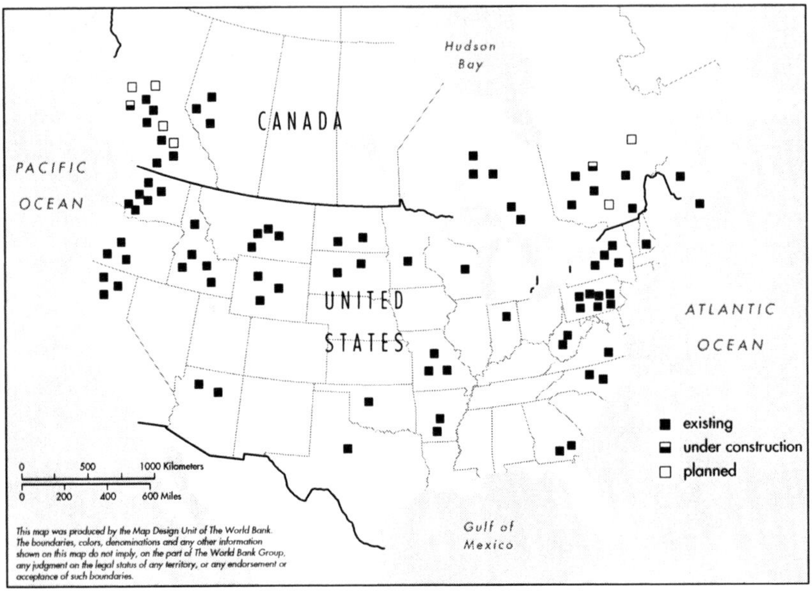

Source: Swann 2006.

Figure 2.9 also presents some statistics on the comparative prices of the three fuels in 2000–07. These are indicated by the thin lines, with the later years toward the right-hand side of the figure. The figure shows that wood pellets were a less expensive source of energy than propane and heating oil for the whole period, although the differences between wood pellets and heating oil were small in earlier years. Over the period, the cost of using wood pellets did not change much. In contrast, the price of heating oil increased by a factor of 2.5, and the price of propane doubled. As a result of these increases in prices, by 2007 the cost of heat and power production from wood pellets was less than half the cost from heating oil and propane.

Rising prices have also resulted in a change in the comparative costs of pellets and natural gas. In 2002–03 domestic natural gas prices in the United States were just over $8/thousand cubic feet (EIA 2008c). At that price, the cost of wood pellets was marginally higher than the cost of gas (per unit of energy content). By 2007–08 gas prices had reached about $13/thousand cubic feet. As a result, the cost of using wood pellets fell to about one-third lower than the cost of using an equivalent amount of gas.

Statistics for the cost of pellets and alternative fuels in Europe are not readily available, but it is likely that similar trends occurred there. The rapid

Figure 2.9   Wood Pellet, Propane, and Heating Oil Costs in the
United States, 2000–07

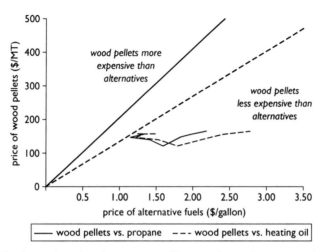

Source: Authors' compilation based on propane and heating oil prices from EIA 2008b and wood
pellet prices from Peksa-Blanchard and others 2007.
Note: Fossil fuel prices are residential prices for U.S. No. 2 Heating Oil and propane (excluding
taxes). Wood pellet prices are based on a delivered price of $150 per U.S. ton in 2007 (as reported
in Peksa-Blanchard and others 2007); prices are estimated using annual changes in U.S. wood chip
trade prices (as reported in FAOSTAT).

growth in the use of wood pellets in Europe has been encouraged by subsidies.
However, these subsidies have largely been directed toward the replacement of
existing appliances with ones that use wood pellets.

The use of wood pellets already appears to be economically feasible for certain applications in many developed countries. Growth in this sector is likely
to continue if fossil fuel prices remain high.

Economic Impact

As with other types of solid biomass used for energy, the main impact of pellet use on employment is in the growing of the biomass feedstock. There is
additional employment in pellet manufacturing. Pellets can be produced on a
modest scale, suggesting that there may be opportunities for small and
medium-size enterprises (with pellet production near or linked to wood or
agricultural processing facilities). There appear to be no major economic
impacts from pellet use other than those associated with the production of the
biomass feedstock.

Impact on Land and Other Resources

Heat and power production from pellets could have significant impacts on land and other resources as a result of growing the biomass feedstock. There appear to be no other effects on land or other resources.

Environmental Impact

Greenhouse gas emissions from the use of biomass pellets are likely to be slightly higher than emissions from primary solid biomass for heat and power production, because the use of pellets introduces another processing stage (that is, pellet production) between growing the biomass and its eventual conversion into heat or power. Pellets can also be transported over longer distances, which could result in more emissions from transportation. The effect of this will depend on the modes of transport used. For similar reasons, the fossil fuel intensity of pellet use is likely to be slightly higher than that of other types of primary solid biomass (table 2.10).

The one area in which the use of biomass pellets for heat and power production is clearly superior is the cost of emissions reductions. Because pellets are economically attractive (that is, they have lower energy costs than the most likely fossil fuel alternatives), emissions reductions can be achieved at no cost by installing pellet-burning appliances. Even where incentives are available to encourage early replacement of existing appliances with new equipment that uses pellets, these costs (incentives) are likely to be negligible per MT of reduced CO_2 emissions over the lifetime of an appliance.

Table 2.10 Summary of Issues and Impacts Related to Energy Production from Solid Biomass

	Traditional biomass	Modern and industrial systems		
		Co-firing biomass	Heat and power production	Wood pellet systems (for domestic heat)
Economic				
Production cost	Generally cheaper than most likely alternatives (kerosene, LPG, and so forth)	Biomass: $3.50–$4.50/mBTU Coal: $1.50–$3.50/mBTU (fuel cost/net unit of input)	Biomass: $0.05–$0.12/kWh Coal: $0.02–$0.04/kWh Gas: $0.04–$0.07/kWh Oil: $0.05–$0.10/kWh (variable cost/unit of output)	Biomass: $15–$25/mBTU Coal: $8–$12/mBTU Gas: $25–$35/mBTU Oil: $20–$25/mBTU (variable cost/unit of output)
Socioeconomic				
Employment/unit of energy	0.30–0.50 years/TOE Much higher than fossil fuels (FTE/unit of input)	0.02–0.04 years FTE/TOE Much higher than fossil fuels (FTE/unit of input)	0.02–0.04 years FTE/TOE Much higher than fossil fuels (FTE/unit of input)	0.02–0.04 years FTE/TOE Much higher than fossil fuels (FTE/unit of input)
Potential for smallholders	High: Small-scale production is the norm.	Low: generally requires very large volumes of wood	Medium: small-scale production is feasible in some circumstances.	Medium: small-scale pellet production is feasible.
Land and other resources				
Efficiency of land use	Not applicable–traditional biomass production is not generally an exclusive land use.	Temperate forest plantations: 2.6–5.2 TOE/ha/yr (10–20 m^3) Temperate energy crops: 5.2–7.8 TOE/ha/yr (20–30 m^3) Tropical forest plantations: 5.2–7.8 TOE/ha/yr (20–30 m^3) Field/forest/processing residues are also possible		
Potential for improvement of degraded land	High: Small-scale planting and agroforestry has potential for traditional biomass production	Low: the very large volumes of wood required are unlikely to make this feasible.	Medium: Yields on degraded land are likely to be lower than those given above and quite large volumes are required. Bioenergy production will only be feasible in places where significant areas of degraded land are available for production.	

(continued)

Table 2.10 (Continued)

		Modern and industrial systems		
	Traditional biomass	**Co-firing biomass**	**Heat and power production**	**Wood pellet systems (for domestic heat)**
Impact on natural forests	Variable: traditional biomass collection can lead to forest degradation and deforestation in some circumstances. It has also been shown to occasionally aid in reforestation (tree planting for biomass collection)	High: the very large volumes of wood required are likely to require large-scale plantation development.	Low: If processing residues are utilized (likely to be the most attractive biomass source in many locations). High–If forest plantation or energy crop development is required, and large-scale heat and power generation is planned.	
Impact on agriculture	Variable–fuelwood collection is often integrated into cycles of shifting cultivation. However, collection of field residues can have a negative impact on soil fertility.	Low–medium to large-scale production of biomass for energy is likely to result in conversion of forest into energy crops rather than conversion of agricultural land.		
Resource competition	Not applicable–traditional collection of biomass does not divert food crops or utilizable wood fiber to bioenergy.	Variable–medium to large-scale production of biomass for energy does increase competition for industry and small-size wood uses. The impact of this depends on whether such resources are currently utilized by the forest processing industry. Currently, these impacts are felt in developed countries; however, if production shifts to developing countries there could be competition for resources.		
Environmental				
Energy intensity (fossil fuel input/unit of energy output)	Not applicable–traditional biomass production uses few or no fossil fuel inputs.		6.25 percent (Mann, 1997)	8.83–12.76 percent (Katers)

Carbon intensity (carbon-dioxide emissions/unit of energy output)	Variable–depends on whether the biomass is harvested sustainably.	46g/kWh (Mann, 1997) Coal: 910g/kWh (DoE 2000) *Update with IEA emissions report*	120–210kilograms/mBTU (Katers)
Cost/tCO2e avoided	Not applicable	$34–92 (replacing coal)	
Impact on water resources	Not applicable	Medium/high water-demand tree and energy crops generally have a much higher water demand than pasture and agricultural crops with a few exceptions (for example, rice, sugarcane). This is particularly true for some of the higher-yielding crops such as eucalyptus, willow, poplars. Water availability and demand is likely to be a limiting factor in biomass crop expansion. Variable impact on water quality–forest plantations and other biomass energy crops can have positive impacts on water quality where they replace agricultural crops, but the overall impact varies greatly by site.	
Impact on Soil Resources	Medium–traditional biomass collection generally leads to some land degradation unless it is within the limits of land and forest productivity.	Variable; forest plantations and other biomass energy crops can have positive impacts on soil erosion and increase soil nutrients. However, intensive production of biomass crops for energy is likely to degrade soils and require artificial inputs in many cases.	
Impact on biodiversity	Medium; traditional biomass collection is likely to lead to some negative effects on biodiversity. The magnitude of these effects will depend on the extent to which it leads to forest degradation.	Variable; forest plantations and other biomass energy crops are likely to have some negative impacts on biodiversity unless they replace agricultural crops. In addition, the most productive biomass energy crops are likely to be introduced species in many locations.	

NOTES

1. According to the IEA (2007, p. 5), "Primary solid biomass is defined as any plant matter used directly as fuel or converted into other forms before combustion. This covers a multitude of woody materials generated by industrial process or provided directly by forestry and agriculture (firewood, wood chips, bark, sawdust, shavings, chips, sulphite lyes also known as black liquor, animal materials/wastes and other solid biomass). Charcoal is included here."

2. The FAO definition of woodfuel (that is, the use of wood for energy) includes the wood used to manufacture charcoal.

3. The developed regions used in this study are North America (Canada and the United States); the 27 members of the European Union (EU) plus Iceland, Norway, and Switzerland; and Australia, Japan, and New Zealand. The developing regions are as defined by the World Bank at http://go.worldbank.org/9FV1KFE8P0. The Europe and Central Asia region excludes EU members.

4. The price of these materials is increasing in some regions (such as Europe), as a result of competition between the forest-processing and energy sectors. In the near future, the cost of these materials could be similar to the cost of agricultural and forest residues.

5. Where there is an opportunity cost of using forest thinnings as a source of energy (for example, for pulp and panel production), that cost rather than its production cost is the more appropriate measure of its actual cost. Where this demand is high, the opportunity costs may be higher than the production costs shown here. (For further discussion, see the section on the economic viability of liquid biofuels production in chapter 3).

6. The use of processing residues is likely to create much less employment than growing energy crops or collecting residues on site, but in most cases the employment generated is probably still greater than in other forms of energy.

7. Most of these studies examine situations in which biomass is co-fired with fossil fuels. The greenhouse gas reductions reported here are converted to compare only the emissions from the biomass components against the fossil fuels they replace. Emissions of other greenhouse gases in these studies have also been converted to CO_2 equivalents.

8. Higher reductions are generally achieved when biomass is compared with coal rather than natural gas.

9. Woodfuels may not always be the least expensive option. A study in Tanzania, for example, finds that in addition to the upfront cost of stoves, the total monthly cost for consumers is about $18 for a refill of LPG or $20.80 to purchase charcoal. The advantage of charcoal is that a household can phase its purchases, whereas the expenses for LPG have to be made upfront. Consumption choices often depend on cash availability, supply reliability, and supplier ability to portion energy supplies (World Bank 2009).

10. Anecdotal evidence suggests that woodfuel combustion may have some positive health benefits, including the ability of smoke to act as a mosquito repellant, thereby reducing the incidence of malaria. A 2007 review of the question finds that there is insufficient scientific evidence to support the theory (Biran and others 2007).

11. Although the study includes the use of coal as well as solid biomass for energy, coal use is relatively small, suggesting that almost all of this impact is caused by traditional uses of solid biomass for energy.

12. Note that this is an overestimate, as it does not include the energy required to produce and transport the kerosene.

13. There are probably numerous small-scale power stations producing heat and power in rural areas in some developing countries. Statistics for India in 2004, for example, show more than 1,900 power stations using biomass, with an average generating capacity of 0.4MW (Indian Ministry of Non-Conventional Energy Sources, quoted in Abe 2005). In addition, almost all large-scale forest-processing facilities in developed countries (and in developing countries such as Brazil) produce heat (and sometimes electricity) for their own operations, and heat and power generation is common in some agricultural-processing facilities worldwide (for example, sugar refineries).

14. Most of these studies examine situations in which biomass is co-fired with fossil fuels. The greenhouse gas reductions reported here are converted to compare the emissions from only the biomass components against the fossil fuels they have replaced. Emissions of other greenhouse gases in these studies have also been converted to CO_2 equivalents.

15. The efficiency of transformation (energy output as a proportion of energy content) is not very different for coal and biomass in modern facilities; both types of fuel are less efficient than heat and power production fuelled by natural gas.

16. Combustion efficiency is the proportion of the energy content of the fuel that is converted into usable heat and this is now about 80-85 percent in modern appliances.

CHAPTER THREE

Liquid Biofuels

Key Messages

- Liquid biofuels are expected to have mainly indirect effects on forests, stemming from the displacement of agriculture and ranching activities.
- Based on current targets, significant increases in the consumption of liquid biofuel are projected, with the largest growth in the United States (bioethanol) and the European Union (biodiesel), followed by Latin America and the Caribbean (bioethanol) and India and China (biodiesel).
- Bioenergy production from liquid biofuels can have both positive and negative effects on the poor. Production can create employment and raise income, but it can increase food insecurity if staple crops are used for energy production.
- Climate change impacts are highly uncertain and have the potential to be both positive and negative, depending on the crop used to produce biofuels and the type of land use present before development.

Liquid biofuels are produced principally from agricultural crops. They consist of the following alcohol and biodiesel fuels:

- *Alcohol production from sugar crops.* This is currently the main type of liquid biofuel production in developing countries. It consists principally of ethanol production from sugarcane.
- *Alcohol production from starch crops.* This is currently the main type of liquid biofuel production in developed countries. It consists principally of

alcohol production from corn. This system could be considered in developing countries. Because it has implications for poverty (with respect to food prices) and natural resource management, it should be examined separately.

- *Biodiesel production from edible oils.* This is currently the main type of biodiesel production. It has important implications for poverty (in terms of its impact on food prices and food security). The main source of biodiesel in this category comes from oil palm.
- *Biodiesel production from nonedible oils.* Production from nonedible oils is currently insignificant, but interest in Jatropha is developing rapidly. Because it is based on nonedible feedstocks, it has different implications for poverty and natural resource management from the other agricultural options for biofuel production.
- *Alcohol production from cellulose (wood and grasses).* Efforts are under way to develop higher-energy yields per unit of land, increase energy efficiency, and address concerns about diverting food crops to bioenergy. Alcohol production from cellulose is often referred to as a second-generation biofuel technology.
- *Higher alcohols, biodiesel, and other oils from cellulose.* A variety of thermo-mechanical technologies (biomass-to-liquid [BTL] processes) are being examined. These sources are second-generation biofuel technology.
- *Third-generation biofuels.* More efficient and advanced technologies for bio-fuel production are also at an early stage of development. They are briefly described in appendix D.

BIOETHANOL FOR FUEL

Most countries currently produce all of the bioethanol required to meet their needs. The main exceptions are the United States (which imports 5–10 percent of its consumption requirements) and Japan and the Republic of Korea (which rely primarily on imports).

Production in the United States is based mostly on corn; production in the European Union is based on a mixture of grains and, on a smaller scale, sugar beet. Production of bioethanol from nonfood crops is being tested on a small scale; it is just beginning to be developed on a larger scale. One facility (Range Fuels in the state of Georgia, in the United States) is being constructed with a first-phase capacity of about 60,000 MT/year and eventual capacity of 300,000 MT/year. The plant, which will use wood as feedstock, is currently under construction. Several other plants are operating on a trial basis. Other plants under construction use diverse feedstocks, such as straw, citrus waste, and poplar wood (see appendix table C.2 for a list of biofuel facilities in the United States).

Brazil is by far the largest exporter of bioethanol for fuel use. Its production is based on sugarcane. Production in other developing countries is based on a mixture of sugarcane, molasses, tubers, and grains, including corn, sweet sorghum, and wheat.

Argentina and some developing countries (for example, Indonesia, Pakistan, and South Africa) are also significant ethanol exporters. Because international trade statistics do not break out ethanol exports by use, it is not possible to identify how much of their exports is used for fuel.

Long-Term Trend

Consumption of bioethanol for fuel has increased markedly since 1975 (figure 3.1). Brazil and the United States are the two major bioethanol consumers; each has a long history of bioethanol consumption for fuel. Consumption in Brazil increased rapidly during the 1980s to reach about 10 million MT a year; it remained at this level between the mid-1980s and 2006. In 2007 and 2008, rising sales of flex-fuel vehicles increased consumption, which surpassed 15 million MT in 2008 and is expected to continue to grow strongly in the

Figure 3.1   Annual Bioethanol Consumption for Fuel, by Region, 1975–2008

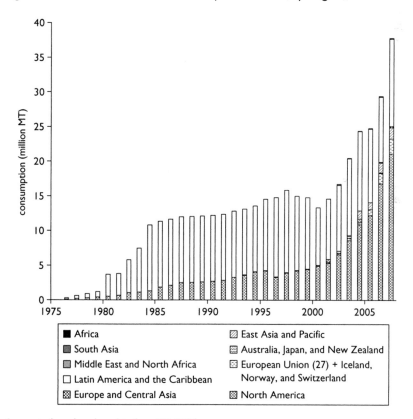

Source: Authors, based on data from IEA 2006b.
Note: One MT of bioethanol equals about 0.64 MT oil equivalent.

future, as flex-fuel vehicles replace conventional vehicles. Consumption in the United States increased gradually until 2000. It has increased almost fivefold since then, to about 28 million MT in 2008, making the United States the world's largest consumer.

Canada consumed about 1.3 million MT of bioethanol in 2008. In the European Union, the main consumers are France, Germany, Spain, and Sweden. Australia, Japan, and New Zealand consume very small amounts of bioethanol for fuel (table 3.1). In developing regions, the main consumers of bioethanol for fuel are Brazil, China, India, Colombia, and Thailand. There is currently no significant consumption of bioethanol for fuel reported in any other developing countries.

Outlook

Bioethanol consumption is projected to increase sevenfold, from about 25 million MT in 2005 to 170 million MT in 2030 (figure 3.2). The United States accounts for the majority of projected consumption and most of this increase. The impact of the U.S. Renewable Fuel Standard (EPA 2008) has been officially projected only to 2022; these projections assume that no increases will occur after 2022.

Latin America and the Caribbean accounts for the next-largest share of projected bioethanol consumption, led by Brazil but including consumption in several other countries. Its share of global consumption does not increase markedly compared with the projections for the European Union and East Asia and Pacific, where significant growth is expected a result of the implementation of blending mandates. Other regions account for only a small share of projected consumption, although significant growth in consumption in Japan could occur if a blending mandate were introduced there.

Table 3.1 Bioethanol Consumption for Fuel, by Region, 2005–08				
Region	**2005**	**2006**	**2007**	**2008**
North America	12.2	16.8	21.1	29.7
European Union (27) + 3	0.9	1.5	2.2	3.1
Australia, Japan, New Zealand	0.0	0.1	0.0	0.2
East Asia and Pacific	1.0	1.4	1.6	1.8
Europe and Central Asia	0.0	0.1	0.2	0.3
Latin America and Caribbean	10.6	9.4	12.6	16.0
Middle East and North Africa	0.0	0.0	0.0	0.0
South Asia	0.1	0.1	0.1	0.2
Sub-Saharan Africa	0.0	0.0	0.0	0.1
Developed countries	13.2	18.3	23.4	33.0
Developing countries	11.6	11.0	14.5	18.4
World total	24.8	29.3	37.9	51.4

Source: Authors, based on IEA 2006b.

Figure 3.2 Projected Annual Bioethanol Consumption for Fuel, by Region, 2010–30

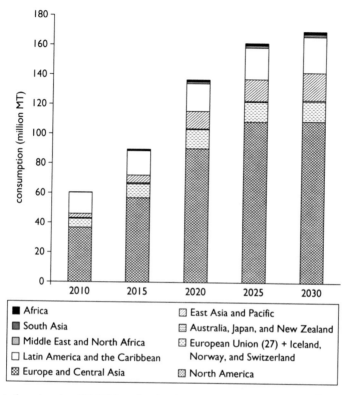

Source: Authors, based on IEA 2006b and national policy targets.

The official projection for bioethanol production in the United States includes a cap on production from corn of 15 billion gallons in 2015 (equal to roughly 45 million MT). Additional production increases are expected to come from cellulose and other sources (which are still speculative).

BIODIESEL FOR FUEL

As with bioethanol, most countries produce their own biodiesel to meet domestic demand. Biodiesel production in Brazil and the United States is largely based on soybeans. Production in China and Japan is based mostly on waste vegetable oils (although China is examining rapeseed and Jatropha for future development). The main feedstock in Canada is rapeseed. Rapeseed is also the main feedstock in Europe, along with imported oil or oilseeds (for example, palm oil); waste animal fats; and vegetable oils. Production in

Indonesia and Malaysia is based on oil palm (although Indonesia is also considering Jatropha).[1]

Long-Term Trend

The use of biodiesel for fuel is much more recent than the use of bioethanol, with significant consumption starting only in the late 1990s. Total consumption is only about 1/10th that of bioethanol (figure 3.3).

The European Union is by far the largest consumer of biodiesel, with consumption in 24 EU countries in 2007 (table 3.2). The largest EU consumers are Germany, France, Italy, Spain, the Netherlands, and the United Kingdom, which together account for about 80 percent of all consumption in the European Union. Consumption in the United States amounted to about 1.5 million MT in 2007, a strong increase from the 800,000 MT consumed in 2006.

Figure 3.3   Annual Biodiesel Consumption, by Region, 1970–2008

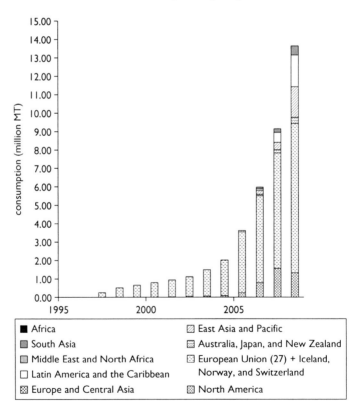

Source: Authors, based on biodiesel statistics from government agencies, trade associations, and consulting firms.
Note: One MT of biodiesel equals about 0.90 MT oil equivalent.

Table 3.2	Annual Biodiesel Consumption, by Region, 2005–08 (thousand MT)			
Region	**2005**	**2006**	**2007**	**2008**
Africa	0	0	0	0
Australia, Japan, and New Zealand	0	84	172	330
East Asia and Pacific	126	210	404	1,655
Europe and Central Asia	0	0	0	0
European Union (27), Iceland, Norway, and Switzerland	2,702	4,705	6,267	8,107
Latin America and the Caribbean	22	84	534	1,724
Middle East and North Africa	0	0	0	0
North America	268	791	1,568	1,331
South Asia	0	100	200	500
Developed countries	2,970	5,579	8,007	9,768
Developing countries	148	394	1,138	3,879
World total	3,118	5,974	9,145	13,647

Source: Authors, based on IEA 2006b and national policy targets.

Consumption in Canada is negligible, but production capacity amounts to about 1.3 million MT.

The sharp rise in the price of vegetable oil in the first half of 2008 resulted in a drop in demand in the European Union and the United States, as even with price incentives, biodiesel was uncompetitive with diesel fuels. Demand has recovered since the return of vegetable oil and biodiesel prices to competitive, but still uneconomic, levels. On the basis of government mandates, 2009 consumption in these major markets is expected to exceed 2007 levels.

Consumption of biodiesel in developing countries is relatively low: in 2007 significant consumption was recorded only in Argentina, Brazil, Colombia, China, India, Indonesia, and Malaysia. Brazil increased consumption in 2006 (to 45,000 MT) and 2007 (to 430,000 MT). India consumed about 200,000 MT of biodiesel in 2007, and Indonesia and Malaysia together consumed about 220,000 MT.

Outlook

Biodiesel consumption is projected to increase, from less than 5 million MT in 2005 to almost 65 million MT in 2030 (figure 3.4). Initially, the European Union is expected to account for the majority of the projected increase, but growth in developing countries (particularly India and China) is likely to account for most of the expected growth in consumption after 2020. The forecast assumes that the proposed biodiesel blending mandates in India and China will be implemented by 2020; continued high growth after this is expected as a result of continued high growth in total diesel consumption in

Figure 3.4   Projected Annual Biodiesel Consumption, by Region, 2010–30

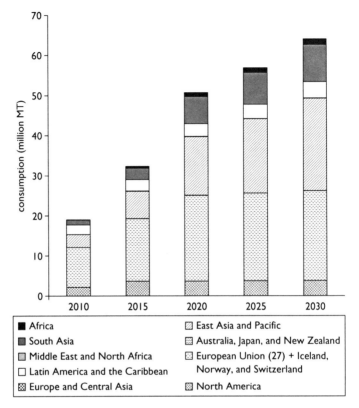

Source: Authors, based on IEA 2006b and national policy targets.

these countries. Developing countries are expected to overtake developed countries in biodiesel consumption in 2020.

ECONOMIC VIABILITY OF LIQUID BIOFUEL PRODUCTION

The cost of liquid biofuel production is determined by the cost of the biomass feedstock and the cost of its conversion into liquid biofuels. These costs are, in turn, determined by the cost of growing, harvesting, and transporting the feedstock plus the capital and operational costs associated with processing. The local or export market values of crops used to produce liquid biofuels (their opportunity costs) are often a more appropriate measure of the feedstock costs than actual costs, because most of these crops have significant alternative uses (most are major food commodities). Except for production from cellulose (discussed below), feedstock costs account for the major share of total production costs for liquid biofuels.

For comparison with the price of gasoline or diesel, the feedstock cost per liter of liquid biofuels can be calculated as the market price of these crops (per MT) divided by the biofuel yield per MT. For a proper comparison on an energy basis, this conversion should also take into account the relative energy content of the liquid biofuel (negligible for biodiesel but about 50 percent for bioethanol, a result of its lower energy content compared with gasoline).

Ethanol and gasoline yields from crops vary widely (table 3.3). For example, 1 MT of maize can produce roughly 400 liters of bioethanol, equivalent to 260 liters of gasoline in terms of its energy content. The differences between these two measures for the same crop reflect the oil content of the crop (the oil content of rapeseed, for example, is roughly twice that of soybeans). Most vegetable oils have similar specific gravities (about 1,100l/MT); the conversion of oil to biodiesel and biodiesel to fossil diesel results in negligible losses in terms of yield and energy content.

The main area of uncertainty about yields in liquid biofuel production concerns cellulosic liquid biofuel production. The theoretical yields are known, but actual yields depend on the production processes chosen and their costs. It is not yet clear whether more expensive production processes will be adopted to achieve higher yields or whether simpler technologies will be adopted on a

Table 3.3 Typical Yields for Main Crops Used to Produce Liquid Biofuels, 2008

Feedstock	Yield		Comments
Crops for bioethanol	Ethanol (l/MT)	Gasoline equivalent (l/MT)	
Maize	400	260	Ethanol yield range narrow (370–410 l/MT)
Cassava	180	120	
Cellulose	150	100	Ethanol yield range wide (100–300 l/MT)
Sweet sorghum	108	70	
Sugarcane	70	45	
Crops for biodiesel	Oil (l/MT)	Diesel equivalent (l/MT)	
Rapeseed oil	1,100	1,100	
Soybean oil	1,100	1,100	
Palm oil	1,100	1,100	
Rapeseed	440	440	Yield with good oil extraction technology
Soybeans	210	210	
Cellulose	—	125	Biodiesel yield range wide (75–200 l/MT)

Source: Authors, based on calculations from FAO 2008b.
Note: — = Not available.

large scale. Significant research and development on these technologies is being conducted, with the aim of reducing some of these costs.

The cost of converting feedstocks into liquid biofuels depends on labor costs, the cost of energy and other inputs, the scale of operations, and the processing technology. In the United States, the nonfeedstock cost of producing ethanol is about $0.15/l for maize and about $0.25/l for sugarcane (the figure is slightly lower in Brazil) (FAO 2008b). Processing costs for the other crops are uncertain, although some studies in China and Thailand are reporting non-feedstock production costs of about $0.20/l for cassava (FAO 2008b). Processing costs to convert vegetable oils into biodiesel may be about $0.15/l. The cost of production is also affected by whether markets exist for some of the by-products of the conversion processes and the values of those by-products.

The cost of liquid biofuel production for 2005–09 is estimated based on the liquid biofuel yields shown above, international commodity prices, and current nonfeedstock processing costs (figure 3.5). These figures were converted to the cost per liter in gasoline or diesel equivalent; for comparison purposes world prices for gasoline and diesel are also shown in figure 3.5.

Figure 3.5   World Prices of Gasoline, Diesel, Maize, Rapeseed Oil, and Palm Oil, 2005–09

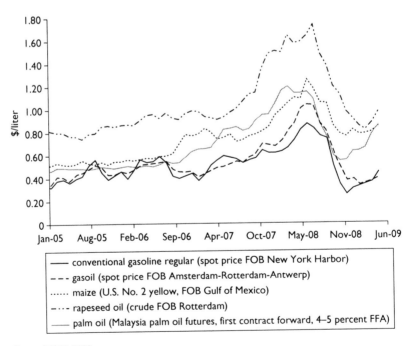

Source: USDA 2009.
Note: Costs of liquid biofuel feedstocks were adjusted for energy content to allow comparison in terms of energy equivalent.

Throughout 2005–09 the costs of liquid biofuels were almost always higher than the cost of their fossil fuel alternatives. The cost per liter of bioethanol from maize and gasoline was roughly similar over the period, but bioethanol was more expensive in terms of its energy content. The cost of bioethanol production from sugarcane was generally lower than the cost of production from maize, but it was still slightly more expensive (in economic terms) than gasoline in almost all countries other than Brazil.[2]

The cost of biodiesel production was also higher than the cost of diesel produced from fossil fuels. In this case, a more direct comparison can be made, because the energy content of the two alternatives is roughly the same. Biodiesel production from palm oil was slightly more expensive than diesel (on a few occasions, it was broadly comparable in cost). In contrast, biodiesel production from rapeseed oil was far more expensive than diesel (by about $0.40/l).

Under very specific circumstances, liquid biofuels may be an economically viable alternative to fossil fuels. However, given the demands placed on these feedstocks for their use as food and feed, it seems likely that their use as biofuel feedstocks is not economically viable now or in the near future; they will continue to require subsidies and other policy measure to encourage their use.

SOCIAL AND ENVIRONMENTAL IMPACTS

Impact on Food Security

The impact of biofuels on global food prices is highly variable. It depends on the feedstock used and whether agricultural land is diverted for production. Historically, agricultural prices have been affected by energy prices, especially in countries that employ intensive farming practices, because the increased cost of fossil fuel–based inputs, such as diesel, fertilizers, and pesticides, eventually reduces output. With the growing use of agricultural commodities for bioenergy production, energy prices and feedstock prices are increasingly being linked (Raswant, Hart, and Romano 2008).

Over the course of 2008, global food prices were highly volatile. During the same period, liquid biofuel feedstock prices also experienced wide fluctuations. Although food (and fuel) prices have fallen from their 2008 peaks, major grain prices remain above average, and prices for most major food crops are projected to remain well above 2004 levels through 2015 (World Bank 2008a).

Price volatility and high prices of key commodities can have devastating consequences on the poor. In developing countries, urban and rural landless households, wage-earning households, rural households that are net purchasers of food, and urban consumers suffer most from high food prices (Raswant, Hart, and Romano 2008; Rossi and Lambrou 2008). The countries that are most vulnerable to food price increases are typically those that rely on imported petroleum. Increasing production of biofuels is likely to exacerbate this vulnerability (CGIAR 2008). Those that are most likely to benefit from increasing prices include producers actively involved in the cultivation and sale of agricultural commodities or biofuel feedstocks.

In response to these concerns, some countries (including China and Mexico) have placed a moratorium on using edible grains (especially corn) as a fuel source. In contrast, in the United States (the leading global producer) almost one-third of total corn production is expected to go toward ethanol production in 2009 (USDA 2009). In developing countries, staples such as cassava are also being considered as feedstock. Given that cassava is the primary source of nutrition for much of Africa, such a step could have serious implications for food security.

Also of concern is the diversion of resources, including land, water, fertilizers, and pesticides, into fuel rather than food production. Food security may be compromised if high-quality agricultural lands are used for energy crops, pushing agriculture and ranching onto more vulnerable, lower-quality lands. Converting forest into bioenergy plantations or clearing forests for biofuel feedstocks could increase the food insecurity of forest-dependent communities (Rossi and Lambrou 2008).

These impacts are often short term, and there is some potential for biofuel developments to have less impact on food security over the long term. A 2008 report notes that biofuel production can be beneficial to small producers when production takes place far from large cities, inputs are expensive, and food prices low. Under these conditions, food production tends to be uncompetitive, making biofuels a better option (Raswant, Hart, and Romano 2008). Higher feedstock prices and higher volumes of marketable produce can supplement rural producer income and create jobs (CGIAR 2008).

Impact on Land Tenure/Access

Rising demand for bioenergy may lead to rapid expansion of large plantations. If the expansion moves into areas where land rights are not well defined, conflict can result. Conflicts may include land appropriation by large private entities, forced reallocations by the government in places where the land is owned by the state, or government mandates to plant certain crops (box 3.1). The poor may be tempted to sell their land at low prices; those without clear land titles may lose their livelihood if the lands they use for farming are repurposed for biofuel production (Raswant, Hart, and Romano 2008). In Indonesia and Colombia, there are reports that smallholders have been forced from their land. In 2000 land disputes with local communities were reported by each of the 81 oil palm plantation companies in Sumatra, Indonesia. Large plantation areas have been cleared without adequate resettlement provisions for displaced communities (Vermeulen and Goad 2006).

In some cases, restriction to land access has resulted in violence. In Colombia there have been reports that increasing demand for biofuels has resulted in land grabs in rural areas, resulting in the expulsion of subsistence farmers from their land and in some cases even deaths (Carroll 2008).[3]

Box 3.1   Forcing Farmers to Plant Jatropha in Myanmar

In 2005, in response to rising energy costs and protests over cuts in diesel subsidies, the government of Myanmar established a project to produce biodiesel from Jatropha. Various reports estimate that the planting area ranges from 200,000–400,000 hectares, with a planned expansion to 3 million hectares.

Production has occurred on large, centrally planned plantations, on military sites, and in rural villages. Farmers with more than 1 acre of land have been directed to plant Jatropha on their landholdings and often required pay for the seeds. Human rights groups have claimed that farmers who refuse to plant Jatropha may be jailed. Other reports suggest that military rulers have confiscated land and used forced labor in some locations. Another concern is that the required planting of Jatropha crops is displacing food production in the very poor, rural areas of Myanmar.

The directive has not been matched by adequate infrastructure (collection mechanisms, processing plants, distribution systems) to process the crop. As a result, Jatropha seed production has not translated into increased fuel production. In response, on February 27, 2009, a Japanese company, the Bio Energy Development Corp (JBEDC), announced that it will establish a joint venture with a Myanmar private company for biofuel development. The new company, Japan-Myanmar Green Energy, aims to export 5,000 MT of seeds in 2009 and start operating its first oil mill plant in 2010. It also plans to distribute and export Jatropha-derived fuel in addition to its seeds.

Source: Aye 2007; Lane 2008; *Time* 2009.

Rising demand for biofuels is likely to increase the value of land—with possible negative consequences for the poor. Higher land values may displace poor people from their land. Women may face additional hardship if they are displaced to lower-quality lands (Cotula, Dyer, and Vermeulen 2008).

Impact on Livelihoods

As a result of economies of scale, many bioenergy crops must be produced in large monocultures to be profitable.[4] One of the risks of large-scale bioenergy development is that land will be concentrated and that small farmers will lose their land, much of which has weak tenancy systems. It is a major social risk of biodiesel development.

Also of concern is the fact that small-scale farmers may have limited or no access to the capital required for large bioethanol or biodiesel operations. Oil processors and other intermediaries, rather than small and marginal farmers, often receive most of the profits from biofuels (Pahariya and Mukherjee 2007). For many peasant farmers, leasing their land to producers is the only way of benefiting at all from the industry—and even this is an option only for peasant farmers with larger areas of land (Roundtable on Responsible Soy 2008). In Indonesia, where 44 percent of productive palm oil plantations are managed by smallholders, there have been persistent reports that such farmers face difficult conditions, including minimal remuneration for their produce and indebtedness to palm oil companies (Colchester and others 2006).

Large plantations may offer an alternative to subsistence farming for some rural poor. In addition, plantations can provide amenities for employees and their families, including housing, water, electricity, roads, medical care, and schools (Koh and Wilcove 2007). Certain biofuel feedstocks can be used for food products, alcohol, livestock fodder, housing materials, and other uses.

Livelihood issues can also arise on plantations targeted for marginal and degraded lands, such as Jatropha plantations. In some countries, including India, a majority of the wastelands targeted for these plantations are collectively owned by villages and supply a wide variety of commodities, including food, fuelwood, fodder, and timber. Planting Jatropha or other crops on these lands may cause hardship, because the plantations could decrease available livestock fodder and other commodities (Rajagopal 2007).

Impact on Employment and Labor

Growing global demand for biofuels raises feedstock prices, which in turn raises producer income and land value. This may translate into an inflow of capital to rural areas, and it has the potential to create jobs (CGIAR 2008). In Brazil, for example, formal employment in the extended sugar-alcohol sector rose 52.9 percent between 2000 and 2005 (from about 643,000 to about 983,000) (table 3.4). Most of these jobs were located in the center-south of the country. Ethanol industry employees in São Paulo received wages 25.6 percent higher than the average Brazilian; wages of workers who worked directly on the sugarcane crop were 16.5 percent above average in 2005, according to the Brazilian Ministry of Labor and Employment (Moraes 2007).

Table 3.4 Formal Employment from Sugarcane, Ethanol, and Sugar Production in Brazil, 2000–05

Year	North-northeast[a]	Center-south[b]	All regions of Brazil
2000	250,224	392,624	642,848
2001	302,720	433,170	735,890
2002	289,507	475,086	764,593
2004	343,026	557,742	900,768
2005	364,443	618,161	982,604

Source: Moraes 2007.
a. Includes states of Alagoas, Bahia, Ceará, Maranhão, Pará, Paraíba, Pernambuco, Piauí, Rio Grande do Norte, Sergipe, and Tocantins.
b. Incudes states of Espírito Santo, Goiás, Paraná, Mato Grosso, Mato Grosso do Sul, Minas Gerais, Rio de Janeiro, Rio Grande do Sul, Santa Catarina, and São Paulo.

As biofuel plantations become larger, the processes for harvesting feedstocks can become more mechanized, reducing the number of jobs for rural workers (Greenergy 2008b). Mechanisms could be developed to ensure that small producers benefit from bioenergy production and markets. One example would be to create specific institutional arrangements to ensure participation by small producers and rural communities in decentralized production and processing through contract farming arrangements or cooperatives (WWF 2008).

Jobs associated with bioenergy production tend to provide more stability and better benefits than other rural jobs (Greiler 2007; Rossi and Lambrou 2008). However, there are some concerns regarding the quality and safety of these jobs. Many of the jobs are for migrant workers, who earn low wages and face poor, even dangerous, working conditions (Greiler 2007; Rossi and Lambrou 2008).

Gender Concerns

In many developing countries, women have fewer opportunities for land ownership and lack the necessary access to the resources (land and water) and inputs (chemical fertilizers and pesticides) biofuel plantations require. In addition, women, who are often unable to use land as collateral, generally lack access to formal credit schemes, thus limiting their ability to acquire such productive inputs. Because of these constraints, female-headed households may face more barriers to accessing the market for these external inputs and thus participating in biofuels production (Rossi and Lambrou 2008).

Particularly in Africa, women are allocated low-quality lands for agricultural activities. Biofuel production targeting these lands can move women's agricultural activities toward increasingly marginal lands, minimizing their household contributions and forcing them to spend more time performing household duties, such as collecting fuelwood and water. When directly working on biofuel plantations, women are usually paid less than their male counterparts, especially when they are drawn into unpaid work in order to help their husbands meet production targets (Rossi and Lambrou 2008).

Health Concerns

Studies of the air quality benefits of liquid biofuels versus fossil fuels yield conflicting results. A 2009 study published in the *Proceedings of the National Academy of Sciences* finds that as a result of fertilizer and fossil fuel inputs, corn ethanol has higher health costs from particulate matter than gasoline ($0.09 per liter for gasoline versus $0.24 per liter for corn ethanol produced with coal for process heat) (Hill and others 2009).[5] In contrast, initial research from the ongoing Life Cycle Impact Assessment (funded by a joint project by the University of California–Berkeley, the University of Illinois, the Lawrence Berkeley National Laboratory, and BP) suggests that biofuels substantially reduce health damages from primary fine particle emissions (DOE 2009). Direct health risks are associated with all forms of agricultural labor. These risks stem primarily from the inappropriate use of agrochemicals, but injuries and the effects of working long hours performing strenuous work also make agricultural work risky (Greiler 2007).

Adaptation Challenges

Farmers are more likely to adapt bioenergy feedstocks that are familiar to them or those that have already been proven to be profitable. The maturation phase of several years for tree species or uncertainties in cultivation and returns on investments present significant barriers to adoption, especially for small farmers (Rajagopal 2007). Additional challenges may also limit farmers' abilities to adapt to new biofuel crops, both on and off the farm (box 3.2).

Box 3.2   On-Farm and Off-Farm Adaptation Challenges

A variety of challenges may make it difficult for farmers to adapt to new biofuel crops. On-farm challenges include the following:

- Institutional structures: adapting to fit production models that allow economies of scale. Large-scale systems are often economically favored; smallholder farmers may need to organize into cooperatives or outgrower schemes to gain access to markets.
- Environmental impacts: increased or decreased soil fertility, water pollution, and downstream effects, such as the draining of wetlands.
- Technology: access to farm technology that increases yields (the Brazilian experience suggests that this can be achieved through the selection of better varieties and irrigation).
- Changes in land use affecting access to land and the effects of biofuels on the cost of land, which are poorly understood.
- Need for flexibility to changes in the prices of feedstocks and to changes in the prices of inputs.

Off-farm challenges include the following:

- Employment patterns: much work in the biofuels sector is unskilled, but requirements for skilled labor are likely to increase.
- Investment: biofuel processing and distribution infrastructure can require substantial upfront investment.
- Need for flexibility: converting current production systems into biofuels production systems; flexibility within processing plants also a constraint.
- Adapting regulations: changing regulation to suit efficient production processes will be needed in some cases (in some countries, increasing efficiency gains in co-generation is not an option, because producers are not allowed to sell into the grid).

Source: Peskett and others 2007.

Impact on Land Use

One percent of the world's arable land is currently dedicated to biofuel production—about 14 million hectares of land (LMC 2008). Land conversion is likely to take place to accommodate the projected increases in bioethanol and biodiesel resulting from current country targets.

The increase in area for bioenergy feedstock cultivation will come from a variety of land uses, principally agricultural production, natural ecosystems (forests), and marginal lands. At a global level, the scale of this demand for land will depend critically on three factors:

- The future level of demand for biofuels, underpinned largely by government policies designed to encourage biofuel consumption
- Future growth in the yields of ethanol and biodiesel per hectare
- The extent to which ethanol and biodiesel are traded internationally (to the extent that cost-competitive producers of biofuels are also the most efficient producers in terms of land use, enhanced trade should moderate future demand for land).

Land-use forecasts vary widely depending on assumptions and methodologies. The figures presented here are therefore indicative, intended only to show broad trends. Analysis by LMC International, a British economic and business consultancy for the agribusiness sector, suggests possible land-use changes resulting from fossil fuel developments. The numbers presented here are indicative of what could happen; they do not reflect an on-the-ground analysis of in-country trends. Its analysis is based on current biofuel production trends and the assumption that current government targets will remain in place through 2020. As countries begin to evaluate the necessary resources and economics of meeting these targets, these numbers may change. The World Bank is currently conducting a land-use analysis that will evaluate large-scale land acquisition in countries resulting from agriculture and forestry investments (including for bioenergy); it will provide much more complete and accurate numbers than those presented here.

Likely potential demand for land is projected through 2020 under three outcomes for liquid biofuel demand and international trade (table 3.5).[6] The analysis assumes that crop yields continue to increase at the annual rates they have since 1990—2.3 percent for carbohydrate crops (weighted by their starch/sugars content) and 1.5 percent for oil-bearing crops (weighted by their oil content).

Three scenarios are examined:

- *Business as usual.* This scenario is designed broadly to reflect the commercial and policy environment that prevails today—that is, governments continue to set ambitious targets for biofuel use and maintain trade barriers

Table 3.5 Assumptions Regarding Potential Demand for Liquid Biofuels, Main Local Feedstocks, and Output from Local Feedstocks in Key Markets to 2020

			Scenario		
Location/fuel	Potential demand for biofuels (billion liters)	Principal local feedstock	Business as usual (percent domestic feedstock)	Enhanced trade (percent domestic feedstock)	Slow growth (percent domestic feedstock)
Brazil					
Ethanol	61	Sugarcane	100	100	100
Biodiesel	5	Soybeans	100	100	100
EU-27					
Ethanol	17	Wheat	90	45	90
Biodiesel	27	Rapeseed	30	15	30
United States					
Ethanol	58	Corn	93	47	93
Biodiesel	4	Soybeans	100	50	100
Rest of world					
Ethanol	78	Pro rata	90	45	90
Biodiesel	26	Pro rata	80	40	80
World					
Ethanol	213	Pro rata	94	61	94
Biodiesel	61	Pro rata	61	34	61
All	275	Pro rata	86	55	86

Source: LMC International 2008.

Note: The United States grants tariff-free entry to 7 percent of its ethanol demand from Caribbean countries, which explains the 93 percent for U.S. ethanol in the business-as-usual column. The European Union grants tariff-free entry to products from developing countries, which explains the 90 percent self-sufficiency ratio in the business-as-usual column. Enhanced trade is assumed to reduce self-sufficiency in biofuel output to 50 percent of its business-as-usual level in all countries/regions except Brazil.

designed to ensure that the vast majority of this demand is supplied with biofuels that are produced using locally grown raw materials. This outcome does not necessarily encourage the most efficient land use, increasing pressure on feedstock supplies and agricultural land.

- *Enhanced trade.* This outcome is intended to reflect a situation in which governments actively encourage biofuel trade by lowering trade barriers, with a view to boosting production from the most land-efficient feedstocks. Under this scenario, 75 percent of biofuel demand is met by the most efficient feedstocks (sugarcane for ethanol, palm oil for biodiesel); the rest is supplied by the current mix of raw materials. By fostering trade, this outcome moderates the demand for agricultural land.

- *Slow growth.* This scenario is designed to illustrate what might happen if a sustained period of low energy prices were to result in slower growth of biofuel production than is envisaged by government targets. Such an outcome would result not because governments lower their biofuel use targets but instead because the prices at which biofuels are supplied are too high to be acceptable to the majority of price-sensitive users of such fuels. This situation may arise because many government policies use tax incentives and buy-out penalties to promote biofuel use. Demand in some countries (notably Brazil) is underpinned by flex-fuel vehicles that allow consumers to choose whether to use gasoline or ethanol. In such instances, governments have created a set of demands for biofuels at prices that are linked to those of gasoline or diesel. The price that stimulates biofuel demand is the gasoline or diesel price plus the tax incentive/buy-out fee. If the price of the relevant biofuel rises above this level in a country, demand for the biofuel will switch off.[7] Under this scenario, governments continue to pursue inward-looking trade policies that are designed to promote the use of biofuels produced from local feedstocks. In this case, low biofuel prices, coupled with high trade barriers, limit crop prices and slow the conversion of land for arable crop production.

Under these scenarios, rising demand for the major carbohydrate and oilseed crops for food/feed uses could potentially increase the global area under these crops to more than 800 million hectares by 2020, an increase of 80 million hectares from 2008 (figure 3.6). Under this scenario, the area under oilseed crops is projected to expand to about 65 million hectares; the area under carbohydrate crops is projected to drop by roughly 25 million hectares. This difference reflects the comparatively high income elasticity of vegetable oils and meal (for animal feed) relative to carbohydrates and the relatively low yield of these crops relative to carbohydrate crops.

One of the greatest environmental concerns related to biofuel expansion is the deforestation and land clearing that comes with increasing capacity and expansion. In addition to direct land conversion, there are possible indirect impacts if land is taken away from other agricultural activities and the displaced farmers and ranchers clear new land to make up for the crop loss. There is also the potential for agricultural lands that have been set aside as conservation areas to be brought back into production if it becomes profitable for farmers to do so.

In this analysis, land use for crops for biofuel production is projected to increase by about 75 million hectares if government targets are to be met by 2020. This comprises about 45 million hectares under carbohydrate crops and 30 million hectares under oil-bearing crops.

Demand for land to grow crops for food and feed uses is the same in each scenario, but the demand for land to meet biofuel production is different. Considerable uncertainty exists over the amounts of extra land that will be needed

Figure 3.6   Global Area Needed to Meet Food/Feed and Potential Liquid
Biofuel Demand, 1980–2014

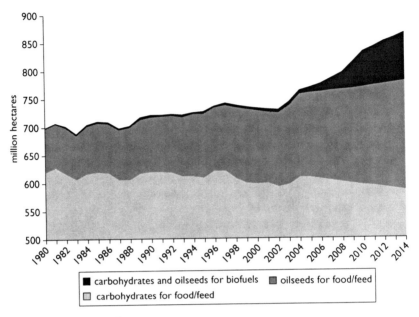

Source: LMC International 2008.

to meet biofuel demand; government policies toward trade and commercial factors—particularly the price of energy and the competitiveness of ethanol and biodiesel (and underlying crop values) as alternative fuels—can exert considerable influence over this demand.

Impact on the Environment

Liquid biofuels may affect the environment, including climate, water and soil resources, biodiversity, and air quality, in a variety of ways. The degree of impact depends greatly on previous land uses, geography, and the type of crop that is planted. Tables 3.6 and 3.7 highlight some of the most critical environmental, social, and economic impacts of liquid biofuels.

Impact on Climate

Estimation of the greenhouse gas balance of a biofuel feedstock requires examination of the entire production chain, including emissions from cultivation, extraction, transport, processing, distribution, and combustion. The main factors that determine whether a particular feedstock has potential to reduce emissions include the previous use of the land, the choice of crop and region

Table 3.6 Issues and Impacts Related to Alcohol Production from Corn, Sugarcane, Sweet Sorghum, Cassava, and Nypa

Issue	Cassava	Corn	Nypa	Sugarcane	Sweet sorghum
Cost					
Bioethanol yield	1,500–4,500 l/hectare (estimated)	3,400 l/hectare (U.S. average)	5,000–20,000 l/hectare (estimated)	6,000 l/hectare (Brazil average)	Estimated yields of up to 6,000 l/hectare (assuming two growing cycles a year); actual yields of 1,250 l/hectare in India
Economic effects					
Employment potential	Variable; some countries have partly mechanized production, but production is labor intensive in other locations	Low; mechanized process requires few laborers	High; production is extremely labor intensive; must be attended to daily for maximum yield	Variable; some countries (including Brazil) have partly mechanized production, but production is labor intensive in other locations	Variable; some countries have partly mechanized production, but production is labor intensive in other locations

(continued)

Table 3.6 (Continued)

Issue	Cassava	Corn	Nypa	Sugarcane	Sweet sorghum
Potential for smallholders	High; easily adapted, as result of global familiarity with crop; can be incorporated into small plots and has multiple uses; already widely planted	Low; economies of scale mean that corn is usually produced on large tracts of land requiring large upfront capital investments	Medium; multiple uses but extremely labor intensive; cultivation success depends on proximity to coastal zones	Medium; economies of scale mean that sugarcane is often produced on large tracts of land requiring large upfront capital investments. In Brazil, however, small producers currently account for roughly 30 percent of production.	High; easily adapted, as result of global familiarity with crop; can be incorporated into small plots and has multiple uses
Land and other resources					
Potential for improvement of degraded land	High; can be cultivated on marginal and degraded lands with low rainfall	Low; not suitable for cultivation on degraded lands	High; can help restore degraded coastal mangroves	Low; not suitable for cultivation on degraded lands	High; can be cultivated on marginal and degraded lands with low rainfall

Impact on natural forests	Low; planting targeted to occur on marginal and previously deforested land	Variable; lands reallocated from set-aside conservation lands may cause deforestation; increased production in United States may displace soy production to tropical countries, indirectly leading to deforestation (shifting cultivation)	Low; cultivated in tidal regions	Variable; although current expansion is targeted for previously cleared lands, there is risk that this will push other agriculture and ranching to clear new lands	Low; planting targeted to occur on marginal and previously deforested land
Impact on agriculture	Low; planting targeted for arid regions where other crops are not cultivated	High; increased production is likely to result in conversion of agricultural lands	Low; cultivated in tidal regions	Low; increased production is likely to result in conversion of ranching pastures rather than gricultural lands	Low; planting targeted for arid regions where other crops are not cultivated

(continued)

Table 3.6 (Continued)

Issue	Cassava	Corn	Nypa	Sugarcane	Sweet sorghum
Resource competition	High; price increases could have a negative impact on what is staple food for rural poor, especially in Africa	High; price increases can drive up global grain prices, affecting poor	Low; cultivated in tidal regions	Low; traditionally does not compete with food crops	Low; crop can provide both fuel and food
Environmental					
Energy intensity (fossil fuel input per unit of energy output)	9–10 (Thailand)	1.34 (United States)	—	8 (Brazil)	8 (12–16 in temperate areas)
Impact on water resources	Low; requires few water or fertilizer inputs	High; high water requirements; fertilizer runoff contributes to eutrophication of water bodies	Low; cultivated in tidal regions	Medium; mainly rain-fed irrigation; some water contamination from fertilizer runoff and effluent discharge from processing	Medium; requires few water inputs; some water contamination from fertilizer runoff
Impact on soil resources	Low; can help improve degraded soils	High; topsoil loss from wind and water erosion; high pesticide/fertilizer use degrades soils	Low; cultivated in tidal regions	High; burning exposes soil to erosion and removes nutrients; removal of bagasse for processing strips nutrients (this impact is avoided in mechanized harvesting)	Low; can help improve degraded soils

Impact on biodiversity	Variable; depends on where production takes place; can be low impact if confined to degraded and marginal lands	Variable; possible effects of shifting cultivation can impact biodiversity	Low; may improve coastal ecosystems	Variable; depends on where expansion takes place and the displacement of agriculture and ranchers, which may result in forest clearing	Variable; depends on where production takes place, can be low impact if confined to degraded and marginal lands
Potential to become invasive outside of native range	Low; not prone to invasion	Low; not prone to invasion	High; a well-established invasive species in Nigeria; known to be invasive in the Caribbean Islands	Low; not prone to invasion	High; known to be invasive in Fiji, the Marshall Islands, the Federated States of Micronesia, and New Zealand

Source: Authors, based on data from O'Hair 1995; Pimentel and Patzek 2005; Eneas 2006; Institute of Pacific Islands Forestry 2006; ICRISAT 2007; IITA 2007; Low and Booth 2007; Nguyen and others 2007; Reddy, Kumar, and Ramesh 2007; FAO 2008; Genomeindia 2008; Shapouri 2009 Global Invasive Species Program 2008 Grassi, n.d.; Repórter Brasil 2008; WWF n.d.

Note: — = Not available.

a. Assumes ideal growing conditions and highest conversion efficiencies.

b. Unless land is uniquely suited for this biofuel crop, diversion of land will always have an indirect impact.

Table 3.7 Issues and Impacts Related to Biodiesel Production from Soy, Oil Palm, Rapeseed, Jatropha, Jojoba, and Pongamia

Issue	Jatropha	Jojoba	Oil palm	Pongamia	Rapeseed	Soy
Cost						
Biodiesel yielda	300 l/hectare in India; global average of 530 l/hectare, estimated best scenario yields of 1,800 l/hectare	1,950 l/hectare (estimated)	3,000–4,500 l/hectare (Malaysia and Indonesia)	2,000–4,000 l/hectare (India)	800–1,200 l/hectare	600–700 l/hectare
Economic impact						
Employment potential	High; seed harvest is very labor intensive, requiring 105 man-days during full maturity stage	High; seed harvest is very labor intensive	High; already a large employer in Indonesia and Malaysia; increase in market likely to increase employment	High; tapping is very labor intensive	Low; highly mechanized process requires few laborers	Low; highly mechanized process and few laborers

Potential for smallholders	High; potential for intercropping in first two years or use as a live fence; multiple uses; prices are low given effort needed to cultivate	Variable; oil prices are currently very high and are used in a wide variety of products ; production requires high upfront and operating costs	Medium; smallholder subsidies in top producer countries provide opportunities, but loans for capital costs create risk of indebtedness	High; smallholder-run enterprises (primarily managed by women) have been very successful in India; high upfront and operating costs; multiple uses	Low; must be produced in large monocultures; production requires large upfront capital investments	Low; economies of scale mean that soy is usually produced in large monocultures and production requires large upfront capital investments

Impact on land and other resource uses

Potential for improvement of degraded land	High; can be cultivated on marginal and degraded lands with low rainfall	High; can be cultivated on marginal and degraded lands with low rainfall	Low; not suitable for cultivation on degraded lands	High; can be cultivated on marginal and degraded lands with low rainfall	Low; not suitable for cultivation on degraded lands	Low; not suitable for cultivation on degraded lands
Impact on natural forests	Low; planting targeted to occur on marginal and previously deforested land	Low; planting targeted to occur on marginal and previously deforested land	High; linked to high levels of deforestation	Low; planting targeted to occur on marginal and previously deforested land	Medium; use of set-aside conservation land can cause direct deforestation; substitution may cause indirect deforestation	High; linked to high levels of deforestation

(continued)

Table 3.7 (Continued)

Issue	Jatropha	Jojoba	Oil palm	Pongamia	Rapeseed	Soy
Impact on agriculture	Low; in first two years, can be intercropped with other agricultural commodities; planting is targeted for arid regions where other crops are not cultivated	Low; can be intercropped with other agricultural commodities; planting is targeted for arid regions where other crops are not cultivated	Low; most land targeted for palm oil expansion in Indonesia identified as unproductive forestland	Low; can be intercropped with other agricultural commodities	High; medium- to large-scale production is likely to result in conversion of agricultural land	High; medium- to large-scale production likely to result in conversion of agricultural land if no expansion occurs into forested areas
Resource competition	Low; not used to produce food oil	Low; not used to produce food oil	High; also used as food oil	Low; not used to produce food oil	High; also used as food oil	High; also used as food oil
Environmental impact						
Energy intensity (fossil fuel input per unit of energy output)	6 (Thailand; includes by-products)	—	9 (Indonesia; excludes land use changes)	—	2.3 (European Union)	3.4 (United States)
Impact on water resources	Low; requires few water inputs; appropriate for dry climates (however, if irrigated may use scarce water resources)	Low; requires few water inputs; appropriate for dry climates (however, if irrigated may use scarce water resources)	High; wetlands (peat lands) may be drained for plantations and residues from processing may pollute water resources	Low; requires few water inputs; appropriate for dry climates (however, if irrigated may use scarce water resources)	High; may require irrigation and relies heavily on use of chemical fertilizers and pesticides	Medium; mostly rain fed and a nitrogen-fixing plant (less fertilizer requirements); field runoff causes pollution

Impact on soil resources	Low; potential to improve soil fertility and slow desertification	Low; potential to improve soil fertility and slow desertification	High; often grown on poor soils; may further deplete soil nutrients; often requires fertilizer inputs	Low; potential to improve soil fertility and slow desertification	High; pesticide and fertilizer use can degrade soils	Medium; low fertilizer inputs and nitrogen-fixing ability can add nutrients to soils, but pesticides use can degrade soils
Impact on Biodiversity	Medium; degraded lands provide habitat for some species	Medium; degraded lands provide habitat for some species	High; deforestation for oil palm plantations has negatively affected endangered species	Medium; degraded lands provide habitat for some species	Variable; can cause clearing of set-aside lands; price increases may cause switch to palm oil, which has affected rare species	High; deforestation for soy may endanger a wide variety of species
Potential to become invasive outside of native range	High; known to be invasive in Australasia, South Africa, North and South America	Low; not identified as invasive in any of the regions where it has been introduced	High; known to be invasive in Brazil, Micronesia, and the United States	Medium; has demonstrated capacity to spread outside of cultivation	High; known to be invasive in Australasia	Low; not prone to invasion

Source: Authors, based on data from Undersander and others 1990; Dalibard 1999; FAO 2002a, 2008b; Corley and Tinker 2003; Gaya, Aparicio, and Patel 2003; Boland 2004; Gunstone 2004; Denham and Rowe 2005; Pimentel and Patzek 2005; Colchester and others 2006; Dalgaard and others 2007; Joshi, Kanagaratnam, and Adhuri 2006; Low and Booth 2007; Pahariya and Mukherjee 2007; American Soybean Association 2008; Fargione and others 2008; GEXSI 2008; Global Invasive Species Program 2008; Greenergy 2008b, 2008c; Henning 2008; Raswant, Hart, and Romano 2008; Selim n.d.; Koivisto n.d.; Lord and Clay n.d.; and Wani and Sreedevi n.d.

Note: — = Not available.

a. Assumes ideal growing conditions and highest conversion efficiencies.

of cultivation, the cultivation method, the transport distance to processing plant and method of transport, and the processing system (Greiler 2007).

Several studies estimate the fossil energy ratio of liquid biofuel feedstocks. They find that corn yields considerably less energy than other crops (figure 3.7).

However, these figures do not take into account emissions from land conversions, nitrous oxide emissions from degradation of crop residues during biological nitrogen fixation (common with soy and rapeseed), or emissions from nitrogen fertilizer (Hill and others 2006). When these emissions are accounted for, the true value of emissions reductions is often significantly lower for many feedstocks—and can even generate greater emissions than fossil fuels. A 2008 study explains how converting rainforests, peatlands, savannas, or grasslands to produce food crop–based biofuels in Brazil, Southeast Asia, and the United States could create a "biofuel carbon debt" by releasing 17–420 times more CO_2 than the annual greenhouse gas reductions these biofuels would provide by displacing fossil fuels (Fargione and others 2008). Unlike previous studies, this study analyzes the life-cycle emissions from biofuels, including land-use changes. The study estimates that conversion of peatland rainforests for oil palm plantations could incur a "carbon debt" of 423 years in Indonesia and Malaysia; it could take 319 years of renewable soy biodiesel production to compensate for the emissions produced by cleaning the Amazon rainforest for soybeans. Although these estimates may not be exact, the message is clear: changes in land use can significantly outweigh any carbon benefits that may result from planting biofuels.

Figure 3.7   Fossil Energy Ratio of Selected Liquid Biofuels

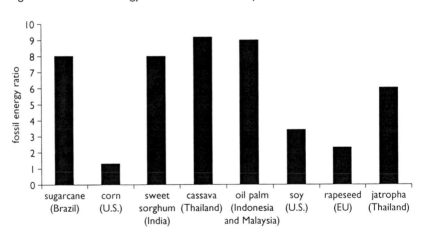

Source: Authors, based on Gunstone 2004; Nguyen and others 2006; Childs and Bradley 2007; ICRISAT 2008;
Prueksakorn and Gheewala 2008; and Shapouri, Duffield, and Wang 2009.
Note: Estimates do not include land-use changes; Jatropha estimates account for use of by-products.

Impact on Water Resources

The effect of biofuels on the availability and quality of water for agriculture is a major concern. Farming consumes around 70 percent of available fresh water globally. Total water consumption for biofuels can be three times that used to produce petroleum diesel on a life-cycle basis (Rutz and Janssen 2008). Water is used for feedstock production, as well as for processing ethanol and biodiesel. Also of concern is the surface water runoff and reduced groundwater availability associated with deforestation.

Water consumption for producing biofuels is especially high if the crop is irrigated. Countries promoting biofuels on a large scale without sustainable management of ground and surface water can experience water scarcity and groundwater salinization (Greiler 2007). Some systems, like Brazilian sugarcane, minimize these impacts by planting crops that have optimal growth under local rainfall conditions.

Some crops are well suited to grow in regions with relatively little rainfall and are capable of withstanding relatively severe drought, making them good candidates for biofuel production on degraded lands, wastelands, and set-aside lands. (Nypa, an estuarine crop, could have the effect of enhancing water quality and restoring damaged mangrove systems, thus offering coastline protection in the event of hurricanes, tsunamis, and other flooding events.) However, because production may be optimized by irrigation, there is a possibility that these crops will use scarce water resources in the already arid countries where they are planted.

In addition, some crops have high nutrient requirements and use large amounts of fertilizer and pesticides. This can lead to contamination of ground and surface waters and eutrophication of water bodies. Bioethanol and biodiesel processing generates effluents; in countries with weak environmental laws, they may be discharged directly into streams. Unlike conventional fossil fuels, ethanol and biodiesel are rapidly biodegradable and pose less risk of water contamination in the case of spilling and leakage (Rutz and Janssen 2008).

Impact on Soil Resources

Intensive agriculture, such as that used for biofuel production, has the potential to lead to soil degradation and nutrient depletion. Chemical inputs, including fertilizers and pesticides, can contaminate the soils and lead to soil erosion. The removal of crop residues for co-firing may cause further declines in soil fertility.

In contrast, perennials (Jatropha and others) suited for marginal and degraded lands could improve soil fertility, reclaiming degraded lands and halting the spread of desertification. However, because planting on productive soils greatly increases oil yields, there are questions regarding whether these crops will actually be produced on marginal and degraded lands.

Impact on Biodiversity

Any time a monoculture replaces a natural area there is a loss of biodiversity. The magnitude of biodiversity loss depends on the type of landscape that is replaced and the crop that is grown. Plantations in tropical countries are more likely to affect high conservation-value forests, which are critical for biodiversity (Greiler 2007). In other countries, especially ones with environmental degradation, increased land pressure from biofuels is likely to affect already fragile ecosystems. There are ways to mitigate some of the impacts to biodiversity, including agroforestry or intercropping systems, but these opportunities are largely limited to small-scale plantations.

Another important consideration is whether a biofuel crop is an invasive species where it is planted. Crops that have demonstrated a propensity to spread beyond cultivated areas (invasives) include Jatropha, Nypa palm, oil palm, Pongamia, and sorghum (Low and Booth 2007).

Impact on Air Quality

It is unclear whether the combustion of biofuels releases more particulate emissions than fossil fuels. Land clearing for large-scale crop production contributes to air pollution, especially if the land is burned. Replacing fossil fuels with liquid biofuels can result in lower emissions of nitrogen and sulfur oxides, carbon monoxide, heavy metals, and carcinogenic substances, such as benzene molecules (GBEP 2005).

NOTES

1. Indonesia and Malaysia have recently started to export biodiesel to the European Union.
2. International trade in refined sugar is significant, but very little sugarcane is traded internationally, so it is not shown in the figure. However, many studies have looked at the cost of ethanol production from sugarcane using local market prices and have come to the conclusion that the production of refined sugar is generally a more profitable use of sugarcane than ethanol production.
3. The president of the National Palm Growers Federation suggests that the conflict is over drug trafficking and these isolated incidents are overshadowing the fact that oil palm brings much needed investment to the rural poor (Carroll 2008).
4. Large, vertically integrated farms have the potential to outcompete smallholders and risk reducing overall employment as a result of mechanization. However, there are opportunities for large-scale farming systems to incorporate smallholders and provide employment; examples are provided elsewhere in this document.
5. This result holds regardless of whether a biorefinery generates process heat from natural gas, coal, or corn stover.

CHAPTER FOUR

Impacts and Issues at the Country and Regional Levels

Key Messages

- Bioenergy production and consumption is projected to increase in Africa and in Latin America and the Caribbean, decrease in East Asia and Pacific, and remain unchanged in South Asia.
- Projected increases in liquid biofuel production and consumption in East Asia and Pacific may have positive effects on income and employment generation. They may increase conflict over land use, however, and increase carbon emissions.
- Latin America and the Caribbean is set to become one of the main global net exporters of liquid biofuels. Expansion in production may indirectly affect forests and create potential conflict over land use as a result of expansion of feedstock production.
- Bioenergy expansion in South Asia may lead to potential conflict over land use, as a result of targeting of already utilized degraded lands. It may also put strain on water resources.
- The continued growth in traditional biomass use in Africa may lead to negative environmental impacts related to soil and forest degradation. Special attention is required to improve sustainability.
- Little bioenergy development is projected in Europe and Central Asia, with the exception of possible opportunities to export wood pellets to the European Union.
- Bioenergy is unlikely to play a large role in the Middle East and North Africa, although some opportunities for small-scale production of biofuels may exist using crops adapted for dry land conditions.

This chapter examines the impacts and issues associated with likely future bioenergy developments in each of the main global regions. Rather than attempt to model an ideal or optimal pattern of future bioenergy developments, it presents a baseline scenario for future developments in each region and then discusses the impacts and issues that may arise and how they may be addressed.

For each region, the text is divided into three parts. The first part presents the baseline, or business-as-usual, scenario for future production and consumption of bioenergy. The consumption figures are taken from the projections in chapter 1. The production projections are based on studies, policy statements, and current trends in production or international trade (where available) or a qualitative assessment of likely developments (where data are not available).[1] Qualitative assessments are based on a range of factors likely to influence future developments (such as land availability, land suitability for bioenergy production, proposed investments, and the general level of agricultural development in countries). The projections of future production include details about the feedstocks likely to be used.

The second part discusses the main impacts and issues that are likely to arise in each of the regions and major countries under this scenario, taking into account the mix of feedstocks and technologies that is likely to be used in each region. The third part discusses how some of these impacts and issues might be addressed.

AFRICA

Primary solid biomass is critical to Africa, where an estimated 76 percent of the population depends on it as the primary source of fuel. Heavy dependence on biomass is concentrated in, but not confined to, rural areas. Well over half of all urban households rely on fuelwood, charcoal, or wood waste to meet their cooking needs (IEA 2006b). This trend is projected to continue.

Baseline Scenario

All types of bioenergy production and consumption are projected to increase in Africa (table 4.1). However, unlike in other regions, almost all of the increase is projected in the primary solid biomass sector.

In 2005 traditional woodfuel production accounted for about 154 MTOE of primary solid biomass used for bioenergy (equivalent to roughly 585 million m³), and another 127 MTOE was produced from agricultural wastes. The remaining 14 MTOE was produced from agricultural and forestry-processing wastes (mostly for own use). By 2030 traditional woodfuel production is projected to increase to 207 MTOE (790 million m³), the use of agricultural wastes may rise to 152 MTOE, and modern uses may increase slightly to 18 MTOE.

Table 4.1 Projected Annual Consumption and Production of Bioenergy in Africa, 2005–30 (MTOE)

Energy type	Consumption				Production			
	2005	2010	2020	2030	2005	2010	2020	2030
Primary solid biomass	295.2	314.1	350.8	377.4	295.2	314.1	350.8	377.4
Biogas	0.0	0.0	0.0	0.0	0.0	0.0	0.0	0.0
Ethanol	0.0	0.0	0.8	1.1	0.3	0.7	2.4	3.2
Biodiesel	0.0	0.0	0.9	1.3	0.0	0.0	1.2	3.5
Total bioenergy	295.2	314.1	352.5	379.8	295.4	314.9	354.4	384.1
TPES	466.1	517.1	625.8	744.7	n.a.	n.a.	n.a.	n.a.
Bioenergy share of TPES (percent)	63.3	60.7	56.3	51.0	n.a.	n.a.	n.a.	n.a.
Transport fuels	35.3	40.7	55.0	75.8	n.a.	n.a.	n.a.	n.a.
Bioenergy share of transport fuels (percent)	0.0	0.1	3.1	3.1	n.a.	n.a.	n.a.	n.a.

Source: Authors, based on IEA 2006b and FAO 2008b.

The relatively high growth projection for traditional bioenergy production in Africa reflects several economic trends. First, population growth will increase overall demand. Second, incomes are not projected to rise sufficiently to result in significant switching from traditional biofuels to other types of fuel. Third, and most important, rising incomes and urbanization are projected to continue the current trend within traditional bioenergy production for charcoal to account for a greater share of future production. The conversion of woodfuel into charcoal results in high transformation losses that magnify the impact of higher charcoal demand on total woodfuel use.

A few African countries have consumption targets for liquid biofuels, but production and consumption are negligible. The competitiveness of biofuel production in Africa is currently uncertain but is likely to be well below that of other net-exporting regions. However, as a result of the world's growing demand for biofuels and the relatively small number of countries with the potential for exports, Africa has already begun to attract investments (for export production).

The projections presented here are based on "demand-pull" as opposed to "supply-push" factors that may stimulate net exports from some other regions. They are based on the assumption that Africa may account for about one-third of future ethanol trade with net-importing regions and half of net imports of biodiesel projected in East Asia and Pacific.

Feedstock production is also uncertain, although a few crops would seem to be the most likely sources of future production. For ethanol production, cassava, sweet sorghum, and sugarcane are all feasible feedstocks. Africa currently accounts for more than half of global cassava production and almost half of global sweet sorghum production; it is a minor producer of sugarcane. However, because sugarcane is likely to be more economically attractive for ethanol production, particularly for large-scale foreign investors, it is assumed here that sugarcane will be a main feedstock used in the future. A very small amount of ethanol is already produced from sugarcane in Africa, accounting for about 7.1 million MT of production. By 2030 sugarcane production for ethanol is projected to increase to 80.5 million MT, which is only slightly less than total sugarcane production in 2005.

For biodiesel production, oil palm and Jatropha are each expected to account for 50 percent of future production. Africa is already the second-largest producer of oil palm in the world (although it accounts for only 10 percent of global production, a result of the dominance of Indonesia and Malaysia in this commodity). A significant expansion of Jatropha is included in this scenario, because it is more suitable for drier parts of the continent and some investments in Jatropha are already moving forward. To meet projected feedstock requirements in 2030, 9.9 million MT of oil palm and 5.7 million MT of Jatropha would be needed.

Impact

Bioenergy production in Africa is likely to have multiple impacts, for which it will be critical to plan an appropriate response. The following sections address potential impacts.

Economic Impact

The above scenario is likely to affect income and employment generation from increased bioenergy production, land use, agricultural markets and food prices, and dependence on traditional biofuels. Biodiesel production from Jatropha is projected to employ about 800,000 people in 2030. Ethanol production could employ about 300,000 people (assuming a rate of labor productivity similar to that of India), and biodiesel production from oil palm might employ a similar number. This projected total of 1.4 million people employed is probably a minimum estimate, because it is based on the assumption that economic factors will encourage large-scale production; greater involvement of smallholders in production would result in much higher employment generation. In addition, employment in charcoal production is likely to increase by a significant amount. Income generation from bioenergy development in Africa is very difficult to estimate but is also likely to be significant.

With respect to food prices, bioenergy developments in Africa are unlikely to have major negative impacts, as a result of changes in agricultural markets and food prices, because the production of feedstocks is projected to be relatively small. The impacts on food prices as a result of bioenergy developments elsewhere may be much more important and potentially harmful, especially to the many food-deficit countries in Africa. The harmful impacts on poverty and food security in many African countries are likely to be "imported" from other regions as a result of changes in global agricultural markets, as occurred in 2008.

Impact on Use of Land and Other Resources

The estimated feedstock requirements (excluding biomass) for Africa indicate a 73.5 million MT increase in sugarcane and much smaller increases in oil palm and Jatropha (table 4.2). The yield of sugarcane could possibly be raised slightly, and there is great potential to increase oil palm yields, which are very low. Given that land speculation for bioenergy development for export is already taking place in some African countries, it is possible that the total feedstock requirements could be much higher than those shown here (see discussion in chapter 3). The estimates here account for the feedstocks that are projected to provide the largest growth in the region.

Overall, the amount of additional land required for bioenergy feedstock production in 2030 is relatively small. However, as elsewhere, oil palm expansion has the potential to occur in forest areas, and Jatropha production could occur on degraded land and degraded forest. Production of biofuels from sugarcane would require a significant expansion in sugarcane production, but the area required is relatively small.

The increased traditional collection of agricultural and forest biomass for energy and charcoal production may have negative impacts. Moreover, there is potential for land and forest degradation associated with this increase.

Table 4.2 Projected Annual Bioenergy Feedstock Requirements in Africa, 2005–30

Commodity	Production in 2005 (million MT)	Amount required for bioenergy (million MT)			Average yield in 2005 (MT/hectare)	Additional area in 2030 at 2005 yield (million hectares)
		2005	2030	Increase		
Sugarcane	93.0	7.1	80.5	+73.5	57.0	1.3
Oil palm	17.6	0	9.9	+9.9	3.6	2.8
Jatropha	0	0	5.7	+5.7	4.0	1.4

Source: Production and yields from FAOSTAT; other figures from authors' own calculations.
Note: Estimates do not take into account all possible feedstocks being considered in the region or account for all countries in the region that may produce bioenergy in the future. They may therefore underestimate the total amount of land needed to meet these targets.

The potential for land-use conflict as a result of increased bioenergy production in Africa will depend on current circumstances and the scale and type of bioenergy developments in each country. Large-scale intensive production (similar to that in Latin America) would likely result in some land-use conflict, and it would create fewer economic job opportunities than small-scale production (similar to that planned in South Asia). Success in this area will depend on the bioenergy policies in each country, the capacity of national institutions to implement those policies, and the ability of local people to adapt to changing market conditions.

Environmental Impact

The environmental impacts of bioenergy developments in Africa will be mixed and, on balance, negative. The main negative environmental impact is likely to be the soil and forest degradation and biodiversity losses arising as a result of continued growth in traditional biomass use. Similar impacts are projected to occur as a result of the expansion of oil palm for biodiesel production. Jatropha production has the potential to improve soils and reduce land degradation, but this depends on the types of land used for this crop and whether irrigation is used to increase yields, which is likely. The expansion of sugarcane production can have the negative environmental implications associated with this crop (described elsewhere) as well as a negative impact on water resources, depending on where it is planted.

The impacts on climate change will be mixed but probably negative overall. In places where traditional biomass collection results in deforestation and forest degradation (that is, the biomass is not replaced by forest regrowth), net greenhouse gas emissions will be high. Conversion of forest to oil palm is also likely to lead to an increase in net emissions. Production of Jatropha and sugarcane for liquid biofuel production has a low energy intensity and high emissions reduction potential, but these positive impacts are likely to be outweighed by the negative development described above.

Discussion

The contribution of bioenergy to TPES is projected to fall slightly (a result of the projected increase in overall TPES) and its contribution to transport fuels to increase slightly. These developments may make a modest contribution to rural development, but they also may have some negative environmental impacts.

The outlook for bioenergy development in Africa is different from that of other regions, because traditional biomass use is likely to increase in importance in this region and the prospects for liquid biofuel developments remain very unclear. Several issues should be addressed, including the potential to improve the sustainability of traditional biomass use (or even substitution of this by other appropriate forms of rural energy supply); the appropriate level and scale of bioenergy development (especially with respect to land tenure issues and economic opportunities); feedstock choice (for example, sugarcane or other crops such as cassava and sweet sorghum); and land-use planning.

EAST ASIA AND PACIFIC

East Asia and Pacific is likely to be a major net exporter and importer of biodiesel. China accounts for most of the developments in the region, but Indonesia, Malaysia, the Philippines, Thailand, and Vietnam are also likely to play important roles.

Baseline Scenario

The baseline scenario for bioenergy production and consumption in East Asia and Pacific projects a decline in total bioenergy production and consumption, a result of a drop in traditional uses of primary solid biomass for energy as incomes rise (table 4.3). However, liquid biofuel production and consumption is projected to increase significantly over the next two decades. In addition, the region is projected to become the world's largest net importer of liquid biofuels.

In the primary solid biomass sector, production of bioenergy within the forest and agricultural processing sectors is projected to increase from

Table 4.3 Projected Annual Consumption and Production of Bioenergy in East Asia and Pacific, 2005–30 (MTOE)

Energy type	Consumption				Production			
	2005	2010	2020	2030	2005	2010	2020	2030
Primary solid biomass	346.6	333.9	313.9	283.4	346.6	333.9	313.9	283.4
Biogas	3.5	3.5	3.6	3.8	3.5	3.5	3.6	3.8
Ethanol	0.8	1.8	7.4	11.9	0.5	1.1	4.5	7.1
Biodiesel	0.1	3.0	13.2	20.9	0.1	3.0	12.6	16.4
Total bioenergy	350.9	342.1	338.2	320.0	350.6	341.4	334.6	310.8
TPES	2,574.9	3,076.2	4,057.1	4,938.6	—	—	—	—
Bioenergy share of TPES (percent)	13.6	11.1	8.3	6.5	—	—	—	—
Transport fuels	189.3	231.8	343.5	506.8	—	—	—	—
Bioenergy share of transport fuels (percent)	0.4	2.0	6.0	6.5	—	—	—	—

Source: Authors' compilation based on IEA 2006b and FAO 2008b.
Note: — = Not available.

43 MTOE in 2005 to 60 MTOE in 2030; heat and power production is projected to increase from 2 MTOE to 33 MTOE. In contrast, traditional uses of forest and agricultural biomass are projected to fall from about 300 MTOE to 190 MTOE over the same period. China accounts for the majority of the increase in heat and power production (18 MTOE), a result of plans to install 30GW of heat and power production from biomass by 2020 (REN21 2008). The main feedstock for this is expected to be pellets made from agricultural residues, with eventual production of 50 million MT of pellets a year. Indonesia is also projected to increase heat and power production from biomass by a significant amount.

In the liquid biofuels sector, China accounts for the majority of growth in production and consumption, although the Philippines and Thailand also have targets for ethanol and biodiesel and Indonesia and Malaysia have targets for biodiesel. China expects to import about half of its ethanol requirements in the future. Production in the region is likely to use sugarcane and possibly small amounts of cassava and sweet sorghum (Preechajarn, Prasertsri, and Kunasirirat 2007; Corpuz 2009).

Biodiesel production in China is currently limited, based mainly on the use of waste cooking oils. Future production is likely to be based on oil palm, cashew, Jatropha, and rapeseed, and imported biofuels are projected to supply half of total consumption. Oil palm is likely to be the main feedstock used in the rest of the region, possibly with some small amounts of Jatropha. Indonesia and Malaysia have agreed to each devote 6 million MT of crude palm oil production to biodiesel production (Associated Press 2008). This level of biodiesel production is projected to exceed domestic needs and result in exports of biodiesel to other countries.

Impact

The environmental impacts in this region have the potential to be substantial given the large forest area. This is especially true if bioenergy is produced in an unsustainable manner.

Economic Impact

Given the scale of projected bioenergy developments in this region, the economic impacts of these developments could be significant. Positive developments are likely to include income and employment generation from increased liquid biofuel production and health benefits from the declining traditional use of bioenergy.

The level of job creation will depend on the mix of feedstocks used and the scale of production. Detailed studies of the employment and income-generation effects of bioenergy developments in this region are not available. Small-scale production of highly labor-intensive crops such as Jatropha, sugarcane, and cassava can employ large numbers of people per unit of output; large-scale oil palm plantations and highly mechanized sugarcane production are likely to result in less employment.[2] The overall impact of these developments remains uncertain but is likely to be quite large.

The global slowdown caused commodity and fossil fuel prices to fall. Despite the decline, many countries, including China and Indonesia, are moving forward with their biofuel agenda in order to meet future energy demands. Indonesian producers are selling biofuels at a loss in order to meet state-mandated requirements. However, it is expected that both demand and prices will rebound as the global economy recovers.

Impact on Use of Land and Other Resources

Given the uncertainty about the future mix of feedstocks that will be used, estimated feedstock requirements (excluding biomass) are only rough estimates based on policies and past trends (table 4.4).[3] The estimates assume that production of ethanol will be split evenly among corn, sorghum, cassava, and sugarcane in China and that 95 percent of production in other countries will come from sugarcane, with the remaining 5 percent coming from cassava. For biodiesel, they assume that oil palm use as a feedstock will account for 70 percent of production,[4] rapeseed will account for 10 percent, and Jatropha will account for 20 percent.

Table 4.4   Projected Annual Bioenergy Feedstock Requirements in East Asia and Pacific, 2005–30

Commodity	Production in 2005 (million MT)	Amount required for bioenergy (million MT)			Average yield in 2005 (MT/hectare)	Additional area in 2030 at 2005 yield (million hectares)
		2005	2030	Change		
Wheat and corn	267.5	1.4	5.9	+4.6	4.5	1.0
Sugarcane	213.9	3.7	86.3	+82.6	59.9	1.4
Oil palm	146.0	0.4	65.9	+65.4	18.9	3.5
Cassava	50.0	0.4	13.1	+12.7	15.7	0.8
Rapeseed	13.1	0.0	9.4	+9.4	1.8	5.2
Sweet sorghum	2.7	0.0	10.5	+10.5	4.3	2.4
Jatropha	—	0.0	10.8	+10.8	4.0	2.7

Source: Production and yields from FAOSTAT; other figures based on authors' calculations.
Note: Figures include estimates only for countries in table. Estimates do not take into account all possible feedstocks being considered in the region or account for all countries in the region that may produce bioenergy in the future. They may therefore underestimate the total amount of land needed to meet these targets. — = Not available.

By far the largest increases in competition for land and other resources a result of bioenergy developments are likely to occur in China, Indonesia, and Malaysia. Increasing land requirements for bioenergy has the potential to convert natural forests into plantations for biofuels. In Indonesia natural forests have already been converted into oil palm plantations; a recent government decree will allow for further development on peat lands that were formerly off limits. In China the government has emphasized that a key element of bioenergy development is that ethanol feedstocks should not compete with food and should be grown on nonarable land (Latner, O'Kray, and Junyang 2007; Bezlova 2008). Development of Jatropha, cassava, and sweet sorghum is thus targeted to occur on land that is marginal, arid, or degraded and to have a minimal impact on food production. By 2030 production of these crops could require as much as 6.3 million hectares of land at current yields, possibly more given the quality of land that is likely to be used. This is a relatively small proportion of the estimated 250 million hectares of degraded land in China (Wang, Otsubo, and Ichinose 2002).

Rapeseed production for biodiesel is likely to require the largest amount of arable land in the future. This demand could reportedly be met without a serious impact on food production by planting rapeseed in the off season in the central region of China (Latner, O'Kray, and Junyang 2006). The other main bioenergy feedstocks in China that may compete with food uses are corn and sugarcane. Some production of these crops may be used for biofuels in the future. However, given the current yields of these crops, it is possible that a significant proportion of any additional demand caused by bioenergy developments could be met by improvements in yield rather than expansion or diversion of crop areas (up to 100 percent in the case of corn and slightly less than 50 percent in the case of sugarcane). It is unlikely that increased production of these crops will lead, directly or indirectly, to forest clearance to obtain more agricultural land in China (this may not be the case in other countries producing sugarcane).

Based on the above scenario and current yields, the area of oil palm required to produce biodiesel feedstock could reach 3.5 million hectares, with most of this production occurring in Indonesia and Malaysia. Commercial yields of oil palm are already relatively high, so the potential for yield increases may be limited. However, there may be potential to increase smallholder yields. Indonesia has 4.3 million hectares and Malaysia 5.5 million hectares of oil palms, so an expansion of 3.5 million hectares would represent a significant increase in current areas. These increases would be in addition to current trends of expanding oil palm areas to meet rapidly growing demand for nonfuel uses of oil palms.

The relationship between the expansion of palm oil production and deforestation is debated; it is unclear exactly how much deforestation is caused directly by palm oil expansion and how much of this expansion occurs on land already deforested or degraded as a result of other causes. However, the majority of palm oil plantations are located on land that was once tropical forest. In view of this, it seems likely that the expansion in palm oil areas suggested above could occur in places with some forest cover.

With respect to biomass demand, the decline in traditional uses of biomass should result in improved soil productivity and reduced pressure on tree and forest resources, leading to improvements in tree cover in some areas. The projected 33 MTOE production of heat and power in 2030 would require about 60 million MT of biomass, with most of this demand coming from China and Indonesia. Agricultural residues alone in these two countries probably amounted to at least 500 million MT in 2005 (assuming 1 MT of residues for every 1 MT of cereal production), and there are significant volumes of biomass residues from forest harvesting and processing and plantation crops. Although it will be economically feasible to harvest only a proportion of this material, it seems possible that primary solid biomass demand in 2030 can be satisfied from the collection of biomass wastes.

The projected changes in land use and impacts on agricultural markets and food prices are likely to have some negative impacts. Population densities in some countries in this region are among the highest in the world, and land ownership and land tenure are not very secure in many places. Land-use changes in some countries could be significant; the potential for conflict depends upon how these changes occur. Small-scale developments that include the participation of local people in production and development may not result in significant conflict; large-scale oil palm plantation development or intensive sugarcane production may lead to problems in this area.

Environmental Impact

The environmental impacts of bioenergy developments in East Asia and Pacific are likely to be significant. They will depend very much on the mix of feedstocks used as well as where and how they are produced. At the regional level, the projections for bioenergy production from primary solid biomass are likely to have significant and positive impacts on the environment a result of the effects of reduced traditional biomass collection on soils and forest resources. This is unlikely to occur in the few countries in which traditional uses are projected to increase in the future. Biomass production for heat and power generation is likely to focus on the use of residues, so this is likely to have a minimal environmental impact (or a positive impact in some cases), as long as sufficient biomass residues are left in forests and fields to maintain soil fertility.

In the liquid biofuels sector, the environmental impact of increased bioenergy production is likely to be more complicated and uncertain. Several of the crops targeted for biofuel production can be grown on marginal or degraded land, where their use may have beneficial effects in terms of reversing land degradation and possibly a small positive effect on biodiversity. These impacts could be negative in areas in which intensively managed crops such as corn and sugarcane are used. Recent research suggests that biofuel developments in China could place a significant strain on water resources there (CGIAR 2007). Expansion of production of biodiesel from oil palm could result in losses of biodiversity and adversely affect soil and water quality. The extent of these impacts will depend on the area and types or quality of forest replaced by such crops. In 2009 the Indonesian government announced that it would allow palm oil plantations to be developed on peatlands less than 3 meters deep (Butler 2009), a practice that will significantly increase carbon emissions. As in Europe, the high level of biodiesel and ethanol imports projected in the future could lead to environmental impacts both inside and outside the region.[5]

The projections for bioenergy production from primary solid biomass indicate that there is potential for a generally positive and significant impact, a result of the relatively low energy intensity and high emissions reductions from biomass heat and power production compared with coal (the major fuel used for power production in China). For liquid biofuels, the impacts are likely to be mixed. Some feedstocks (for example, Jatropha, sweet sorghum, cassava, and sugarcane) have a low energy intensity and potentially high emissions reductions; other feedstocks (for example, corn and rapeseed) perform less well. Biodiesel produced from oil palm has low energy intensity and potentially lower emissions than fossil diesel, but the replacement of forest with oil palm crops can lead to significant emissions from land-use change, which results in a significant increase in net emissions.

Discussion

The contribution of bioenergy to TPES in East Asia and Pacific is likely to decline by more than half by 2030, although its contribution to transport fuels is projected to increase significantly. This overall decline is a result of a projected decrease in traditional uses of primary solid biomass for bioenergy combined with a doubling of TPES as the region develops. Within the primary solid biomass sector, a significant increase in modern uses of biomass for energy (own use and heat and power) is projected.

Overall, these developments are likely to make a significant contribution to rural development and probably have a positive impact on climate change. With respect to climate change, the main potentially negative effect is likely to be the increased use of oil palm and forest conversion/ peatland development for biodiesel production. Energy security in the region is expected to increase somewhat, but a high level of liquid biofuel imports is projected, which is likely to replace some of the current dependence on oil imports with dependence on biofuel imports.

There is a risk of negative economic and environmental outcomes as a result of the above developments. The main economic impacts that may arise are higher food prices and, possibly, conflicts over land-use change. Environmental impacts will vary by feedstock, with generally positive impacts where biofuel feedstocks are planted on degraded land and negative impacts where they are planted on forest land. One other element of uncertainty will be the sustainability of biofuel or feedstock imports.

To address some of these issues, where possible, policy makers should steer bioenergy development toward nonfood crops grown on marginal or degraded land (some countries already encourage this in their bioenergy policies). Another possibility (not included in the scenario above) is production of second-generation liquid biofuels from biomass. The region has an abundance of biomass residues that are currently underutilized; there may be potential for expansion in this area beyond what is currently planned for heat and power production. Although declining, traditional uses of biomass for bioenergy will remain significant and deserve attention.

Small-scale production involving local farmers would also seem appropriate. Although such farming may be more expensive from both a production and transportation standpoint, it may reduce the potential for land-use conflict and could increase the benefits of these developments for the rural poor.

The replacement of some forest areas with crops for bioenergy feedstock production seems inevitable. These areas should be chosen carefully to reduce negative macroeconomic and environmental impacts. At a minimum, peatlands should not be converted for oil palm plantations, given the very large amounts of carbon dioxide emissions that result from peatland conversion.

EUROPE AND CENTRAL ASIA

Very few countries in the Europe and Central Asia region have liquid biofuel targets, so consumption of liquid biofuels is not projected to increase much. However, as a result of high demand elsewhere (particularly in Western Europe), the region is projected to become a net exporter of biodiesel and wood pellets to other regions.

Baseline Scenario

Bioenergy consumption in Europe and Central Asia is projected to decline throughout the period as a result of reductions in the use of primary solid biomass (table 4.5).

Total primary solid biomass use in this region is currently about 115 million m^3, with 95 million m^3 used as traditional woodfuel and the remainder used in modern production of bioenergy and a small amount of wood pellet exports (about 500,000 MT of pellets). By 2030 traditional woodfuel consumption is projected to decline to 65 million m^3 and modern uses are projected to increase slightly to 30 million m^3. In addition, as a result of high demand in Western Europe, wood pellet exports are projected to increase to about 20–25 million MT, requiring an additional 40 million m^3 of biomass. The amount of biomass required for these uses is projected to increase to 135 million m^3 in 2030.

Energy type	Consumption				Production			
	2005	2010	2020	2030	2005	2010	2020	2030
Primary solid biomass	30.4	28.7	26.8	24.9	30.6	29.3	33.5	36.0
Biogas	0	0	0	0	0	0	0	0
Ethanol	0	0	0	0	0	0	0	0
Biodiesel	0	0	0.1	0.1	0	0.2	1.0	2.1
Total bioenergy	30.4	28.7	26.9	25.0	30.6	29.5	34.6	38.1
TPES	1,082.6	1,158.5	1,292.9	1,405.8	—	—	—	—
Bioenergy share of TPES (percent)	2.8	2.5	2.1	1.8	—	—	—	—
Transport fuels	77.1	85.0	97.5	105.9	—	—	—	—
Bioenergy share of transport fuels (percent)	0	0	0.1	0.1	—	—	—	—

Source: Authors, based on IEA 2006b and FAO 2008b.
Note: — = Not available.

As of 2005, Croatia was the only country in this region with a liquid biofuels target. The baseline scenario therefore assumes that liquid biofuel consumption remains negligible. However, as a result of increased demand in Western Europe, this region is projected to become an exporter. (It is assumed here that all of these exports will be biodiesel, although exports of biodiesel feedstocks may occur instead.) These exports will most likely be produced from rapeseed and would require annual production of about 4.2 million MT by 2030.

Impact

Bioenergy is a small contributor to TPES in this region. As a result, bioenergy developments are unlikely to have a significant impact.

Economic Impact

With the relatively modest level of future bioenergy developments projected above, the economic impacts of these developments are likely to be small and limited to some income and employment generation in the production of wood pellets and biodiesel (or biodiesel feedstocks) for export. Rapeseed production in the region is projected to have minimal impact on income and employment generation. These developments may have some impact on food prices, as the projected increase in rapeseed production is significant. The final impact is uncertain, however, because as rapeseed prices increase, the food industry could create demand for less expensive substitute oils, including palm oil.

Impact on Use of Land and Other Resources

The estimated feedstock requirement for biodiesel production in 2030 (4.2 million MT of rapeseed) is much higher than 2005 production of 0.7 million MT. However, yields (1.4 MT/hectare) are much less than half those achieved in developed countries with similar growing conditions (for example, Western Europe). At current yields, the projected feedstock production would require about 3 million hectares of land devoted to rapeseed; yield gains could reduce this amount by half. Furthermore, with or without yield gains, the area of land required for this production is very small compared with the total area used for agriculture in these countries, and although there may be some crop substitution, it is unlikely to have a significant impact on land resources (and is unlikely to shift current agricultural production toward clearing new lands). Similarly, the amount of primary solid biomass required in the future is far below what could be produced from forest industry residues, forest and agricultural residues, and sustainable production of wood from forests in this region (even after taking into account likely future growth in the forestry sector). Therefore, biodiesel production is not projected to have a significant detrimental effect on forests in the region.[6]

Environmental Impact

The environmental impacts of bioenergy developments in Europe and Central Asia are likely to be modest and are likely to be related to expanded or intensified production of feedstocks for biodiesel production. Production of primary solid biomass could have some environmental impact, but there will be opportunities to increase the use of wastes to meet future demands with low impacts.

These developments are projected to have a modest positive impact on climate change. The reduction in traditional uses of woodfuel combined with expansion in modern uses (including wood pellets) may reduce the energy intensity of heat and power production (including in importing countries) and reduce net greenhouse gas emissions. Liquid biofuel production is likely to be focused biodiesel production from rapeseed, which also tends to have a relatively low energy intensity and high emissions reduction potential.

Discussion

The scenario for Europe and Central Asia suggests that the contribution of bioenergy to TPES will decline and its contribution to transport fuels remain negligible. These developments may thus make only a modest contribution to rural development and have a small positive impact on climate change. The main focus of future bioenergy developments in this region should be to examine the scope for increases in bioenergy feedstock yield and the potential to use wastes for primary solid biomass supply. Development of cellulosic ethanol (not considered here) may also be worth pursuing.

LATIN AMERICA AND THE CARIBBEAN

Latin America and the Caribbean is the world's largest producer, the second-largest consumer (after North America), and only net exporter of ethanol. Brazil accounts for the majority of production; other countries are planning or starting to increase production. Biodiesel production and consumption in this region is currently very limited, but nine countries have or are planning to introduce biodiesel targets. In addition, some countries are targeting biodiesel production as an export opportunity.

Baseline Scenario

All types of bioenergy consumption in Latin America and the Caribbean are projected to increase in the future, a result of policies and targets for renewable energy and liquid biofuels as well as general economic trends (table 4.6). This region is already a significant net exporter of ethanol; higher net exports of ethanol and biodiesel are projected in the future, as a result of the competitiveness of production in this region.

Primary solid biomass accounts for most bioenergy production and is projected to increase by almost one-third by 2030. Traditional biomass use (mostly woodfuel) accounts for almost three-quarters of production and is projected to increase from 75 MTOE (285 million m³) in 2005 to 89 MTOE (340 million m³)

Table 4.6 Projected Annual Consumption and Production of Bioenergy in Latin America and the Caribbean, 2005–30 (MTOE)

	Consumption				Production			
Energy type	2005	2010	2020	2030	2005	2010	2020	2030
Primary solid biomass	105.9	112.3	124.4	134.0	105.9	112.3	124.4	134.0
Ethanol	7.6	9.1	11.9	15.4	8.2	10.8	15.6	20.4
Biogas	0.0	0.0	0.0	0.0	0.0	0.0	0.0	0.0
Biodiesel	0.0	2.1	2.9	3.6	0.0	2.1	3.2	5.9
Total bioenergy	113.5	123.5	139.3	153.1	114.1	125.2	143.3	160.3
TPES	676.4	756.0	926.7	1,114.9	—	—	—	—
Bioenergy share of TPES (percent)	16.8	16.3	15.0	13.7	—	—	—	—
Transport fuels	149.2	164.4	203.2	255.1	—	—	—	—
Bioenergy share of transport fuels (percent)	5.1	6.8	7.3	7.5	—	—	—	—

Source: Authors, based on IEA 2006b and FAO 2008b.
Note: — = Not available.

in 2030 (IEA 2006b). Although rising incomes may reduce per capita woodfuel consumption slightly as people switch to alternative fuels, this should not be enough to outweigh increased overall demand as a result of population growth in the region.

Modern uses of biomass for energy (heat and power and own use) are projected to increase by about 50 percent, from 30 MTOE to 45 MTOE. Much of this is recorded in IEA statistics as commercial heat and power production rather than own use, although it is produced from wastes generated in the forestry and agricultural processing sectors (Barros 2007) and is unlikely to have a major impact in terms of demand for wood and fiber from forests and agriculture. The main impact on forests is likely to be the growth in traditional biomass use.

Sugarcane accounts for almost all ethanol production in the region (about half of Brazil's sugarcane production is used for ethanol production) and is likely to remain the main feedstock used in the future. Ethanol production in 2005 used about 205 million MT of sugarcane production in the region (about one-third of the total); by 2030 the requirement for ethanol production is projected to increase to about 510 million MT.

The feedstocks used to produce biodiesel are mostly oil palm and soybeans. The future mix between these two feedstocks is uncertain, but assuming that about half will be produced from soybeans and half from oil palm, the projected production in 2030 would require about 16.8 million MT of each commodity.

Impact

Latin America is planning major increases in bioenergy production. The impacts are likely to be substantial.

Economic Impact

The large expansion of bioenergy production projected in this region in the future is likely to lead to significant economic impacts in several areas. Sugarcane production provides opportunities for job creation. In Brazil more than 980,000 people were employed in the extended sugar-alcohol sector (for both producing regions and the whole country) during 2000–05. Soybean production is also labor intensive: it is estimated that 1–4 people are employed per 200 hectares of soybean production (Repórter Brasil 2008), which would suggest employment of 150,000–500,000 people in soybean production for conversion to biodiesel in 2030 (plus additional jobs in processing and support services). Figures for employment in oil palm production are not readily available, but based on figures from Southeast Asia, this component of the biodiesel sector could employ another 150,000 people by 2030.

Based on the above, a minimum estimate of total employment in liquid biofuel production in 2030 would be 2 million people (the majority in sugarcane and ethanol production). This estimate assumes that most production occurs in large-scale and mechanized operations (this is currently the case for soybean and sugarcane production in this region and is quite common in oil palm production in many parts of the world). Employment could be higher if production is more labor intensive. The income generated by the above developments is likely to be significant; its level depends on the intensity of production.

Impact on Use of Land and Other Resources

Another issue that is likely to be important in this region is the potential for land-use conflict. The baseline scenario suggests that an additional 12.3 million hectares of agricultural and forest land may be required for feedstock production. Given the emphasis currently placed on large-scale, intensive production, such changes could exacerbate an already complicated and difficult situation with respect to land use, land tenure, and land rights in some countries in the region.

Except for liquid biofuels, the scenario for bioenergy production from primary solid biomass is unlikely to have much impact on income, employment, or land-use change, as long as expansion in modern use of biomass in this region uses wastes generated by the forestry and agricultural processing sectors. If large-scale cultivation of forest crops for biomass is pursued, the impact on land use could be significant. Increased traditional use of biomass will continue to result in some adverse economic impacts such as health effects from poor indoor air quality and the large amount of time required collecting biomass.

These developments may have some impact on food prices, because the projected increases in feedstock production are significant (resulting in part, from government support programs). However, as production of most of these feedstocks is already strongly oriented toward exports, the impact is likely to be indirect, either through land-use changes affecting the production of other crops or through the more general increase in global commodity prices occurring as a result of bioenergy developments.

Yields of all three main feedstocks are already high, so the potential for yield gains to meet the additional demand for biofuel production is limited; most of the increase in demand is likely to be satisfied by land-use change, which could include pasture land (table 4.7).

Environmental Impact

Before the 2006 moratorium (put in place to stop deforestation of the Brazilian Amazon), soybean production was recognized as a driver of deforestation in this region; oil palm expansion has been linked to deforestation in other regions. Thus, it seems likely that the additional 8 million hectares required for biodiesel production has the potential to put some forest areas at risk of clearance. Expansion of sugarcane production has been a driver of deforestation in the past (through displaced cattle ranching), but forest land is not generally able to support intensive sugarcane production and government policies in countries such

Table 4.7 Projected Annual Bioenergy Feedstock Requirements in Latin America and the Caribbean, 2005–30

Commodity	Production in 2005 (million MT)	Amount required for bioenergy (million MT) 2005	2030	Increase	Average yield in 2005 (MT/hectare)	Additional area in 2030 at 2005 yield (million hectares)
Sugarcane	622.3	206.0	510.1	+304.1	70.3	4.3
Soybeans	96.0	0.0	16.8	+16.8	2.4	7.0
Oil palm	0.6	0.0	16.8	+16.8	17.1	1.0

Source: Production and yields from FAOSTAT; other figures from authors' own calculations.
Note: Estimates do not take into account all possible feedstocks being considered in the region or account for all countries in the region that may produce bioenergy in the future. They may therefore underestimate the total amount of land needed to meet these targets.

as Brazil are starting to target underutilized or underdeveloped arable land (see appendix A). The 2006 moratorium targeting soy expansion in the Brazilian Amazon has reduced forest clearing for soy production by up to 99 percent, according to a 2009 study (WWF 2009). Thus, the direct impact of ethanol and biodiesel production can be minimized. Increased sugarcane and soy production may indirectly affect forests if, by replacing other crops or pasture, it pushes the agricultural frontier farther into the forest. This may occur, but it would be extremely difficult to identify and quantify this impact and separate the impact caused by biofuels from other more general trends in land-use change.

Increased traditional use of fuelwood in most countries is likely to cause some forest degradation. This impact is expected to be minor compared with other factors affecting forests in the region, however.

The environmental impacts of bioenergy developments in this region have the possibility to be significant if related to expanded production of biodiesel feedstocks. If previous patterns of land-use change persist, much of the expansion of soybean and oil palm production is likely to occur in forest areas, resulting in losses of biodiversity and adverse effects on soil and water quality. The extent of these impacts will depend on the types of land uses and the area and quality of forest that may be replaced by such crops.

The impacts on climate change could be both positive and negative. Ethanol production from sugarcane is expected to account for a major share of bioenergy production; as long as this does not result in direct or indirect forest clearance, this production system has a low energy intensity and high potential to reduce net greenhouse gas emissions. Biodiesel production also has a relatively low energy intensity and potential to reduce greenhouse gas emissions. If forests are cleared for this production, however, the net impact on greenhouse gas emissions will be negative and could be substantial. Given the uneconomic nature of many of these fuels, countries may reduce their targets.

The impacts of increased bioenergy production from primary solid biomass are also complicated. Increased traditional uses of biomass are likely to result in some forest degradation and possibly increased greenhouse gas emissions (where woodfuel is not collected sustainably), but the increased production of heat- and power-using industry residues is likely to have a positive impact on climate change.

Discussion

The outlook for Latin America and the Caribbean suggests that the contribution of bioenergy to TPES will decline slightly and its contribution to transport fuels will increase slightly. These developments are likely to contribute to rural development and have a small positive impact on energy security. Land-use change is expected be a major factor affecting the environmental and macroeconomic impacts of these developments.

The impacts of land-use change in this region will depend on a number of factors, such as the intensity of feedstock production, the conversion of forests for feedstock production, and the existing situation with respect to land tenure and land rights. Bioenergy development in this region is based mostly on expansion of large-scale, intensive feedstock production. There is thus a very clear trade-off between the economic returns to bioenergy development (most of them low or negative) and the economic and environmental impacts of such development. Policy makers should consider these factors very carefully. In particular, the factors favoring large-scale expansion may reduce the potential for these developments to benefit the rural poor.

One option not considered above is the possibility of large-scale expansion of second-generation liquid biofuels. Several countries in this region have had excellent experiences in developing planted forests; this option may be more economically attractive than first-generation biodiesel production (cellulosic ethanol production is unlikely to be competitive with ethanol production using sugarcane). Such a development could address some of the environmental issues associated with biodiesel expansion in this region, although some of the other issues related to land-use change would probably remain important.

MIDDLE EAST AND NORTH AFRICA

Bioenergy is unlikely to play much of a role in this region, given the dry geography and the large quantities of oil in the region. However, some countries (including Egypt and the United Arab Emirates) have expressed some interest in using crops adapted for dry land to produce bioenergy.

Baseline Scenario

Currently, there is no liquid biofuel production or consumption in the Middle East and North Africa, and there are no targets for the future. The baseline scenario therefore assumes that consumption and production will remain at zero (table 4.8). Production and consumption of primary solid biomass are projected to increase.

Traditional woodfuel use accounts for most bioenergy production from primary solid biomass (most of this is woodfuel use in North Africa). This is projected to increase very slightly by 2030. Most of the increase shown is projected to occur from increased heat and power production from biomass in the few countries in the region that have renewable energy targets. Most production will come from organic waste material.

Impact

The expansion of bioenergy production in the Middle East and North Africa is likely to have a negligible economic impact and little or no impact on land use. As bioenergy development is likely to focus on the use of wastes, it may have a modest positive impact on climate change and the environment in the region.

Discussion

Bioenergy currently makes an insignificant contribution to TPES and transport fuels in this region, a situation projected to continue. Given existing land uses and climatic conditions in much of this region, bioenergy development

Table 4.8   Projected Annual Consumption and Production of Bioenergy in the Middle East and North Africa, 2005–30 (MTOE)

Energy type	Consumption				Production			
	2005	2010	2020	2030	2005	2010	2020	2030
Primary solid biomass	11.2	12.9	16.0	19.0	11.2	12.9	16.0	19.0
Biogas	0	0	0	0	0	0	0	0
Ethanol	0	0	0	0	0	0	0	0
Biodiesel	0	0	0	0	0	0	0	0
Total bioenergy	11.2	12.9	16.0	19.0	11.2	12.9	16.0	19.0
TPES	641.7	771.9	1,029.7	1,262.9	—	—	—	—
Bioenergy share of TPES (percent)	1.7	1.7	1.6	1.5	—	—	—	—
Transport fuels	104.1	124.4	157.7	178.8	—	—	—	—
Bioenergy share of transport fuels (percent)	0	0	0	0	—	—	—	—

Source: Authors, based on IEA 2006b and FAO 2008b.
Note: — = Not available.

beyond that projected here seems unlikely. However, small-scale development of drought-tolerant bioenergy feedstocks (for local use) on degraded or arid land may be worth considering as part of broader rural development initiatives.

SOUTH ASIA

Total bioenergy production in South Asia is projected to remain about constant through 2030. Primary solid biomass use is projected to decline slightly, and liquid biofuel use is projected to increase significantly (table 4.9).

Baseline Scenario

The role of traditional biomass, which already plays a large role in this region (in India it provided energy for more than 700 million people in 2004) is projected to increase as a result of population growth.

Traditional woodfuel collection accounts for about 101 MTOE of primary solid biomass used for bioenergy (equivalent to roughly 380 million m^3) in 2005, and another 91 MTOE is produced from agricultural wastes. The remaining 18 MTOE is produced from agricultural and forestry-processing wastes (for example, burning of bagasse for heat and power in sugar refining mills), most of it produced for own use. By 2030 traditional uses of bioenergy are projected to fall by about 10 MTOE to 180 MTOE and modern uses to

Table 4.9 Projected Annual Consumption and Production of Bioenergy in South Asia, 2005–30 (MTOE)

Energy type	Consumption				Production			
	2005	2010	2020	2030	2005	2010	2020	2030
Primary solid biomass	209.4	212.8	210.2	200.8	209.4	212.8	210.2	200.8
Biogas	0.0	0.1	0.1	0.1	0.0	0.1	0.1	0.1
Ethanol	0.1	0.2	0.9	1.2	0.1	0.2	0.9	1.2
Biodiesel	0.0	1.1	6.1	8.4	0.0	1.1	6.1	8.4
Total bioenergy	209.6	214.1	217.2	210.4	209.6	214.1	217.2	210.4
TPES	657.6	755.4	974.5	1,229.7	—	—	—	—
Bioenergy share of TPES (percent)	31.9	28.3	22.3	17.1	—	—	—	—
Transport fuels	42.7	49.5	66.7	89.8	—	—	—	—
Bioenergy share of transport fuels (percent)	0.2	2.6	10.5	10.6	—	—	—	—

Source: Authors, based on IEA 2006b and FAO 2008b.
Note: — = Not available.

increase marginally to 21 MTOE. Traditional bioenergy production per capita is projected to fall, as a result of rising incomes, but the effect on total consumption will be muted by population growth in the region. India accounts for about three-quarters of bioenergy production from primary solid biomass in this region, with Pakistan a distant second.

India has a target for ethanol consumption, and three countries in the region (India, Pakistan, and Nepal) have or are planning biodiesel targets. The small amount of ethanol currently produced in the region is made from sugarcane, which is likely to remain the main feedstock for ethanol production. Countries in the region aim to be self-sufficient in ethanol production, so the projected production of 1.2 MTOE of ethanol in 2030 would require almost 30 million MT of sugarcane in 2030. For biodiesel production, Jatropha appears to be the main feedstock attracting government support and attention from investors (although a small amount of Pongamia is also expected to be used). At current conversion rates, projected biodiesel production in 2030 would require 27.4 million MT of Jatropha seeds.

Impact

Many of the bioenergy developments in this region will take place in areas with high populations and on fragile lands. It will therefore be critical to determine lands that are best suited to meet targets.

Economic Impact

The economic impacts of the above scenario are likely to be similar to those elsewhere in Asia. Positive developments may include income and employment generation from increased liquid biofuel production and health benefits from the declining traditional use of bioenergy. Changes in land use and impacts on agricultural markets and food prices could have some minor negative impacts.

Sugarcane production is less intensive than in Brazil and is believed to employ more people per unit of output: according to Genomeindia (2008), roughly one person is employed for every 300 MT of sugarcane produced in India, two-thirds more employment than in Brazil. This figure includes those employed in sugar refining. Assuming that the conversion of sugarcane to ethanol would result in a similar employment multiplier, ethanol production could employ about 100,000 people in 2030.

Future employment in biodiesel production from Jatropha is very difficult to estimate and will depend on the scale of production. With intensive large-scale production, biodiesel production in 2030 could employ as few as 400,000 people, although this outcome seems unlikely. Using the assumptions of the Planning Commission of India (2003) of 32 days employment per MT of biodiesel production, employment in 2030 could amount to 1.5 million.

Employment in bioenergy production from primary solid biomass is very difficult to estimate (because so much is produced for subsistence needs or in the informal sector), but little change is expected. Therefore, employment creation as a result of bioenergy development could amount to a total of 1.3 million jobs.

Income generation from bioenergy development is also difficult to estimate. Based on the Planning Commission's assumptions, the level of biodiesel production projected for 2030 would create about $1.5 billion gross annual income for farmers (at current prices and exchange rates), plus additional income in the conversion of oilseeds to biodiesel. Income from ethanol production is likely to represent only a fraction of this, however.

Expansion of feedstock production for liquid biofuel production creates the potential for land-use conflict. The government of India is focusing biofuel production on degraded and underutilized land and expects to encourage smallholder participation to meet the majority of production needs; other countries in this region are likely to take similar approaches. The scenario presented here suggests that 7.3 million hectares of land may be required for feedstock production (more if Jatropha yields are lower). India expects to plant these feedstocks on several different land types, including degraded forests, field boundaries, fallow land, road/river/canal boundaries, and other marginal lands. However, most land in India is already used in some fashion (even so-called wastelands and marginal lands), so there is opportunity for conflict.

These developments may have some negative impact on food prices. The effect is likely to be small, however, because the required increase in sugarcane production is relatively small and Jatropha is not a food crop.

Impact on Use of Land and Other Resources

The estimates presented here account for the feedstocks that are projected to provide the largest growth in the region (table 4.10). The yield of sugarcane in South Asia is already high, but there may be some potential to meet the

Table 4.10   Projected Annual Bioenergy Feedstock Requirements in South Asia, 2005–30

Commodity	Production in 2005 (million MT)	Amount required for bioenergy (million MT) 2005	2030	Increase	Average yield in 2005 (MT/hectare)	Additional area in 2030 at 2005 yield (million hectares)
Sugarcane	299.7	2.5	29.6	+27.1	60.8	0.4
Jatropha	—	0	27.4	+27.4	4.0	6.8

Source: Production and yields from FAOSTAT, other figures based on authors' own calculations.
Note: Estimates do not take into account all possible feedstocks being considered in the region or account for all countries in the region that may produce bioenergy in the future. They may therefore underestimate the total amount of land needed to meet these targets.
— = Not available.

additional demand for biofuel production through higher yield gains. Whether or not this is possible, the additional area required at current yields is small.

The yield of Jatropha is uncertain; a wide range of yield estimates are available in the literature (from 0.5 MT/hectare/year to 12 MT/hectare/year [see appendix B]). The oil and biodiesel yields per MT of seeds are also uncertain. It is assumed here that seed yields will be 4 MT/hectare/year and oil yield will be 350 kg/MT. This is somewhat higher than the calculations used by the Planning Commission of India, which assume a yield of 3.75 MT/hectare/year and an oil yield of 310 l/MT (285 kg/MT). Using their lower figures, the amount of land required for biodiesel production would be roughly 30 percent higher than shown above.

With respect to primary solid biomass, the projections are expected to have a limited positive impact in terms of slightly reduced land and forest degradation a result of decreased traditional collection of agricultural and forest biomass for energy. The slight increase in modern uses of primary solid biomass for bioenergy is likely to use processing wastes and therefore not to have a major impact on land or other resources.

Environmental Impact

Most of the environmental impacts of bioenergy developments in this region are likely to be positive. Increased use of biomass wastes and reduced traditional collection of biomass may slightly reduce soil and forest degradation and can improve biodiversity. Jatropha production in some areas could also improve soils and have a small positive impact on biodiversity. However, some of the land targeted for Jatropha production is projected to be degraded forest, where the environmental impact is less certain.[7] The expansion of sugarcane production may be small, but there are some negative environmental implications associated with this crop.

A major environmental concern in the region is likely to be the impact of these developments on water use and water resources. India is the other major country (along with China) in which bioenergy developments may put a strain on water resources (CGIAR 2008).

The overall impacts on climate change are likely to be positive. As long as no significant forest conversion occurs, liquid biofuel production will have a low energy intensity and high potential to reduce net greenhouse gas emission. Projected developments in the use of primary solid biomass for bioenergy are likely to have similar positive impacts.

Discussion

The outlook for South Asia suggests that the contribution of bioenergy to TPES will fall by almost half, to 17 percent, in 2030 (largely a result of the projected increase in TPES) but that its contribution to transport fuels will increase significantly, to about 11 percent. These developments are likely to contribute to rural development, improve energy security slightly, and have few negative environmental impacts.

The sustainability of soil and water use in bioenergy feedstock production seems to be the main area that should be examined as these developments unfold. Current plans appear to have a sharp focus on poverty alleviation, but this impact should be monitored during implementation. As traditional uses of primary solid biomass for bioenergy are expected to remain important, efforts to improve the sustainability of this production should continue.

NOTES

1. Although the projections presented here reach 2020 or 2030, the estimates are based on mandates and targets as of 2005. Given that the bioenergy continues to be uneconomic in most cases, and the impacts are just being realized, some of these mandates may change, affecting the projections.

2. Based on current employment in oil palm production in Malaysia, for example, 1 TOE of biodiesel production from intensively managed oil palm plantations would create 0.03 full-time jobs in oil production plus a little additional employment in biodiesel production. At the other end of the scale, small-scale biodiesel production in Africa from Jatropha employs about 0.85 people per TOE of output (Henning 2008).

3. An ongoing World Bank study is assessing the impact of large-scale agriculture and forestry projects (including bioenergy) on land resources in countries. The analysis presented here is based on trends, including past and future production yields and current country targets; it is not an in-depth analysis of what is happening on the ground in these regions. The figures presented here are therefore strictly indicative.

4. Some consumption of oil palm in China could be displaced by the use of cashew nuts, but this is not included here, because it is still at the experimental stage.

5. China is especially likely to import biofuels to meet fuel demand. Before prices became too high in 2008, it had begun negotiations with Indonesia and Malaysia on biodiesel trade (APEC 2008).

6. This analysis accounts only for rapeseed growth in key countries. It may therefore underestimate the total impact to the region.

7. In India planting Jatropha on these lands is viewed as "upgrading" deforested land.

CHAPTER FIVE

Conclusions

his chapter draws both general and regional conclusions about the use of bioenergy. It then offers some brief policy recommendations.

GENERAL CONCLUSIONS

Developments in bioenergy are likely to have significant impacts on both the forest sector and poverty alleviation. Bioenergy may provide opportunities for income and employment generation, and it can increase poor people's access to improved types of energy. But concerns remain about the effect of bioenergy on combating climate change and the environment; on agriculture, food security, and sustainable forest management; and on people, particularly the poor people in developing countries who will be affected by the changes in land use, land tenure, and land rights it will bring about.

Finding 1: Solid Biomass Will Continue to Provide a Principal Source of Energy and Should Not Be Overlooked

Globally, primary solid biomass accounted for 95 percent of TPES from bioenergy in 2005; biogas and bioethanol accounted for about 2 percent each and biodiesel the remaining 1 percent. Biogas and liquid biofuels are important in North America (15 percent of total bioenergy consumption), the European Union (10 percent), and Latin America and the Caribbean (5 percent). They represent an extremely small share of bioenergy outside these three regions.

Solid biomass has various uses. Traditional biomass energy (wood, charcoal, dung, and crop residues) is used primarily by the poor for heating, cooking, and artisanal purposes. Modern uses of wood biomass (co-firing, heat and power installations, and pellets) are generally used at an industrial scale for heat and power generation, although there are applications for small-scale use.

Globally, traditional uses of biomass are projected to decline slightly, driven by large shifts in energy consumption patterns in East Asia and Pacific toward other fuel sources, including electricity. In other regions, particularly Africa and Latin America, traditional biomass use is likely to grow.

Modern uses of primary solid biomass for heat and energy production are projected to increase significantly. Thus, the share of primary solid biomass in total bioenergy production will remain high.

Finding 2: Bioenergy Developments Will Have Major Implications for Land Use

The impact of bioenergy production on land and other resources is determined by the demand for biomass and the efficiency of land use (that is, energy yield per hectare). An important question is whether the biomass crop can be grown on unused or degraded land or will take land out of agriculture or forestry. In order to meet ambitious global targets, the total area of land used for bioenergy production is likely to increase. Although some bioenergy developments are planned for, and likely to occur on, degraded or unused lands, such lands are not likely to meet the overall requirements. Therefore, agriculture/rangelands and forests/grasslands will need to be used for bioenergy.

The analysis in this report suggests that large changes in land use may occur as a result of solid biomass and liquid biofuel feedstock production in order to meet current government targets. Most of the changes are likely to result from the planting of agricultural crops to produce ethanol and biodiesel, which make up the largest percentage of all government targets. Solid biomass is likely to account for a smaller, but still significant, amount of land conversion.

Finding 3: Tradeoffs—Including Those Related to Poverty, Equity, and the Environment—Must Be Considered When Choosing a Bioenergy System

Bioenergy policies in most countries have a number of (often conflicting) objectives. Increased consumption of bioenergy is likely to result in increased competition for land that has potential to affect agriculture and forestry and could negatively affect the poor in other ways, such as through changes in access to resources and changes in environmental quality. The effect of bioenergy on climate change must also be considered. Many measures and instruments can be used as part of policy implementation; they may have different impacts on different objectives (table 5.1).

Table 5.1 Trade-Off Matrix for Liquid Biofuels

Item	Cassava	Corn	Jatropha	Jojoba	Nypa palm	Oil palm	Pongamia	Rapeseed	Soy	Sugarcane	Sweet sorghum
Employment potential	Medium	Low	High	High	High	High	High	Low	Low	Medium	Medium
Potential for smallholders	High	Low	High	Variable	Medium	Medium	High	Low	Low	Medium	High
Improvement of degraded land	High	Low	High	High	High	Low	High	Low	Low	Low	High
Impact on natural forests	Low	Variable	Low	Low	Low	High	Low	Medium	High	Variable	Low
Impact on agriculture	Low	High	Low	Low	Low	Low	Low	High	High	Low	Low
Impact on resource competition	High	High	Low	Low	Low	High	Low	High	High	Low	Low
Impact on water resources	Low	High	Low	Low	Low	High	Low	High	Medium	Medium	Medium
Impact on soil resources	Low	High	Low	Low	Low	High	Low	High	Low	High	Medium
Impact on biodiversity	Variable	Variable	Medium	Medium	Low	High	Medium	Variable	High	Variable	Variable
Invasiveness	Low	Low	High	Low	High	High	Medium	High	Low	Low	High

Source: Derived from tables 3.6 and 3.7.

Note: All impacts are evaluated based on the minimum necessary inputs and the type of land uses targeted by decision makers. They do not take into account planting on land areas other than those targeted or additional inputs, such as irrigation, which would change the suitability of the crops. The reality on the ground may differ widely from the scenarios presented in this matrix. For example, if Jatropha is planted on degraded lands and is not irrigated, it will have lower impacts on resource competition and water use; if Jatropha is planted on prime agricultural land and irrigated, the impacts are likely to be much higher than presented here.

Policy makers should identify the expected outcomes of a system, choose a system based on the stated program goals for a particular location, and attempt to reduce negative impacts. For example, a country may choose a system because it provides greater employment, even if it does not maximize fuel production. Cost considerations are likely to play a role in making these decisions. It is critical to keep in mind the land-use and environmental implications of each system in the locale in which it is implemented, as production of a particular feedstock may have minimal impacts in one location and very severe impacts in another.

The broad potential impacts indicated in table 5.1 will vary widely depending on site conditions and current land use. There is need for more technical analysis and evaluation of options, measures, and instruments in many countries with respect to bioenergy development. Thorough environmental and social impact evaluations (including strategic evaluations), which can help identify and mitigate potential impacts, should be undertaken before large-scale investments in bioenergy are made.

Finding 4: There Is Considerable Potential for Greater Use of Forestry and Timber Waste as a Bioenergy Feedstock

Although there is considerable variation (depending on local market conditions and average transport distances), the least expensive source of biomass is recovered wood (that is, postconsumer waste) and forest-processing waste (residues from timber mill or timber processing). Agricultural and forest residues (those left over from harvesting operations) are the next most inexpensive sources of waste. Crops specifically managed for biomass production (for example, energy crops such as switchgrass, miscanthus, and short-rotation coppice) are generally more expensive than these wastes, as are forest thinnings produced using traditional forest harvesting systems. In the developed regions of the world, traditional wood energy is already supplied, mostly by forest thinnings, harvesting residues, and trees outside forests; biomass for heat, power, and internal use is supplied largely from industry waste and recovered wood products.

There are opportunities for the private sector (and organizations that invest in private sector development) to develop processing facilities serving more than one purpose. In some developing countries (particularly in East Asia and Pacific), forestry thinnings are underutilized, and the cost of biomass can be low. In situations in which disposal in a landfill is costly, biomass waste presents a disposal problem, and producers may be willing to pay to have this material removed. Some timber and biofuel operations are already energy self-sufficient as a result of co-firing. Logging and milling wastes from traditional timber operations provide additional opportunities for heat and power generation, particularly in developing countries, where waste products are not fully utilized.

Finding 5: The Climate Benefits of Bioenergy Development Are Uncertain and Highly Location and Feedstock Specific

Bioenergy can have both positive and negative effects on climate change. The major liquid biofuel crops in the future are expected to be sugarcane, maize, and oil palm. Ethanol production from sugar cane will account for a large share of bioethanol production. As long as production does not result in forest clearance, this system has a fairly low energy intensity and good potential to reduce net greenhouse gas emissions (ethanol-processing facilities often use sugarcane bagasse for heat generation). In contrast, biofuel production from corn requires fossil fuel inputs at every stage of the process, including conversion into corn ethanol. Corn ethanol has minimal carbon savings versus conventional gasoline and may actually increase emissions. Biodiesel from oil palm can have lower emissions than fossil fuels, but it is highly dependent on the type of land on which it is planted.

The impacts of increased bioenergy production from primary solid biomass are also complicated. Increased traditional uses of biomass are likely to result in some forest degradation and possibly increased greenhouse gas emissions (where woodfuel is not collected sustainably), but the increased production of heat and power using industry residues could have a positive impact on climate change.

If agricultural or forested land is converted for bioenergy production, carbon emissions may actually increase over fossil fuel emissions, especially if the land converted is forested peatlands. Land conversions, nitrous oxide emissions from degradation of crop residues during biological nitrogen fixation (common with soy and rapeseed), and emissions from nitrogen fertilizer should be factored into the analysis. For this reason, life-cycle analyses are the best predictors of total carbon reductions for a fuel source. According to one study (Fargione and others 2008), converting rainforests, peatlands, savannas, or grasslands into agricultural land in order to produce food crop–based biofuels in Brazil, Southeast Asia, and the United States could create a biofuel carbon debt by releasing 17–420 times more CO_2 than the annual greenhouse gas reductions that these biofuels would provide by displacing fossil fuels. Although there are uncertainties regarding the estimated total carbon emissions, the results suggest that changes in land use could significantly outweigh any carbon benefits that may result from planting biofuels.

REGIONAL CONCLUSIONS

A variety of factors—including a region's climatic, economic, and demographic conditions—affect the policy choices it makes regarding biodiversity. The report's main regional conclusions are summarized here.

Africa

Given the high level of interest and investment in acquiring land on which to develop both liquid biofuel and solid biomass fuels, it is important for countries in Africa to evaluate the potential impacts in detail and plan appropriate responses. Where investments are made, they need to be managed in a way that minimizes land conflicts and negative impacts on the poor.

Water use is critical in Africa. Care should be taken to select bioenergy systems that will not create water-use conflicts.

Another important consideration for the region is the need to reduce its dependence on traditional woodfuel as a source of energy. Much progress has been made in this regard through the use of enhanced stoves and fuelwood plantations (including in the forest poor regions of the Sahel). There are opportunities to follow up on some of these programs.

East Asia and Pacific

East Asia and Pacific is likely to contain both large net-exporting biodiesel countries (including Indonesia and Malaysia) and large net-importing counties (China and India are likely to import the principal feedstocks—palm and soy—for food rather than fuel). Concerns in this region relate to forest conversions for biofuel plantations. It will be crucial to identify opportunities to increase production while avoiding the large carbon emissions associated with clearing peatland or felling natural forests.

The potential for land-use conflicts caused by large populations and uncertain land rights in some countries indicates that local participation in bioenergy production and development will be critical. There also appear to be significant opportunities to utilize biomass wastes as an energy source.

Europe and Central Asia

Bioenergy production is low in this region, and it is not forecast to experience much growth. There may be some opportunities to export wood pellets (especially utilizing waste products) to the European Union, however.

Latin America and the Caribbean

Latin America and the Caribbean is poised to become one of the principal global net exporters of liquid biofuels and biofuel feedstocks (both ethanol from sugarcane and oil feedstocks such as palm or soy oil); expansion of production is likely to meet these goals. Growth in production is dependent on high premiums above crop prices paid by countries with biofuel mandates, such as members of the European Union. There is currently too much uncertainty for developers in the region to commit to investment in oil seed production based on external markets and politically determined price premiums.

Sustainability criteria could help ensure that production of biofuels in the region does not come at the expense of forests or other land uses that would cancel out the greenhouse gas benefits. It will also be important to explore opportunities to more fully incorporate smallholders into bioenergy production premiums.

Middle East and North Africa

Given the dry conditions and surplus of oil resources in this region, bioenergy is unlikely to play a large role. However, there may be some opportunities for small-scale production of biofuels as a part of a broader rural development plans that use crops adapted for dry land conditions (which may also help combat desertification).

South Asia

A land-use assessment is critical to determining where bioenergy development is best suited in South Asia. Bioenergy expansion in this region often targets degraded land that is often already being used, potentially leading to land-use conflicts.

Bioenergy production in South Asia should be balanced in the use of water resources. Crops planted on drylands should not be irrigated to increase yields, as this could further deplete resources and create conflicts with other water users.

POLICY IMPLICATIONS

It is important for consumer countries to consider the upstream impacts of their bioenergy mandates and targets, including the social and environmental effects. The European Union has already begun discussions regarding the potential environmental implications its standards will have in producer countries and what this means for the targets. Consumer countries can help drive the development of biofuel production standards (such as those developed by the roundtable on sustainable biofuels). Consumer countries can also agree to purchase biodiesel only from producers that already meet previously established standards (such as those established at the roundtables on sustainable soy and sustainable palm oil).

Wood pellet use is expected to increase in developed and some developing countries. Imports, including imports from the tropics, will be needed to meet this demand. Such production could put new pressures on land and local populations if it is not handled using sustainable production schemes.

In producer countries, it is important to balance production targets with environmental and social concerns, including concerns about food security. The trade-offs associated with bioenergy production should be carefully considered in order to determine the correct feedstock for a particular location, after considering production costs and rural development. Some regional criteria within countries that have established national biofuels promotion policies may also need to be applied, as some areas may have very low environmental risks of expanding biofuels and others have very high risks. Investors and development organizations can play key roles by steering investments into feedstocks that meet best practices for environmental, social, and climate change considerations.

As a result of various initiatives to reduce carbon emissions and environmental degradation (including payments for environmental services, carbon markets, and bioenergy developments), new demands are being placed on environmental goods and services, and lands (including forests) are being assigned a monetary value. These initiatives may provide new opportunities for income generation and job creation, but they are also likely to attract investors. This can result in insecure rights for the poor, including reduced access to land or reduced ability to secure products. New opportunities should ensure the participation and land rights of the people living in the areas targeted for new initiatives.

Bioenergy solutions should strive to be environmentally sensitive and have a positive social impact. Opportunities for doing so appear greater for solid biomass than liquid biofuels (based on current feedstocks and production methods), which tend to have larger environmental risks and mixed benefits for the poor.

The production of conventional bioenergy development (at both large and small scales) can create opportunities for the poor. Other options should also be studied. When produced at a small scale, for example, biochar may help mitigate climate change and help increase rural production (which would yield nutritional and financial benefits).[1] Other opportunities cited in this report include black liquor and the use of modern stoves.

Recent studies suggest that soot (also known as black carbon) released from burning woodfuels, industry, farming, and transportation may contribute more to climate change than originally thought. Further analysis is needed to bring clarity to this potentially important source of global warming.

Given the potential for using wood residues as a source of energy, it would be useful to identify which countries have the greatest potential to use residues and thinnings. Further analysis of the full potential of wood residues for energy generation is also important.

Economies of scale could drive production toward a large scale. There is therefore a need to identify opportunities for small-scale producers into bioenergy production systems.

The future of bioenergy development is unclear. One open question is whether food crops will be the primary feedstock for bioenergy in the future or development of advanced technologies will promote grasses, trees, and residues (lignocelluloses) as the principal feedstocks. Using nonfood crops could reduce concerns about the effect of biofuels on food prices. However, the technology is still uncertain. Both governments and private companies are investing in nonfood bioenergy, but the profitability of such investment is highly dependent on the price of oil. This technology is not expected to be commercially viable for 5–10 years, although major breakthroughs in technology could mean that the fuels become economically feasible much earlier than expected. Shifting production away from food as a biofuel feedstock would have significant implications for the forestry sector.

Even with new developments, however, there will still be a need to use land resources for production. The preliminary estimates of potential changes in land use presented in this report and the large impact that bioenergy may have on natural and agricultural lands suggest that additional land-use analyses should be conducted in countries that plan to implement large-scale bioenergy production.

NOTE

1. Biochar is a by-product of the pyrolysis of solid biomass. When added to the soil on degraded lands, it can improve fertility.

Production of Alcohol Bioenergy from Sugars and Starches

Technologies for conversion of sugar and starch to fuel are the most technologically and commercially mature today; sugarcane and corn supply almost all the bioethanol produced. Developing countries are increasing their use of these crops, along with a variety of alternative sugar and starch crops for fuels, including sweet sorghum, cassava, and Nypa palm.

The major drawback of sugar and starch crops is that they are food crops: their use for fuel can have adverse impacts on food availability and prices. Another drawback is that these crops tend to be intensive in the use of inputs, including land, water, fertilizer, and pesticides, which have various environmental implications (Rajagopal and Zilberman 2007).

SUGARCANE

Sugarcane (*Saccharum*) is a genus of 6–37 species of tall perennial grasses that are native to warm, temperate, and tropical regions of South Asia and Southeast Asia. Sugarcane was rapidly spread by traders throughout the tropics and is a major source of income for many countries, especially in Central and South America and the Caribbean. It is used to produce sugar, syrups, molasses, spirits, soft drinks, and ethanol for fuel.

Economics of Sugarcane Production

Sugarcane harvest yields 50–150 MT/hectare or more, depending on the length of the growing period, the volume of rainfall, and whether it is the first-planted harvest or a ratoon crop.[1] Sugar yield depends on cane tonnage, the sugar content of the cane, and the quality of the cane; it usually represents 10–15 percent of the harvest (FAO/AGLW 2002b). Average ethanol yield is about 70 liters per MT.

An advantage of using sugarcane to produce ethanol is that many sugar and ethanol production plants have the capability to burn residual bagasse for power generation, enabling these plants to become self-sufficient in electricity and even have some surplus for sale into the electricity grid. The molasses by-product of sugar production can be commercially viable for conversion into ethanol, which can further increase revenue (Kojima and others 2007). The average nonfeedstock cost for producing sugarcane is about $0.25/l, with a lower figure for Brazil (FAO2008a).

Brazil is the world's largest sugarcane produces (table A.1); it also produces the largest amount of fuel ethanol from sugarcane. Other large producers include India, China, Mexico, and Thailand, which use sugarcane largely for sugar production. These countries are considering sugarcane ethanol production, but they may have difficulty replicating Brazil's cost-efficient system, for the reasons outlined below.

In crop year 2007/08, Brazil produced 493 million MT; about 35 percent of the global total (FAO 2008a). The majority of Brazil's sugarcane harvest (about 50–60 percent, depending on the year) is converted into ethanol to fuel the transportation industry (figure A.1).

Sugarcane production in Brazil has been increasing at a steady rate for the past 50 years. Of all crops that can be used as fuel, sugarcane represents more than half of potential future supplies available for export to global markets or

Table A.1 Sugarcane Production and Yields by Leading Global Producers, 2007/08

Country	Production quantity (million MT)	Percentage of global production	Yield (MT/hectare)	Area harvested (million hectares)
Brazil	514	33.0	76.6	6.7
India	356	22.8	72.6	4.9
China	106	6.8	86.2	1.2
Thailand	64	4.1	74.5	1.0
Pakistan	55	3.5	53.2	1.0

Source: FAO 2008a.

Figure A.1   Sugarcane, Sugar, and Ethanol Production in Brazil, 1990/1991–2006/2007

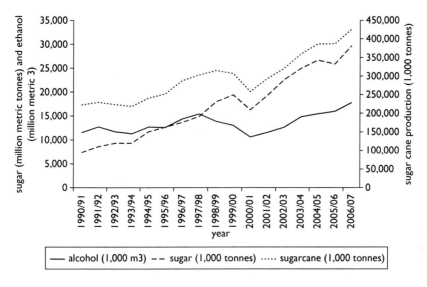

Source: UNICA 2008.

conversion to ethanol (on a gasoline-equivalent basis) over the next two decades (Kline and others 2008).

Brazil has a distinct advantage in sugarcane production, for a variety of reasons:

- Cane cultivation is water intensive, and nearly all cane fields in Brazil are rainfed.
- Sugarcane and other activities need not compete for land in Brazil, because there is still land suitable for growing sugarcane that is not currently forested or used for agriculture.
- Productivity has been boosted by decades of research and commercial cultivation.[2]
- Residual bagasse is used to heat and power distilleries, thereby lowering energy costs.
- Most distilleries in Brazil are part of sugar mill/distillery complexes, capable of changing the production ratio of sugar to ethanol.[3]
- The Brazilian government provided crucial institutional support to get the ethanol industry off the ground by providing incentives, setting technical standards, supporting technologies for ethanol production and use, and ensuring appropriate market conditions (von Braun and Pachauri 2006).

All of these factors give Brazil a significant competitive cost advantage. As a result, the cost of ethanol production in Brazil was about $0.29–$0.35/l in 2008, corresponding to $0.44–$0.53/l of gasoline equivalent.[4] These numbers depend on the exchange rate; costs were high in 2008 compared with earlier years.

One important development in the Brazilian sugarcane-ethanol market came about in 2002, when the first flex-fuel vehicles were released. These vehicles, designed to use any mixture of hydrous ethanol and gasohol, have been extremely popular with consumers (figure A.2). By giving drivers the opportunity to choose from a wide variety of fuel blends based on price, they have allayed fears of ethanol shortages (Green*ergy* 2008a). At the end of 2008, nearly 90 percent of all passenger vehicles sold in Brazil were flex-fuel vehicles (Anfavea 2008).

Social and Economic Impact of Sugarcane Production

Sugarcane production provides opportunities for job creation. Almost 1 million formal sector workers were involved in Brazil's extended sugar-alcohol sector in 2005, a 53 percent increase over 2000 (see table 3.5 in chapter 3).

However, there are concerns regarding the working conditions in the sugarcane industry. In 2007 news stories described conditions at one sugarcane plantation in Brazil that included work days of up to 13 hours a day for as little as $8 a day. Workers may be paid by the amount of cane they cut, they may work until the point of exhaustion, risking serious injury and even death: 17 deaths were reported between 2004 and 2007 in São Paulo alone, according to one report (Raynes 2008). Workers may live in overcrowded conditions without

Figure A.2 Passenger Car Sales in Brazil, 2004–08

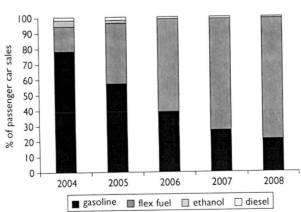

Source: Authors, based on data from Anfavea 2008.

proper sanitation or food storage facilities. They may travel long distances to their jobs and be required to deduct the transportation and lodging costs from their wages, sometimes resulting in negative earnings. Human rights and labor organizations estimate that 25,000–40,000 workers in Brazil could be indebted to sugarcane producers in this way (Biopact 2007b).

Sugarcane harvesting has traditionally involved burning the cane to prepare it for manual harvesting. Workers prefer burning the cane before harvesting, because doing so increases their productivity by as much as 80 percent. It also decreases the risk of injury from sharp cane leaves and insect and snake bites (Greenergy 2008a).

Brazil's government passed a law in 2000 to reduce burning by 55 percent and shift to a mechanized harvest where possible (Law No. 10.547). As a result, more than 100,000 of the nation's 1.2 million seasonal sugarcane workers became unemployed, and many producers relocated their farms in order to avoid regulation (Martines-Filho and others 2006).

Impact of Sugarcane Production on the Use of Land and Other Resources

Eighty-five percent of bioethanol production in Brazil comes from sugarcane grown in the center-south of the country. The state of São Paulo, whose climate is ideally suited to the crop, is the largest producer, producing 65 percent of Brazil's sugarcane. A forthcoming World Bank study estimates that there are about 35 million hectares of available arable land for agricultural "expansion" in Brazil suitable for sugarcane production without promoting further deforestation. There is limited room for expansion of sugarcane production in the Amazon region, where the hot, humid conditions are unfavorable for production (Greenergy 2008a).

Other countries that are making large investments into sugarcane ethanol include Argentina, Colombia, Mexico, Guatemala, Nicaragua, China, and India. All of these countries have more limited opportunities for sugarcane production than Brazil, because of the need to irrigate. Another concern (particularly in China and India) is that the arable land suitable for sugarcane may displace other productive systems and lead to food security concerns (Kline and others 2008). A combination of physical attributes, including soil, slope, climate, water; tenure; prior use; economics; and policies will influence what lands will become available for expansion of sugarcane for ethanol.

Sugarcane has been identified as a cause of deforestation in ecologically sensitive areas, including the State of Alagoas, where only 3 percent of the original rainforest cover remains. A report by the World Wildlife Fund (n.d.) shows an 85 percent reduction in Cerrado vegetation surrounding the cities of Franca, Araraquara, Ribeirao Preto, and São Carlos, caused in part by clearing for sugarcane cultivation. None of the areas targeted for future expansion in Brazil is located in the Amazon or the Pantanal (Greenergy 2008a). However, there are concerns that expanding sugarcane production could lead to indirect deforestation if ranching is displaced into forested lands. In response, the Brazilian government has established technical and environmental criteria for the sustainable expansion of ethanol production and is making an effort to reduce the negative impacts of sugarcane expansion. Approaches include focusing growth in areas of abandoned ranch land and improving the sustainability of production in other areas.

Environmental Impact of Sugarcane Production

Sugarcane grows best at daily temperatures of 22°C–30°C. In order to achieve high yields, a long growing season is required (12–16 months). Production is best suited between the latitudes of 35°N and 35°S. The first sugarcane crop is normally followed by two to four ratoon crops (FAO/AGLW 2002a).

In Brazil carbon dioxide savings from bioethanol made from sugarcane (not counting land-use change) can reach as high as 77 percent (Green*ergy* 2008a). Eight equivalent units of fossil energy are produced for each unit consumed in production, which is much more efficient than most other biofuel feedstocks (Kline and others 2008). Sugarcane production requires relatively low levels of fertilizer input per unit of output, and cane is harvested efficiently on large plantations. Preharvest burning of sugarcane makes harvesting easier and safer for workers, but it raises the levels of greenhouse gases, carbon monoxide, fine particulates, and ozone in the atmosphere (WWF n.d.). According to a World Wildlife Fund report (n.d.), environmental impacts from sugarcane cultivation can be reduced in a variety of ways, including increasing the efficiency of irrigation systems, reducing fertilizer use in cane cultivation systems, adopting integrated pest management (IPM) systems, and reducing soil erosion.

Impact on Water Resources

In some countries with weak environmental laws, sugar mill or ethanol effluent may be discharged directly into streams. This may cause eutrophication or release toxins, such as heavy metals, oil, grease, and cleaning agents. In countries in which irrigation is necessary water resources may be depleted.

Impact on Soil Resources

The preharvest burning of sugarcane may decrease soil quality by killing beneficial microbes and removing as much as 30 percent of nitrogen from the soil (WWF n.d.). Burning also exposes the soil, making it more susceptible to erosion.

Impact on Biodiversity

Sugarcane has replaced natural forests in some tropical regions and islands; it was cultivated in former areas of wetlands across the globe. A 2005 World

Wildlife Fund report notes that if not for sugarcane cultivation, the Caribbean region and islands in Southeast Asia would have greater biological diversity than they do today. However, if expanding sugarcane production meets developing guidelines and standards for better land management practices, it could actually contribute to reforestation and increased protection of natural resources versus previous land uses(Kline and others 2008).

CORN

Zea mays, commonly known as maize or corn, is one of a variety of cereal crops that provide more food energy to humans than any other type of crop. Together, corn, wheat, rice, and barley account for more than 84 percent of all cereal production worldwide; corn alone accounts for close to 11 percent of total global crop production, third only to wheat and rice (FAO 2008a).

Recent genetic evidence suggests that corn domestication occurred about 9,000 years ago, in central Mexico. As it was domesticated, corn spread widely and rapidly, becoming a staple food crop in many countries of the world.

Economics of Corn Production

The United States and China are the world's largest producers of corn (table A.2), accounting for close to 65 percent of the global total (FAO 2008a). Other large producers include Brazil, Mexico, and Argentina.

In addition to providing food and feedstock, corn yields ethanol. The average ethanol yield from corn is about 400l/MT, translating to about 260 gasoline equivalent l/MT. The largest producer of corn-based ethanol is the United States, which accounted for almost 45 percent of global ethanol production in 2006 (table A.3). Other producers include China, Japan, Brazil, and South Africa. Production of corn ethanol has been increasing since about 2001 in the United States; it represents a growing share of U.S. corn production (figure A.3).

Table A.2 Corn Production, Yield, and Area Harvested by Leading Global Producers, 2007/08

Country	Production quantity (million MT/hectare)	Percentage of global production	Yield (MT hectare)	Area harvested (million hectares)
United States	331.2	41.8	9.46	35.01
China	152.3	19.2	5.17	29.48
Brazil	58.6	7.4	3.99	14.7
Mexico	22.7	2.9	3.08	7.35
Argentina	20.9	2.6	6.4	3.26

Source: FAO 2008a; Shapouri, Duffield, and Wang 2009.

Table A.3 Corn-Based Ethanol Production, Yield, and Price by Leading Global Producers, 2006

Country	Production (million MT)	Percentage of global total
United States	1,130,000	52.8
China	174,340	8.1
Japan	101,700	4.8
Brazil	75,200	3.5
South Africa	73,200	3.4

Source: FAO 2008a.

Figure A.3 Total Corn Production and Production of Corn for Ethanol Production in the United States, 1986–2007

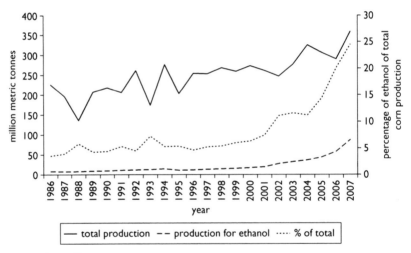

Source: USDA 2009.

The nonfeedstock cost of producing ethanol from corn in the United States is about $0.15/l (FAO 2008a). Based on current production technology, ethanol production in the United States would not be competitive without a federal tax credit.

During 2008 corn prices rose to record levels, largely as a result of the use of corn to produce ethanol fuels, before falling again (figure A.4). The spike created a crisis for low-income countries in which corn makes up the primary dietary staple. In general, the urban poor suffer most when food prices rice (World Bank 2008a).

BIOENERGY DEVELOPMENT

Figure A.4   Average Price for U.S. Corn, 2002–08

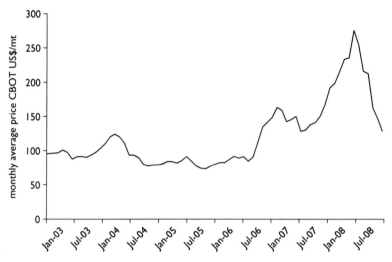

Source: USDA 2009.

Impact of Corn Production on the Use of Land and Other Resources

The impact of corn ethanol production on land-use changes is highly uncertain and variable. In the United States, a portion of the land currently set aside through the Conservation Reserve Program has the potential to be converted into corn in order to meet growing ethanol targets.[5] Concerns have also been raised that if corn prices are high in the United States, soy producers could shift to corn, providing an incentive for other producer countries to meet the global demand for soy (and clearing new lands as a result).

Environmental Impact of Corn Production

The life cycle of E85 corn grain ethanol–gasoline blend yields emissions of five major air pollutants—carbon monoxide, volatile organic compounds, particulate matter, sulfur oxide, and nitrogen oxide (contributors to acid rain)—that are higher than those of gasoline (Hill and others 2006). Moreover, producing corn requires fossil fuel inputs at every stage of the process: transporting and planting the seeds; operating farm equipment; making and applying fertilizers, herbicides, and insecticides; and transporting the corn to market. Several studies have looked at the greenhouse gases emissions from corn ethanol. Estimates range from a 38 percent reduction to a 30 percent increase over the production and combustion of an energetically equivalent amount of gasoline (table A.4). Some of the variation is a result of incorporating producer emissions into the value.

Table A.4 Estimated Change in Greenhouse Gas Emission from Replacing Conventional Gasoline with Corn Ethanol

Study	Percentage change
Levelton (2000)	−38
Levy (1993)	−33
Levy (1993)	−30
Marland (1991)	−21
Delucchi (2003)	−10
Hill and others (2006)	−12
Wang, Saricks, and Santini (E10) (1999)	1
Wang, Saricks, and Santini (E85) (1999)	14–19
Pimentel (1991, 2001)	30

Source: IEA 2004; Kojima and others 2007.
Note: Negative figures indicate reductions in greenhouse gas emissions; positive figures indicate increases in greenhouse gas emissions.

When land-use changes are included, the benefits of using corn for ethanol appear to decrease. A 2008 study in *Science* estimated that ethanol from corn produced on converted U.S. central grasslands or on lands formerly in the Conservation Reserve Program would initially release large amounts of carbon into the atmosphere. It will take many years of biofuel production on the same lands to repay these initial emissions and see carbon reductions (Fargione and others 2008).

Impact on Water Resources

Corn requires a minimum annual rainfall of 500 mm, with the best yields at 1,200–1,500 mm. It is drought tolerant early in the growth cycle, but after about five weeks it becomes extremely susceptible to drought. Because of this, corn is widely irrigated, especially in arid locations. In China it takes an average of 2,400 liters of water to produce enough corn for one liter of ethanol; the figure in the United States is just 400 liters (Rossi and Lambrou 2008).

Large amounts of fertilizer and pesticides go into corn production. They may lead to contamination of ground and surface waters and eutrophication of water bodies. The yearly "dead zone" in the Gulf of Mexico is an example of contamination from fertilizer runoff in the Midwest region of the United States. Release of ethanol effluent from plants into the environment may also cause environmental damage. Plants produce 13 liters of wastewater for each liter of corn ethanol (Pimentel and Patzek 2005).

Impact on Soil Resources

Corn production on sensitive lands may cause soil erosion from wind and water; heavy fertilizer and pesticide inputs can cause soil contamination. When corn is produced using no-till/low-till and soil conservation measures, soil erosion can be kept low.

Impact on Biodiversity

Replacing grasslands and forestlands for monocultures of corn reduces biodiversity. Increasing corn production may also have indirect deforestation impacts, such as the example cited earlier of displaced soy production, which could also affect biodiversity.

SWEET SORGHUM

Sorghum is a genus of a species of grasses, the most familiar of which is a common grain crop cultivated worldwide. Sweet sorghum (*Sorghum bicolor*) is similar to grain sorghum but features more rapid growth, higher biomass production, and a wide adaptability to a variety of conditions, including drought, saline and alkaline soils, and tolerance to waterlogging, which have allowed it to be planted in arid and semiarid regions of the world (Reddy and others 2007). Sweet sorghum is primarily used as animal fodder, although it is also used to produce grains, sugar, and industrial commodities such as organic fertilizers. Its stalk can be used to produce bioethanol (FAO 2008c).

Sweet sorghum can be successfully grown in the semiarid tropics; it has been cultivated for centuries in parts of Asia and Africa. The crop already covers a global area of about 45 million hectares (Reddy and others 2007). Countries that have already begun production of ethanol from sweet sorghum include Burkina Faso, China, India, Mexico, Nigeria, South Africa, and Zambia.

Economics of Sweet Sorghum Production

Sorghum yields average 20–50 MT per hectare. In most places, two crops may be harvested per year, leading to a yearly biomass yield of 40–100 MT per hectare. In Africa sorghum has a higher yield than most other crops commonly used to produce ethanol (table A.5.)

Sorghum is less water intensive than other common grain and sugar crops, using about 300 kg water/kg dry matter (versus 350 kg for corn and 1,250 kg for sugarcane) (DESA 2007). In addition to the stalks, a sweet sorghum crop can have a grain yield of 2.0–2.5 MT per hectare, which can be used as food or feed (Reddy and others 2007).

Pilot studies have indicated that ethanol production from sweet sorghum can be cost-effective. Results for Zambia show that some sweet sorghum varieties are competitive with sugarcane, because three harvests can be produced within 18 months (in contrast to only one sugarcane harvest in the same period). Research by the National Agricultural Research Institute in

Table A.5 Potential Ethanol Yields by Feedstock in Africa

Feedstock	Biomass yield (MT/hectare/year)	Ethanol yield (liters/MT)	Ethanol yield (liters/hectare/year)
Sweet sorghum	92	108	5,000
Sugarcane	50	70	3,500
Wood	20	160	3,200
Cassava	12	180	2,150
Corn	6	370	2,220
Molasses	n.a.	270	n.a.

Source: Hodes 2006.
Note: n.a. = not applicable.

India confirms these findings (DESA 2007). A study in Mexico suggests that sorghum is the least-cost feedstock available (Kline and others 2008). Another benefit of sorghum is that the leftover stillage, which contains levels of cellulose similar to those of as sugarcane bagasse, can be used to power fuel production.

In some places, sweet sorghum may be a better alternative than sugarcane. In addition to using less water, sweet sorghum has a higher fermentable sugar content (15–20 percent) than sugarcane (10–15 percent) (Reddy and others 2007). This means that the annual yield of biofuel per hectare is higher than sugarcane and its cultivation cost can be lower (Rajagopal 2007).

Sweet sorghum's ethanol production capacity is comparable to that of sugarcane molasses and sugarcane. In addition, the cost of ethanol production from sweet sorghum is lower than that of sugarcane molasses at prevailing prices. The stillage from sweet sorghum after the extraction of juice has a higher biological value than the bagasse from sugarcane when used as forage for cattle, as it is rich in micronutrients and minerals. The use of sweet sorghum for ethanol production is being given high priority by many developing countries, including India (Reddy and others 2007).

Some of the challenges of large-scale ethanol production from sweet sorghum include establishing processing facilities that are large enough to process the feedstock within a few weeks of harvest. Building large ethanol production facilities for a single feedstock can mean that the facilities will be underutilized or idle for many months each year if there is no integrated production of several crops and simultaneous processing of the full crop components (DESA 2007).

Social and Economic Impact of Sweet Sorghum Production

Given that sorghum is already cultivated in many of the countries considering ethanol production, there is a high likelihood that small-scale farmers are already familiar with the crop and, therefore, more likely to adopt it. Shorter-duration crops like sweet sorghum allow poor farmers to practice crop rotation and provide them with the flexibility to shift to more profitable crops depending on market conditions, especially during the initial stages of development of the biofuel industry (Rajagopal 2007).

Sweet sorghum for ethanol production can also create jobs (table A.6). Figures are available only for highly mechanized production; there are no good estimates for smaller-scale job creation. Mechanized production is estimated to create 10,000 jobs, with an additional 1,500 jobs created to produce ethanol vehicles and bioethanol fuel.

Impact of Sweet Sorghum Production on the Use of Land and Other Resources

Depending on the scale of production, there is some potential that land could be converted for sweet sorghum production. Sorghum is capable of growing in conditions that other crops are unable to tolerate, including in drought-prone areas with poor soils. Because of this, it is often planted on fragile and marginal lands. In Africa (where sorghum is widely cultivated), this could mean conversion of large areas of dry habitat to cultivation (WWF 2005).

Environmental Impact of Sweet Sorghum Production

Sweet sorghum has a good energy balance, generating eight units of energy for every unit of fossil-fuel energy invested. If land is not converted for production, sweet sorghum ethanol therefore produces fewer greenhouse gas emissions than traditional fossil fuels (ICRISAT 2008).

Impact on Water Resources

Sorghum is suited to grow in areas with annual rainfall range of 400–750 mm. It has the ability to become dormant and resume growth after a relatively severe drought. Sorghum production does not generally compete with other agricultural crops for water resources. However, as irrigation can increase yields, water resources could potentially be diverted into sorghum production for biofuels. This is true for any crop grown in regions with water scarcity.

Table A.6 Estimated Direct Job Creation for Mechanized Bioethanol Production from Sweet Sorghum in Brazil

Type of jobs	Number of jobs created
Jobs in production of sweet sorghum	2,950
Jobs in industrial and related activity	7,000
Total	9,950

Source: Grassi n.d.

Sorghum requires fairly large inputs of nitrogen and moderate amounts of phosphorus and potassium, which can lead to high fertilizer runoff and waterway contamination. It also requires pesticides, which have a high potential to contaminate waterways.

Impact on Soil Resources

Sorghum production has high potential to cause soil erosion, even on relatively shallow slopes. In addition, when the crop is harvested, there is potential for nutrient leaching from the soil, which may be exacerbated if sorghum stillage is removed from the field in order to be processed into biofuels.

Impact on Biodiversity

Sorghum production in Africa is one of the primary causes of dry habitat fragmentation. It changes the composition of flora and fauna that depend on this habitat (WWF 2005). Sweet sorghum is an invasive crop. The U.S. Forest Service's Institute of Pacific Islands (2006) lists it as an invasive species in Fiji, the Marshall Islands, the Federated States of Micronesia, and New Zealand.

CASSAVA

Manihot esculenta, better known as cassava, yucca, manioc, or mandioca, is a perennial woody shrub with an edible root that grows in tropical and subtropical regions. Originally native to Brazil and Mexico, cassava was domesticated by Portuguese explorers and introduced across the globe. Cassava has the ability to grow on marginal lands. Harvest can be delayed for up to two years, meaning producers can wait for favorable market conditions or use the crop as an insurance against food shortages (ITTA 2007). Because of these advantages, cassava has replaced corn as a food staple in parts of Africa.

Fresh cassava roots have many uses. They can be dried and milled into flour or peeled, grated, and washed with water to extract the starch, which hat can be used to make breads, crackers, pasta, and pearls of tapioca. Unpeeled roots can be grated and dried for use as animal feed. Cassava is used in industrial processing procedures and product manufacture including paper making, textiles, adhesives, high-fructose syrup, and alcohol (O'Hair 1995).

Economics of Cassava Production

Africa is the largest producer of cassava, with 54 percent of world output in 2006. Nigeria alone accounts for more than 20 percent of global production (table A.7) (FAO 2007). Asia is the second-largest producer of cassava, accounting for 30 percent of global production. Much of this production takes place in Thailand, which produces cassava principally as a starch for export.

Table A.7 Cassava Production, Yield, and Area Harvested by Leading Global Producers, 2007

Country	Production (million MT)	Percentage of global production	Yield (MT/hectare)	Area harvested (million hectares)
Nigeria	46	20.1	11.9	3.9
Brazil	27	12.0	14.0	1.9
Thailand	26	11.6	22.9	1.2
Indonesia	20	8.6	16.2	1.2
Democratic Republic of Congo	15	6.6	8.1	1.9

Source: FAO 2008a.

Yields of the largest producers varies greatly across regions, ranging from 8 MT/hectare in the Democratic Republic of Congo to 22 MT/hectare in Thailand. Yields are lowest in Africa (FAO 2008a). Typical ethanol yields from cassava are in the range of 180l/MT, a gasoline equivalent of about 100l/MT. Some studies in China and Thailand have suggested nonfeedstock production costs of about $0.20/l for cassava (FAO 2008a). Thailand is the largest producer of cassava for commercial applications. The economic potential for cassava remains largely untapped in Africa, despite annual increases in production (Eneas 2006).

Nigerian cassava growers, in association with the state petroleum company, have set a goal to produce 1 billion liters of cassava ethanol a year (Eneas 2006). In the Philippines, 300,000 hectares have been allotted by a private company to begin in-country production of cassava for ethanol. The company is already purchasing cassava from other countries in order to meet plant capacity (FAO 2007). The Quantum Group of Australia was reportedly planning to invest $250 million to develop four ethanol plants to produce 132 million liters of bioethanol a year; the plan would require 100,000 hectares of land in Indonesia to fuel the plants. Most of the land would come from small farms in one of the poorest regions in Indonesia. The project is expected to provide employment for as many as 60,000 local farmers (Biopact 2008).

As a result of oil price volatility, some countries have begun to evaluate using cassava as a source of ethanol fuel (Eneas 2006). China is already producing biofuel using cassava as a feedstock. Guangxi Province, in the southwest part of the country, has replaced traditional petrol and diesel oil with commercially produced cassava ethanol. However, ethanol producers say they need more government subsidies in order to stay profitable (Bezlova 2008). A leading petroleum refinery in Thailand is finalizing the construction of a cassava-based biofuel plant. Other countries considering cassava biofuels include Indonesia, Nigeria, Papua New Guinea, the Philippines, Swaziland, and Thailand (FAO 2007).

Social and Economic Impact of Cassava Production

Cassava harvesting can begin eight months after planting or left to grow for more than one season. Most cassava is harvested by hand. The shelf life of cassava is only a few days, unless the roots receive special treatment (O'Hair 1995).

Cassava is more difficult to produce than other grain crops, because the stem cuttings are bulky and highly perishable (IITA 2007). Other difficulties include pests and diseases, which, together with poor harvesting practices, cause yield losses that may be as high as 50 percent in Africa (IITA 2007).

Because cassava requires very few nutrient or pesticide inputs, it is frequently cultivated by poor farmers on marginal lands who cannot afford to grow other crops or by women on small plots along with other food crops. It is the staple food of more than 200 million Africans—more than one-quarter of the continent's population (Eneas 2006). In places where land is scarce, cassava serves as food security for villagers vulnerable to malnutrition. For farmers living close to towns, it is a valuable cash crop, with a flourishing market. Market access is difficult for many Africans, however: a study conducted in the 1990s finds that only 20 percent of cassava-producing villages could be reached by motorized transport and that on average farmers had to carry their loads more than 10 kilometers to reach a market (Eneas 2006).

Using cassava as a biofuel feedstock could have a major effect on prices, which are expected to increase 135 percent by 2020, in order to meet current targets (Boddiger 2007). Such increases in food prices could have the dual effect of increasing wages for small farmers while making cassava unaffordable for those who purchase it as food.

Impact of Cassava Production on the Use of Land and Other Resources

Because cassava is a hardy crop produced mostly by the poor, it is often grown on low-value and marginal lands. Cassava does not often replace other agriculture, because it grows where few other food crops can. This implies that increasing demand for cassava for biofuels could lead to conversion of lower (agricultural) value pastures and woodlands.

Environmental Impact of Cassava Production

Cassava is most productive in warm, sunny climates. It requires 8 months to produce a crop under ideal climatic conditions, 18 months when conditions are unfavorable.

One study in Thailand finds that cassava ethanol has a positive energy balance of 22.4 MJ/l and net avoided greenhouse gas emissions of 1.6 $kgCO_2e/l$. It finds a greenhouse gas abatement cost of \$99/T of CO_2. Ethanol from cassava is much less cost-effective than other climate strategies relevant to Thailand in the short term (Nguyen, Gheewala, and Garivait 2007). The study does not factor in changes in land use.

Impact on Water Resources

Cassava is traditionally grown in a savannah climate, but it is tolerant of drought as well as high rainfall. It will not tolerate flooding. Because cassava does not need a large amount of rainfall to flourish or large quantities of fertilizer or pesticide inputs, it has a minimal impact on water resources.

Impact on Soil Resources

Cassava thrives in relatively poor, dry soils and requires few fertilizer inputs. It can be grown in soils with a pH of 4.0–8.0 (O'Hair 1995). Because the plant does not produce enough vegetation to cover the soil well and early crops tend to be harvested within a few months or the first year at the latest, the production of cassava can contribute to soil erosion (WWF 2005).

Impact on Biodiversity

Cassava is often grown on marginal lands, which can be of high value for biodiversity (WWF 2005). It has not been identified as an invasive species in any of the regions where it has been introduced.

NYPA PALM

Nypa fruticans is a palm native to South and Southeast Asia. It is common on coasts and rivers flowing into the Indian and Pacific oceans, from India and Bangladesh to the Pacific Islands and northern Australia. It is known by many different names, including Nypa, nipah, nipa, attap chee, mangrove palm, gol pata, and dani.

The sugar-rich sap from Nypa can be fermented to produce ethanol for biofuel. Malaysia and Nigeria are currently pursuing options to produce bioethanol from Nypa fruticans.

Economics of Nypa Production

One major advantage of Nypa over other ethanol feedstocks is that the trees can be tapped year round, providing a continuous source of sugar. However, the lack of crop residues means that there is a need for external energy inputs to process the ethanol (Dalibard 1999)

Nypa can be tapped for sugar 4 years after planting, after which it provides a continuous yield for 50 or more years (Dalibard 1999). The sap contains 15 percent sugar content. Studies have shown that it is capable of producing 20 MT of sugar/hectare and may yield 6,500–15,600 l/hectare of alcohol fuel (Biopact 2007b). Others studies suggest that with optimal plantation management, this figure may reach as much as 20,000 liters (Biopact 2007b). Given the high-labor intensity of sugar extraction these production levels seem ambitious.

One company that is investing in the production of Nypa ethanol on a large scale is Pioneer Bio Industries Corp. of Malaysia, which claims that when its 15 planned refineries begin operation in 2009, it will be able to produce 6.48 billion liters per year of Nypa palm ethanol from 10,000 hectares of land. Given current yield estimates, this land area would result in a maximum of just 200 million liters of ethanol (Biopact 2007b). Pioneer has reportedly received an order worth more than $66 billion from one of the largest trading companies in the world (whose name is withheld by Pioneer) to buy the Nypa ethanol from 2009 to 2013 (Biopact 2007b).

In Nigeria local NGOs are investigating the feasibility of building a Nypa ethanol industry in the Niger Delta region. The aim of the small project is to bring jobs to the impoverished region and to make use of the invasive Nypa.

Social and Economic Impact of Nypa Production

Nypa is naturally occurring throughout South and Southeast Asia. It does not compete with most other agricultural crops. Because sugar can be tapped year round, production is uninterrupted by replanting and rotation, which means that workers can be continuously employed. However, tapping Nypa palms is labor intensive and costly. In the past, whenever easier jobs became available, laborers abandoned sap harvesting.

Along with commercial production for fuel, Nypa has the opportunity to provide livelihoods and income for villagers because of its wide variety of marketable products. In addition to sugar and ethanol production, Nypa palm has a wide variety of uses throughout the area in which it is found, including food, beverages, and animal fodder; the leaves can also be used as housing materials and weaving. Harvesting the leaves reduces the sugar yield.

Impact of Nypa Production on the Use of Land and Other Resources

Nypa palm is primarily found in coastal brackish waters and does not directly compete with most land uses. Therefore, conversion of agricultural lands for Nypa production is not likely.

Environmental Impact of Nypa Production

No studies have been conducted regarding the effectiveness of Nypa fuel over conventional fossil fuels to reduce greenhouse gas emissions.

Impact on Water Resources

Nypa fruticans is found mostly in brackish tidal areas. It is generally considered a mangrove, although it is not a mangrove in the strict sense, as it cannot tolerate inundation with undiluted sea water for long periods of time. It does not require a saline environment and can withstand freshwater conditions; it will survive occasional short-term drying of its environment (Joshi, Kanagaratnam, and Adhuri 2006).

Nypa requires no freshwater inputs. It is therefore unlikely to have a large impact on water resources.

Impact on Soil Resources

As Nypa grows in coastal tidal regions, it has few direct impacts on soil resources. As part of a mangrove ecosystem, it can protect the coastline from erosion.

Impact on Biodiversity

Planting Nypa for biofuel production could help restore damaged mangrove systems. Such systems offer coastline protection, as demonstrated by the lesser amounts of damage from the 2006 tsunami to areas with intact mangrove systems. Mangrove ecosystems also offer breeding areas for a wide variety of marine organisms and are critical to maintaining marine biodiversity.

In some places, Nypa is considered an invasive species. In Nigeria, where it was introduced in 1906–12, it displaced the native mangrove flora in the Niger Delta (Ita 1993). The Nigerian mangrove system is the largest in Africa and the third largest in the world, covering an area of more than 10,000 square kilometers, of which more than 504,000 hectares are found in the Niger Delta region. Nypa fruticans has become the third most dominant species and now encroaches 45 kilometers inland (Biopact 2007c). Several unsuccessful eradication efforts have been attempted, which is why an NGO in Nigeria is attempting to profit from the plant by using it to produce ethanol.

NOTES

1. A ratoon crop is a crop that matures into an economic crop the year after the lower parts of the cane and the root are left uncut at harvest.
2. Cane growers in Brazil use more than 500 commercial cane varieties that are resistant to many of the 40-odd crop diseases found in the country.
3. This capability enables plant owners to take advantage of fluctuations in the relative prices of sugar and ethanol and to benefit from the higher price that can be obtained by converting molasses into ethanol (Kojima and Johnson 2005).
4. Flex-fuel vehicle drivers switch to ethanol at prices equivalent to 65–70 percent of gasohol, representing the lower energy value of ethanol when used as a blend (pure gasoline is not sold at the pump in Brazil, where all gasoline is mixed with at least 20 percent alcohol).
5. The Conservation Reserve Program provides incentives for farmers to maintain agricultural land under vegetative cover, such as tame or native grasses, wildlife plantings, trees, filterstrips, and riparian buffers.

Production of Bioenergy from Oilseed Crops

Biodiesel is typically produced from oilseed crops, such as palm oil, soybean, and rapeseed. The main sources of edible oils require large quantities of inputs. In contrast, shrubs and trees, such as Jatropha, Pongamia, and jojoba, are low-input sources of inedible oils and suited to marginal lands; they could become major sources of biodiesel, especially in dry and semiarid regions of Asia and Africa. The economic viability of these crops under conditions of low inputs and poor land quality is low (Rajagopal 2007).

OIL PALM

Oil palm (*Elaeis guineensis*) is indigenous to the West African tropical rain forest region. The edible oil from the fruits was traditionally used for cooking, until British traders began to use it in the early 19th century as an industrial lubricant and later as a component of soap.

Oil palm can be found in a variety of products, including cooking oils, margarine, food additives, and detergents and cosmetics. A liquid fraction, olein, obtained by fractionation (the use of heat to separate palm oil into solid and liquid components) is used in chemical processes to produce esters, plastics, textiles, emulsifiers, explosives, and pharmaceutical products.

By far the greatest use of palm oil is as a food oil. It is extensively used in processed foods in Western Europe: 70 percent of all products on supermarket shelves in the United Kingdom are estimated to contain palm oil (Colchester and others 2006). Because of its economic importance as a high-yielding source of edible and technical oils, palm oil is an important plantation crop in countries with high rainfall and a tropical climate (FAO 2002a).

The growing popularity of biodiesel from oil palm has increased demand for it. New plantations are being established in many countries, including Colombia, Costa Rica, Côte d'Ivoire, Ecuador, Indonesia, Malaysia, Papua New Guinea, the Philippines, and Thailand, with the greatest planned expansion in Indonesia.

Economics of Palm Oil Production

Palm oil fresh fruit bunches have an oil content of more than 20 percent and provide a higher yield of oil per hectare than most other crops (MPOB 2009). Palm oil typically produces an average of about 1,100 liters of biodiesel per MT. In 2007/08 Malaysia and Indonesia were the largest producers of palm oil, accounting for more than 85 percent of global production (table B.2). Production in these countries has been steadily increasing for the past 20 years (USDA 2009) (figure B.1).

Palm oil is the most widely traded edible oil, accounting for more than half of foreign trade in edible oils oil (table B.1). Western Europe has historically been the largest consumer of palm oil products (figure B.2). Its demand or palm oil products recently stabilized. Demand from China, India, Pakistan, and Bangladesh has grown rapidly, driving the expansion of production in Southeast Asia. Global demand for palm oil is set to double by 2020, with a projected rate of increase of nearly 4 percent a year—twice the projected rate of growth for soybean oil (Colchester and others 2006).

Table B.1   World Edible Oil Exports, by Type, 2006/07–2008/09

	2006/2007		2007/2008		2008/2009	
Edible oil	Volume (million MT)	Percent of total	Volume (million MT)	Percent of total	Volume (million MT)	Percent of total
Palm	26.91	58.3	30.37	61.1	31.60	61.7
Soybean	10.57	22.9	10.79	21.7	10.32	20.1
Sunflower seed	3.86	8.4	3.54	7.1	4.13	8.1
Rapeseed	1.94	4.2	1.92	3.9	2.10	4.1
Coconut	1.82	4.0	2.03	4.1	1.99	3.9
Olive	0.70	1.5	0.69	1.4	0.75	1.5
Cottonseed	0.16	0.3	0.19	0.4	0.15	0.3
Peanut	0.16	0.3	0.18	0.4	0.20	0.4
Total edible oil	46.12	100.0	49.70	100.0	51.25	100.0

Source: USDA 2009.

Table B.2 World Palm Oil Production, 2006/07–2008/09

Country	2006/2007 Volume (million MT)	2006/2007 Percent of total	2007/2008 Volume (million MT)	2007/2008 Percent of total	2008/2009 Volume (million MT)	2008/2009 Percent of total
Malaysia	15.3	41.1	17.5	41.2	17.7	40.8
Indonesia	16.6	44.7	19.2	45.2	19.9	46.0
World total	37.2	100.0	42.4	100.0	43.2	100.0

Source: USDA 2009 and LMC International 2008 estimates.

Figure B.1 Production of Palm Oil by Indonesia and Malaysia, 1990/91–2008/09

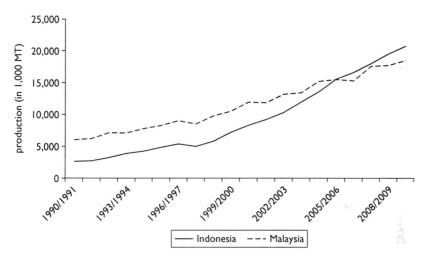

Source: USDA 2009.

Palm oil is the lowest-cost feedstock for producing biodiesel today, but future demand will continue to determine prices (Kojima and others 2007). The price of crude palm oil is closely correlated to that of crude oil. Its average price fluctuated widely in 2007 and 2008, increasing by 68 percent in 2007 and dropping sharply in the second half of 2008, from more than $1,000/MT to $425/ MT (figure B.3) (MPOB 2009).

In part because of the increasing use of palm oil as biodiesel, production is likely to more than double in the next 20 years, implying that at least another 5–10 million hectares of new palm oil plantations will be established (Vermeulen and Goad 2006). These projections are speculative, based more on estimates of biofuel mandates (most of which are flexible) than the

Figure B.2   Main Consumers of Globally Traded Palm Oil, 2007/2008

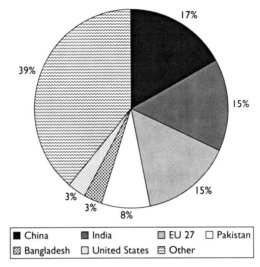

| ■ China | ■ India | ▨ EU 27 | ☐ Pakistan |
| ▨ Bangladesh | ▨ United States | ▨ Other | |

Source: USDA 2009.

Figure B.3   Monthly Price of Crude Palm Oil, 2002–09
($/MT)

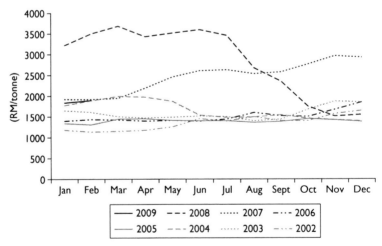

Source: MPOB 2009.

economics of biodiesel from palm. The value of biodiesel (represented by the value of diesel) has almost never been above the cost of producing biodiesel from palm (represented by the opportunity cost of the palm oil). Some estimates have suggested that biodiesel production capacity could reach 3–4 million MTs in Malaysia and 2 million MTs in Indonesia (Kline and others 2008).

These estimates assume high demand from the European Union, which could change because of sustainability concerns and the economics of biodiesel from palm.

Colombia is the largest palm oil producer in Latin America, although its output is only 4 percent that of Malaysia. It has recently begun biodiesel production. In 2007 Ecodiesel Colombia (a subsidiary of the state-owned Ecopetrol), jointly with local palm oil producers, invested $23 million in a new palm oil biodiesel plant. The plan is expected to open in 2010, with an output of 100,000 MT of biodiesel/year (2,000 barrels/day) (Biodiesel 2008). Other plants under construction in Colombia will lift total biodiesel capacity toward 0.5 MT.

Social and Economic Impact of Palm Oil Production

Along with employment, large oil-palm plantations provide a variety of amenities for employees and their families, including housing, water, electricity, roads, medical care, and schools. In some rural communities, palm oil plantations offer the only livelihood option (Koh and Wilcove 2007). In Malaysia, according to the Malaysian Palm Oil Board, oil-palm plantations directly employ more than half a million people, including Malaysians and foreign workers, as well as provide opportunities for smallholders (box B.1).

Large palm oil plantations have also been associated with corruption of community members, the decline of cultural traditions (the result of large inflows of immigrant workers), dependence on palm oil plantations and companies, and the loss of biodiversity. The loss of biodiversity is reducing opportunities for hunting, fishing, gathering, use of forest products, and access to clean water (Colchester and others 2006).

In response to social concerns associated with palm oil production (as well as legal, economic, and environmental issues), the Roundtable on Sustainable Palm Oil was formed in 2004 to develop and implement global standards for sustainable production. Membership in the group now includes 257 ordinary and 92 affiliate members, who represent about 35 percent of palm oil production in the world (Roundtable on Sustainable Palm Oil 2009).

Impact of Palm Oil Production on the Use of Land and Other Resources

Palm oil production has been increasing in Indonesia, and the trend is expected to continue. As a result, new land will need to be allocated to palm oil plantations. In 2004 the government determined that there were about 32 million hectares of suitable land for plantation development. In 2000–09 the government issued about 10 million hectares of new land-use licenses to individuals and companies interested in developing palm plantations. The Indonesian Palm Oil Commission estimates that 6.6 million additional hectares are available for purchase. New laws have increased the life of the

Box B.1 Smallholder Opportunities for Palm Oil Production in Indonesia

Substantial upfront costs in both labor and cash—of about $8,000/hectare—are often required to establish new palm oil plantations in Indonesia. This initial investment includes, among other items, the cost of mechanized land preparation; the purchase of seedlings, fertilizers, and pesticides; and access to vehicles for rapid product transport. Palm oil plantations do not become economically solvent for up to eight years after planting, making the crop unaffordable for many small farmers (defined as those with holdings of less than five hectares).

To address the problem, over the past decade, the Indonesian government has subsidized expansion for noncommercial farmers through preferential interest rate loans and improved seed and fertilizer programs. As a result of the program, 44 percent of productive palm oil plantations in Indonesia are managed by smallholders. In a typical new plantation, the government or private owner will underwrite the entire establishment cost of the farm, with land prepared and planted. Smallholders, who occupy a portion of the plantation, essentially take out a subsidized loan and are obliged to pay the owner back for a portion of the establishment costs over a 15-year period. The Indonesian Palm Oil Commission (IPOC) indicates that roughly 98 percent of all smallholder palm farmers have successfully paid off their loans in the past 10 years.

These small-scale farmers include independent land owners, community members (contracted by companies to plant palm oil on their own lands and supply the products to the same companies), and transmigrants or local people relocated to palm oil areas, where they are assigned lands in palm oil estates. Whereas farmers in the first category can choose to whom they sell their produce, smallholders in the second two categories are typically tied into monopsonistic relations with the companies they supply. These two categories of smallholders may gain minimal remuneration for their produce, be trapped into debt to the companies, defrauded of their lands, and suffer human rights abuses if they protest their circumstances.

Source: Colchester and others 2006; USDA 2009.

licenses from 25 years to 95 years. This change resulted in much greater long-term security for foreign investors and contributed to massive new investment in Indonesian palm oil and land speculation by large private companies (USDA 2009).

In Indonesia there has been a lack of clarity of ownership over forested land, leading to widespread disagreements over land tenure. Land disputes with local communities were reported by each of the 81 palm oil plantation companies in

Sumatra in 2000. One of the most important issues is related to the displacement of communities in order to clear large plantation areas. The company may not provide adequate resettlement provisions for the displaced communities (Vermeulen and Goad 2006).

Deforestation in Indonesia is occurring at a rate of 1.8 percent per year and accounts for 13 percent of annual global deforestation (WRI 2008). The relationship between the expansion of palm oil production and deforestation is currently debated, and it is unclear exactly how much deforestation is caused directly by palm oil expansion or how much of this expansion occurs on land already deforested or degraded as a result of other factors.

The majority of palm oil plantations are located on land that was once tropical forest. In view of this, it seems likely that expansion in palm oil areas will occur in places with some forest cover. Because plantations cannot be harvested for several years after planting, there is an incentive to clear forested land and sell the timber to subsidize the capital costs.[1] In addition to destroying forests, new plantations may displace local subsistence agricultural communities, often because land rights, land-use, and compensation negotiations are often expensive and arduous to complete.

Conservation organizations in Indonesia estimate that there are opportunities for future palm oil development to occur on already degraded land (lands cleared for timber or wood fibers that have not regenerated) rather than in rainforests. It is estimated that about 15–20 million hectares of degraded lands exist in Indonesia, concentrated on the islands of Sumatra and Borneo. There is also an opportunity to reduce land-use requirements by focusing on increasing yields rather than expanding the overall area, especially by targeting smallholders. Investment in high-yield seeds has the potential to increase smallholder production by 47 percent over current levels (USDA 2009).

In Colombia serious human rights concerns have been related to palm oil production. There are reports that increasing demand for biofuels has resulted in land grabs in rural areas, resulting in the expulsion of subsistence farmers from their land, and in some cases, even deaths.

Environmental Impact of Palm Oil Production

Biodiesel from palm oil is estimated to reduce CO_2 emissions by 30–70 percent over fossil diesel fuels. This translates into savings of up to 10 MT of CO_2 per hectare. However, if land-use changes are factored into these calculations, the savings may be very different. About one-quarter of palm oil concessions are planted on peatlands. This means that these lands are drained. As the peat begins to dry out, it decomposes, releasing large amounts of stored carbon. The land is then often burned, releasing CO_2 and causing air pollution. Forests often undergo a similar clearing and burning process. Clearing forest and peatlands for biofuels emits so much CO_2 that it would take a many years of producing biofuels from that land to reduce carbon emissions (Fargione and others 2008). In 2009 the Indonesian government announced that it would allow development of palm oil plantations on peatlands less than 3 meters deep, bringing an end to a 15-month moratorium on conversion of peatlands (Butler 2009).

Impact on Water Resources

Palm oil requires an average annual rainfall of at least 2,000 millimeters, without a marked dry season. Palm oils cannot survive in waterlogged soils: if plantations are placed on peat soils, the water must first be drained. As most palm oil plantations are rain fed, water inputs for irrigation are not usually an important concern.

Nitrogen, potassium, and magnesium fertilizer applications increase palm oil production and yield (Corley and Tinker 2003) and may contribute to contamination of ground and surface water. Use of chemical pesticides and the release of large quantities of palm oil effluent into rivers can cause water pollution.

Impact on Soil Resources

Some soil erosion occurs during forest clearing and plantation establishment, when the soil is left uncovered. More important is the construction of roads for access, the greatest contributor to soil erosion. For example, in Papua New Guinea, 100 meters of unpaved road may produce as much sediment as one hectare of oil palm. Because roads are often built to access the plantations, the issues are closely related. Paving the roads can make a large difference in reducing the amount of soil erosion (up to 95 percent) (Lord and Clay n.d.).

Impact on Biodiversity

Palm oil plantations provide a habitat for 15–25 percent fewer mammals per hectare than natural tropical forests. Plantations cause habitat fragmentation and cut off corridors for species and genetic migration.

The Global Invasive Species Program (2008) classifies palm oil as an invasive species in parts of Brazil, Micronesia, and the United States.

SOYBEAN

Soybean (*Glycine max*) is a legume originating in Asia, where it is known to have been cultivated for more than 4,000 years. It was first introduced to Europe and North America as a forage crop in the early 1800s.

Soybean yields two principal products: soybean oil and soybean meal. Soybean oil, which accounts for 20 percent of the physical output, can be used for human consumption (cooking oil, margarine) or as an input for industrial products, such as plastics and biodiesel fuel. After removal of the soybean oil, the remaining flakes can be processed into various edible soy protein products or used to produce soybean meal for animal feeds.

Soybean meal is by far the world's most important protein feed, accounting for nearly 65 percent of world protein feed supplies. Livestock and fish feed accounts for 98 percent of U.S. soybean meal consumption, with the remainder used in human food (Ash, Livezey, and Dohlman 2006).

Economics of Soybean Production

Soybean makes up 56 percent of total global oilseed production (table B.3). The largest soybean producers in 2008/09 were the United States (34 percent of global production), Brazil (26 percent), Argentina (21 percent), China (7 percent), and India (4 percent) (table B.4).

Table B.3 World Oilseed Production, 2006/07–2008/09

	2006/2007		2007/2008			2008/2009
Oilseed	Volume (million MT)	Percent of total	Volume (million MT)	Volume (million MT)	Percent of total	Volume (million MT)
Soybean	237.3	58.7	220.9	235.7	56.4	235.7
Cottonseed	45.8	11.3	46.0	43.4	11.8	10.4
Rapeseed	45.2	11.2	48.4	54.4	12.4	13.0
Peanut	30.7	7.6	32.0	33.5	8.2	8.0
Sunflower seed	29.8	7.4	27.2	33.2	7.0	7.9
Palm kernel	10.2	2.5	11.1	11.8	2.8	2.8
Copra	5.3	1.3	5.7	5.9	1.5	1.4
Total edible oil	404.3	100.0	391.3	417.8	100.0	100.0

Source: USDA 2009.

Table B.4 Soybean Production, Yield, and Area Harvested by Leading Global Producers, 2007/08

Country	Production quantity (million MT/hectare)	Percentage of global production	Yield (MT/hectare)	Area harvested (million ha)
United States	79.5	33.7	2.3	30.6
Brazil	60.0	25.5	2.8	20.6
Argentina	50.5	21.4	2.8	16.1
China	16.8	7.1	1.8	8.9
India	9.2	3.9	1.1	8.6
World total	235.7	100.0	2.3	94.9

Source: FAO 2008a; USDA 2009.

In the United States, soybean is the second most important crop after corn. Almost half of soybean production is exported, in the form of beans (76 percent), meal (21 percent) and oil (3 percent). The United States is the world's top exporter of soybeans; Argentina is the largest global exporter of soybean oil and soybean meal (table B.5). China is the fourth-largest soybean producer and the largest global importer. Mexico is also a large importer of U.S. soybean and soybean oil (American Soybean Association 2008).

The volume of soybeans traded globally grew from 48 million MT in 1985 to 236 million MT in 2008–09. The global soybean harvest expanded from 32 million hectares in 1975 to 97 million hectares in 2008–09 (USDA 2009), mostly in Argentina and Brazil (Simino n.d.).

In the United States, only 17 percent of total soybean oil consumption is for industrial products (including biofuel). The rest is for human consumption (table B.6).

Soybeans produce about 210 liters of biodiesel per MT. In Argentina and Brazil, growing amounts of soybean are used to produce biodiesel. Argentina produced about 200 million liters of soybean-based biodiesel in 2007; by the end of 2008, more than 20 soy-based biodiesel projects were expected, with a potential capacity of 2 billion liters (Ash and others 2006). In Brazil production of biodiesel is modest compared with sugar ethanol, but total output increased from 40 million liters in 2005 to close to 1 billion liters in 2008.

Social and Economic Impact of Soybean Production

Soy oil is one of the most widely used vegetable oils. It is added to a variety of food products, including margarine, bread, mayonnaise, salad dressings, and

Table B. 5 Soybean, Soybean Oil, and Soybean Meal Exports by Argentina, Brazil, and the United States

		2006/2007		2007/2008		2008/2009	
Country	Product	Volume (million MT)	Percent of total	Volume (million MT)	Percent of total	Volume (million MT)	Percent of total
Argentina	Bean	9.6	23.2	13.8	30.0	15.2	31.3
	Oil	6.0	14.5	5.7	12.4	5.8	11.8
	Meal	25.6	62.3	26.4	57.6	27.7	56.9
Brazil	Bean	23.5	60.7	25.4	63.6	25.7	63.5
	Oil	2.5	6.4	2.4	6.0	2.3	5.7
	Meal	12.7	32.9	12.1	30.4	12.5	30.9
United States	Bean	30.4	77.5	31.6	76.5	27.8	75.8
	Oil	0.9	2.2	1.3	3.3	1.0	2.8
	Meal	8.0	20.4	8.3	20.2	7.8	21.3

Source: USDA 2009.

Table B.6 Soy Oil Consumption in the United States, 2006/07–2008/09

Type of consumption	2006/2007 Volume (million MT)	2006/2007 Percent of total	2007/2008 Volume (million MT)	2007/2008 Percent of total	2008/2009 Volume (million MT)	2008/2009 Percent of total
Industrial domestic consumption	1.3	14.9	1.4	16.3	1.4	17.1
Food use domestic consumption	7.2	85.1	6.9	83.7	6.8	82.9
Total domestic consumption	8.4	100.0	8.3	100.0	8.2	100.0

Source: USDA 2009.

various snack foods. In the United States it accounts for nearly 71 percent of edible oil consumption. Soy oil is also increasingly being used in nonfood products, such as soap, cosmetics, resins, plastics, inks, solvents, and biodiesel.

As a result of economies of scale, small and medium-size producers find soy production difficult. It requires considerable capital to buy genetically modified seeds and to make large investments in pesticides and machinery.[2] Peasant farmers have limited or no access to the level of capital required for viable soy biodiesel operations.

To counteract the trend of larger, more mechanized farms and reduced employment, the Brazilian government launched the ProBiodiesel program in 2004. The program seeks to produce biofuel under conditions that benefit small farmers. A program called Social Fuel guarantees ownership by small farmers (Biopact 2007b).

Research shows that rotating leguminous nitrogen-fixing crops such as soybean with cereals may enhance the overall productivity of the system (Koivisto n.d.). Such rotations are widely practiced, and double cropping (soybean followed by corn) is common in Brazil. As soy is an important food and feed crop, large price increases resulting from diversion of yields into biodiesel could have a strong impact worldwide.

Impact of Soybean Production on the Use of Land and Other Resources

Soy cultivation has been a cause of deforestation in Brazil, affecting the ecologically sensitive Brazilian Amazon and Cerrado. About 20 million hectares are under soy cultivation in Brazil. According to Greenpeace (2006), 2 million hectares of Amazon rainforest were destroyed in 2004–05 as a result of soy expansion. In Argentina it is estimated that more than 40 percent of the lands for soybean production have come from forests and savannahs (Dalgaard and others 2007).

In response to pressure from environmental organizations, major soy traders operating in Brazil announced a two-year moratorium, which went into effect in July 2006, halting trade in soy grown on newly deforested land. The moratorium was extended for an additional year in 2008. Field evaluations show that even with high soy prices in 2007 and 2008, the moratorium significantly reduced the amount of deforestation in Brazil resulting from soy cultivation (figure B.4).

Environmental Impact of Soybean Production

It takes a large number of acres (17) to produce 1,000 gallons of soybean biodiesel (Currie 2007). Soybean biodiesel production is land intensive, because far more meal than oil is produced (20 percent oil versus 80 percent meal) when the oilseeds are crushed. However, the energy demand ratio for the production of soybean biodiesel is less than that for other oilseed crops.

Soybean biodiesel has the potential to reduce greenhouse gas emissions over petroleum diesel by an average of 65 percent. This estimate is based on carbon reductions from temperate areas, such as the Netherlands and the United States; it does not take into account emissions from land conversions (Kojima, Mitchell, and Ward 2007). If soybean biodiesel is produced on converted forest lands, the carbon emissions resulting from deforestation greatly outweigh any reductions from biofuels (Fargione and others 2008). Soy also contributes

Figure B.4   Soy Prices and Deforestation in the Brazilian Amazon

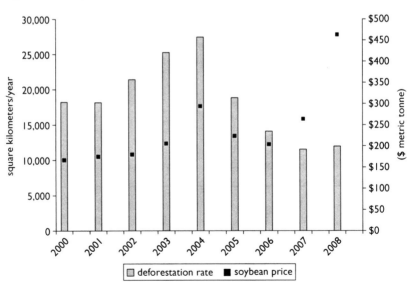

Source: FAO 2008; INPE 2009; USDA 2009.

N$_2$O emissions (a greenhouse gas) from degradation of crop residues and nitrogen fixation, which lessens the greenhouse gas reductions from soybean biodiesel (Hill and others 2006).

Impact on Water Resources

After establishment, soy can withstand short periods of drought. Water requirements for maximum production are 450–700 millimeters annually, depending on climate and length of growing period.

Soy production can have direct impacts on water resources from herbicide and fertilizer runoff and as a result of land clearing. One interesting connection between soy production and water resources is that of "virtual water" exports. In 2004/2005 Argentina used 42,500 million cubic meters of water to produce 39 million tons of soybeans, 25 percent of which was exported. Argentina is a net exporter of virtual water, largely as a result of soybean production (Roundtable on Responsible Soy 2008).

Impact on Soil Resources

Soy can be grown on a wide range of soils, except those that are very sandy. Moderately fertile soils are particularly suitable. Optimum soil pH for soybean is 6.0–6.5 (FAO/AGLW 2002a).

Large-scale monocultures eventually experience decreasing soil productivity, as fertile soil is washed away by rain and wind. Fertilizers and pesticides cause contamination. Soybean production can also cause soil compaction.

Impact on Biodiversity

Soy has been a cause of tropical rainforest deforestation. Soybean farming can contribute directly to forest clearing; it has had an even greater indirect impact by consuming productive farm and grazing lands, and ranchers and slash-and-burn farmers are displaced and move deeper into the forest frontier. Soybean farming may also provide a key economic and political impetus for new highways and infrastructure projects, which can lead to deforestation by other actors.

RAPESEED

Rapeseed (*Brassica napus* and *Brassica rapa*), also known as canola (in the case of one particular group of cultivars), is a bright yellow flowering member of the mustard/cabbage family that is suited for a moderate to cold climate. *Brassica* crops are one of the oldest cultivated crops, dating back to 5000 BC.

Rapeseed has two varieties, winter and spring, and two main types, double-zero varieties (such as canola) and high-erucic rapeseed. Canola refers to the edible oil crop that contains significantly less than 2 percent of erucic acid and no glucosinolate in its meal. High-erucic (industrial) rapeseed has an erucic acid content of at least 45 percent in the oil. Canola is the variety generally used for food oil production and biodiesel; high-erucic rapeseed is used for industrial purposes (lubricants, hydraulic fluids, and plastics) (Boland 2004).

Social and Economics of Rapeseed Production

Rapeseed is an important source of vegetable oil globally. It is the most widely produced vegetable oil after soybean and palm oil (Sovero 1993). Rapeseed oil is used for a variety of purposes, including include food products (cooking oil, mayonnaise, margarine) and industrial uses (hydraulic and heating oils, lubricants, plastic manufacturing, cosmetics, and soaps). Rapeseed seeds contain 40–44 percent oil (Sovero 1993). When refined, it can produce about 440 liters of biodiesel per MT. The use of rapeseed oil as a biodiesel is well established, particularly in the European Union.

Some estimates suggest that about 60–70 percent of rapeseed oil in the European Union is used to produce biodiesel (Harman 2007). Outside Europe, in countries such as China and India, rapeseed is produced primarily for use as food oils, although that is beginning to change, especially as China searches for fossil fuel alternatives.

China is the world's largest single national producer of rapeseed oil (table B.7), although it produces less rapeseed oil than the European Union. Nearly 85 percent of China's rapeseed is grown in the Yangtze River basin. Within Europe, Germany is the largest producer and consumer of rapeseed oil, which it uses primarily as a biodiesel to meet the European Union's CO_2 reduction targets (Yokoyama 2007). As of 2003, about 11 percent of all land in Germany was designated for rape cultivation (Gaya, Aparicio, and Patel 2003). Other large rapeseed producers include India, Canada, Ukraine, Australia, and the United States.

Table B.7 World Rapeseed Oil Production, by Producer, 2006/07–2008/09

Country	2006/2007 Volume (million MT)	2006/2007 Percent of total	2007/2008 Volume (million MT)	2007/2008 Percent of total	2008/2009 Volume (million MT)	2008/2009 Percent of total
EU-27	6.5	38.0	7.6	41.5	8.1	42.0
China	4.1	23.7	3.9	21.2	4.0	20.5
India	2.1	12.5	2.0	10.8	2.0	10.3
Canada	1.5	8.8	1.7	9.2	1.8	9.0
Japan	0.9	5.2	0.9	4.9	0.9	4.8
World total	17.1	100.0	18.3	100.0	19.4	100.0

Source: USDA 2009.

Trade in seeds means that rapeseed oil is often produced far from the country in which seeds are grown. Japan, for example, is a large rapeseed oil producer, but the vast majority of its seeds are imported from Canada.

In Europe there are about 220 plants capable of producing about 17 million MT of biodiesel annually. The rapeseed biodiesel industry in China is still in its early stages, with only two or three companies capable of production. The Chinese Ministry of Agriculture's Administration of Plantation Industry has stated that China will work to increase acreage and yield, as well as improve mechanized production and technology. There is also high potential for rapeseed to play an increasingly important role in China's domestic energy sector (Harman 2007).

Social and Economic Impact of Rapeseed Production

Aside from producing oil, rapeseed is a beneficial cover crop, and the winter variety provides livestock fodder (Boland 2004). The meal by-product of rapeseed for oil production provides a high protein oil cake that can be used for animal feed. Some rapeseed varieties have edible leaves and stems and are sold as greens, primarily in Asian cuisine.

In India 80 percent of rural consumers use rapeseed oil as their staple edible oil. As a result, fluctuating prices can adversely affect the rural poor. Small and marginal farmers do not often benefit from high prices, because most sell their seeds to oil processors and other intermediaries (Pahariya and Mukherjee 2007).

A 2005 World Bank report notes that the German Federal Environmental Agency (UBA) concluded that from an environmental point of view, the use of rapeseed methyl ester (RME) in diesel engines had no distinct advantages over the use of modern diesel fuel made from mineral oil. In addition, because RME requires subsidies to remain competitive, it does not make much sense as a fossil fuel substitute (Kojima and Johnson 2005). Increased taxes on biodiesel for sale as pure biodiesel in Germany (scheduled to increase from $0.09 per liter in 2008 to more than $0.65 in 2012) and high rapeseed oil prices cut into producer profits, forcing plant closures and consumers to switch to conventional diesel fuels. This has left France poised to take over from Germany as the leading rapeseed biodiesel producer in Europe. In order to offset the impact of the tax increases, Germany has made blending of biodiesel by refineries compulsory, but companies argue that this has had the effect of increasing the amount of subsidized biodiesel imported from the United States and other countries (Soyatech 2007).

Impact of Rapeseed Production on the Use of Land and Other Resources

In the event that rising demand for rapeseed from the biofuel sector drives up feedstock prices, it is expected that the food industry will create demand for less expensive substitute oils in the food and cosmetics industries, with palm oil expected to fill much of the gap. This means that rapeseed may be indirectly connected with land-use issues in other countries. There is also growing concern that increasing rapeseed production for biofuels is moving onto lands in Europe that had been "set aside," or taken out of agricultural production. Some of these lands are dedicated for approved environmental uses, known as a "green set-asides." Agricultural activities on these lands may reduce wildlife (especially songbird) habitat (Clover 2007).

Environmental Impact of Rapeseed Production

One of the main environmental advantages of rapeseed biodiesel (and biodiesel in general) over petroleum diesel is its faster rate of biodegradation. A 1995 study shows that blending rapeseed biodiesel with petroleum diesel also increases the biodegradation rate, which has positive indications for wildlife in the event of a leak or spill (Kojima and Johnson 2005).

Greenhouse gas emissions from rapeseed oil are lower than those from fuel (table B.8). The average of greenhouse gas emissions savings of rapeseed diesel is estimated to be 49 percent over petroleum diesel fuels, with estimates raging from 21 to 66 percent, although this does not account for any land use changes.

A 2008 study investigating the potential of rapeseed biodiesel to reduce greenhouse gas emissions finds that for biodiesel derived from rapeseed, nitrous oxide (N_2O) emissions are on average 1.0–1.7 times larger than the cooling effect from reduced CO_2 emissions, leading to an estimated increase in global warming (Crutzen and others 2008).[3] Critics of the study claim that the authors overlooked decreases in greenhouse gas emissions from using biodiesel byproducts as animal feed or as additional biofuel feedstocks (Biopact 2007e).

Table B.8   Estimated Greenhouse Gas Emission Reductions from Rapeseed Biodiesel versus Conventional Diesel

Study	Percentage reduction
Altener (1996)	66
Levington (2000)	58
ETSU (1996)	56
Altener (1996)	56
Levelton (1999)	51
GM and others (2002)	49
Noven (2003)[a]	38
Armstrong and others (2002)	21

Source: IEA 2004; Kojima and others 2007.
a. CO_2 emissions only.

Impact on Water Resources

Rapeseed production requires energy inputs, including fertilizer and pesticide applications as well as oil extraction and processing (Yokoyama 2007). These inputs can affect water use and quality.

Impact on Soil Resources

Rapeseed grows on well-drained soils and is moderately tolerant of saline soils. A no-till approach can minimize soil erosion from rapeseed production.

Impact on Biodiversity

Like corn, rapeseed may indirectly contribute to biodiversity loss if palm oil produced from cleared rainforest land is used as a substitute in products that currently use rapeseed oil (as a result of increasing rapeseed prices).

JATROPHA

There are about 175 variations within the genus *Jatropha. Jatropha curcas* (Physic nut), an inedible (and mildly toxic) plant, is being widely promoted and cultivated for bioenergy production. Jatropha is thought to have originated in Latin America; it is now present throughout much of the world. It can grow in areas with marginal to poor soils and survive with little rainfall. This has led to its use as a live fence around homesteads, gardens, and fields and interest in its use as a biofuel (DESA 2007).

More than 41 countries worldwide have developed Jatropha test projects or cultivation systems for the purpose of making biodiesel. Countries with more developed and larger cultivation systems include Brazil, China, Ghana, India, Kenya, Mali, Mozambique, Myanmar, Nicaragua, and the Philippines.

Economics of Jatropha Production

Jatropha is of great interest as a biofuel feedstock, particularly in Africa and Asia. Most Jatropha plantations are located in Asia, with the East Asia and Pacific region accounting for 62 percent of all plantations and production in India accounting for 23 percent. Worldwide the number of hectares dedicated to Jatropha is targeted to grow from 936,000 in 2008 to an estimated 12.8 million hectares in 2015 (GEXSI 2008) (figure B.5). Much of the growth through 2015 is expected to occur in Asia (figure B.6).[4] Brazil is also expected to increase Jatropha production by more than 1 million hectares by 2015 (GEXSI 2008).

Unlike sugar and starch crops, Jatropha does not yield a full harvest for at least three to four years. The economic life of the plant is about 35–40 years (DESA 2007), although declines in productivity have been reported as plantations age (Francis, Edinger, and Becker 2005).

Figure B.5   Scale of Jatropha Plantations

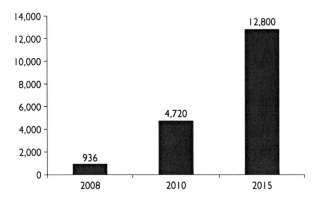

Source: GEXSI 2008.

Figure B.6   Distribution of Jatropha Plantations, 2008

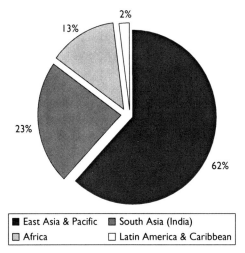

■ East Asia & Pacific   ▨ South Asia (India)
▤ Africa   □ Latin America & Caribbean

Source: GEXSI 2008.

Depending on the soil, rainfall, and nutrient conditions, Jatropha plantations may yield 0.5–12.0 MT of seed/hectare/year, with lower seed production
in the first few years. Average annual seed productions in the range of 3–5
MT/hectare are common in areas of good soil with rainfall of 900–1,200 millimeters a year (DESA 2007). However, a yield of 1 MT/hectare/year is a realistic yield estimate if rainfall is within the range of 500–600 millimeters a year
(Jongschaap and others 2007). This number is unlikely to be economically
viable, at least on a large scale.

Multiple scientific analyses show an oil content of Jatropha seeds of 25–40 percent. Total oil yield estimates also vary a great deal depending on climatic and soil conditions. Research on total oil yields is ongoing, and production estimates are still mostly guesswork (Fairless 2007). India's Planning Commission estimates that 1 hectare of Jatropha has the potential to produce about 1,300 liters of oil; researchers with the Central Salt and Marine Chemicals Research Institute (Bhavnagar, India) estimate the figure at about half that.[5] Marginal lands will have lower yields than lands of higher quality.

The estimated production cost of biodiesel from Jatropha is about $0.50/l. This price assumes that plantations are sited on marginal lands and no farmer subsidies are provided. The sale of by-products (including glycerin and seed cake) can bring in additional profits, reducing the selling price of biodiesel to an estimated $0.40/l (Francis, Edinger, and Becker 2005).[6] Case studies, such as one in Sumbawa, Indonesia, find the real price to be closer to $0.90/l, with the retail price as much as $2.20 (because of the plant's remote location) (Rismantojo 2008).

In most countries where Jatropha is being considered as a biofuel feedstock, the processing infrastructure is being developed in a decentralized manner. In India, for instance, seed collection and oil-pressing centers with a capacity of 4–5 MT/day have been built throughout the country in order to encourage investment in remote areas (Francis, Edinger, and Becker 2005).

Jatropha can also be converted to a biofuel on a commercial basis (Francis, Edinger, and Becker 2005). Although no biofuel from Jatropha is currently being produced on a commercial scale, some companies are beginning to evaluate what is needed to achieve the required fuel standards, provide for storage, and set up distribution facilities.

Social and Economic Impact of Jatropha Production

Jatropha is a labor-intensive crop that is harvested by hand. In some parts of the world, the labor requirements are regarded as having a positive social impact on local communities (Greenergy 2008b). In an ideal situation, farmers could make about $375 per hectare, a 50 percent increase over harvests of other cash crops, such as tobacco. The market for Jatropha is far from established, and both small-scale and commercial production earnings are still largely theoretical. In the 1990s, large plantations of Jatropha were developed in Central America but subsequently abandoned as a result of low yields and higher than expected labor costs (Jongschaap 2007). This suggests that large-scale production of Jatropha could have negative implications for local farmers as well as investors (Greenergy 2008b). The three- to four-year maturation phase, coupled with uncertainties in cultivation and marketing, presents significant barriers to adoption, especially by small farmers (Rajagopal 2007).

Impact of Jatropha Production on the Use of Land and Other Resources

Although Jatropha has the potential to grow on dry marginal lands that would reduce competition with traditional agriculture, it is potentially more profitable to grow the crop on prime land. Doing so can displace food crops.

In some countries, such as India, a majority of the wastelands targeted for Jatropha plantations are collectively owned by villages. These lands supply a wide variety of commodities, including food, fuelwood, fodder, and timber. Planting Jatropha on these lands may cause hardship, because plantations could decrease livestock fodder without offering a replacement, as Jatropha is unsuitable for a livestock feed without detoxification. Moreover, as Jatropha yields an insignificant amount of wood per tree, it may lead to a decline in fuel sources if the biofuel produced from the plant is not used within the community in which it is grown (Rajagopal 2007).

Environmental Impact of Jatropha Production

Early studies indicate that biodiesel from Jatropha may reduce carbon emissions by up to 5 tons of CO_2 per hectare of plantation if it is located on barren land (table B.9); if vegetative cover is cleared, carbon emissions can increase significantly. The biomass produced after the oil extraction will result in carbon reduction based on the amount of electricity generated from it. The seedcake left over from biofuel production has value as an organic fertilizer a result of its high mineral content.

Impact on Water Resources

Jatropha can survive on as little as 400–500 millimeters of rainfall per year and is able to withstand long periods of drought (DESA 2007). The ideal water requirements for maximum possible seed yields are not well researched. Studies in India have indicated that fertilizer applications greatly increase seed production (Jongschaap and others 2007).

Table B.9 Carbon Content of Natural Vegetation and Jatropha Plantation under Alternative Land-Use Scenarios

	Carbon content of natural vegetation (t C/hectare)	Carbon content of Jatropha plantation (t C/hectare)	Carbon change (t C/hectare)
No vegetation	0	5	+ 5
Scarce vegetation	5	5	0
Medium vegetation	25	5	–20

Source: IFEU 2008.

For these reasons, Jatropha is considered to have good potential for marginal and degraded and arid lands and is targeted for these areas. However, as yields increase considerably with more water, there is a possibility that Jatropha may be irrigated. In arid climates (such as India and parts of Africa) in which the crop is being considered, this may have very large impacts on scarce water resources.

Impact on Soil Resources

Jatropha is been used to reclaim lands that were degraded as a result of overgrazing or topsoil loss. The aim is to convert the land into productive land and halt the spread of desertification, especially in parts of Africa.

Impact on Biodiversity

Because it can be planted on marginal and degraded lands, Jatropha may have fewer impacts on biodiversity than other bioenergy crops. However, these types of land may hold value for biodiversity, which may be diminished if cleared for Jatropha.

There is also concern that, if widely planted, Jatropha could become a problem species. Jatropha is not listed in the Global Invasive Species database, but the Department of Agriculture in Western Australia has classified it as an invasive species and banned its use in biodiesel production there (ARRPA 2004).

JOJOBA

Simmodsia chinensis, commonly known as jojoba, is a perennial woody shrub native to the semiarid regions of the southwestern United States and northwestern Mexico (Undersander and others 1990). Jojoba is now cultivated throughout South America, as well in the Middle East and North Africa.

Jojoba has been used for centuries. The most common use was by Native Americans, who extracted the seed oil to treat wounds. Large-scale processing began in the 1970s, when a ban on products from sperm whales led to the discovery of the high utility of jojoba for cosmetics and other products (Undersander and others 1990). The Arab Republic of Egypt and the United Arab Emirates are the principal countries investigating the possibility of using jojoba as a source of fuel.

Economics of Jojoba Production

Jojoba oil is used in a wide variety of products, including cosmetics, pharmaceuticals, food products, manufacturing, and automobile lubricant. The major world producers of jojoba are the United States and Mexico, with the largest exports of oil going to Europe and Japan.

Jojoba lives 100–200 years and is very tolerant of high temperatures and low moisture. Cold temperatures and frost significantly reduce seed yield. Jojoba generally does not produce an economically useful seed yield until the 4th or 5th year after planting, and yields are maximized around the 11th year. Unlike conventional oilseed crops, jojoba seed contains a liquid wax. The wax makes up 50 percent of the seed's dry weight and is used to produce jojoba oil (Selim n.d.). Jojoba is unique as a fuel, because unlike other oils it does not break down under high temperature or pressure or turn rancid (Selim n.d.). It is also relatively pure, nontoxic, and biodegradable (Undersander and others 1990).

Seed production is widely variable in a stand and can vary greatly in a plant from one year to the next, making it difficult to predict total yields. One hectare of jojoba yields about 950–2,000 liters of oil per year (Undersander and others 1990).

In 2003 scientists at the United Arab Emirates University were able to develop an alternative to diesel fuel using jojoba oil. Their research indicates that jojoba can be used pure or in a diesel mixture and can run diesel engines with few modifications (Landais 2007).

Farmers in Egypt have begun planting jojoba shrubs in order to use the oil as a fuel (Sample 2003). The development of fuel from jojoba is still in very early stages, however, and many uncertainties remain regarding production potential. Moreover, the price of jojoba oil is extremely high, making its use as a fuel uneconomical (Denham and Rowe 2005).

Economic Impact of Jojoba Production

Like other arid land crops, jojoba provides a good opportunity for communities with marginal lands unsuitable for agriculture to produce an income-generating crop. Jojoba is a palatable plant and thus could be used as a livestock feed, although grazing results in lower seed production.

Impact of Jojoba Production on the Use of Land and Other Resources

There is less concern about competition with food crops than with other bio-fuel crops if jojoba is grown in very arid regions and on marginal lands. However, marginal lands can sometimes have a high value to communities, and there is a possibility that jojoba production could disrupt traditional land uses.

Environmental Impact of Jojoba Production

Fuel from jojoba oil contains no sulfur emissions and produces lower emissions of CO_2 and soot than conventional diesel fuels, while matching them in efficiency (Selim n.d.). There are no statistics regarding the net CO_2 savings from using jojoba oil as a fuel.

Impact on Water Resources

Jojoba is well adapted to areas with annual precipitation in the range of 300–450 millimeters. Irrigation and fertilization can produce more growth. Whether this increased growth results in higher seed yield is not known.

Impact on Soil Resources

Jojoba is ideally suited to very hot conditions and can thrive in temperatures up to 46°C. This ability to survive in a harsh, dry environment combined with high oil output is one of the reasons why jojoba is considered a potential source of biofuel in countries with these climatic conditions.

Impact on Biodiversity

Jojoba has not been identified as an invasive species in any region in which it has been introduced.

PONGAMIA

Pongamia is a medium-size, nitrogen-fixing tree native to India, Indonesia, Malaysia, and Myanmar. It is known by several names, including Panigrahi, Indian beech, Honge, and Karanja. It has been successfully introduced to humid tropical lowlands worldwide and to parts of Australia, China, New Zealand, and the United States (Daniel 1997; Scott and others 2008).

Pongamia is most often planted as an ornamental and shade tree. The seeds are largely exploited for extraction of nonedible oil commercially known as Karanja oil. India has begun to investigate the possibility of using Pongamia as a source of liquid biofuel (Wani and Sreedevi n.d.).

Economics of Pongamia Production

Pongamia seed kernels have a commercial value as a result of their high oil content, which ranges from 27 to 40 percent. The oil has a bitter taste, an unpleasant smell, and is inedible, but it is commonly used as a fuel for cooking and lighting. It is also used as a lubricant, water-paint binder, pesticide, and an ingredient in soap making and tanning. The oil is known to have medicinal value and is used to treat rheumatism and various skin ailments. It has been identified as a viable source of oil for the burgeoning biofuel industry.

Like many trees, Pongamia does not produce seeds immediately. Oil production is not technically feasible until the fourth year after planting. Oil yield using mechanical extraction techniques is reported to be in the range of 24–27 percent (Wani and Sreedevi n.d.); village crushers generally extract an average yield of 20 percent (Daniel 1997). The seed yield from Pongamia is about 10–50 kg/tree, translating into 2,000–4,000 liters of biodiesel/hectare/year (Daniel 1997).

Rural communities have produced Pongamia biofuels at a very small scale (10–12 kwh/day); production has not yet been tested on a larger scale (box B.2). This species may have a higher value for smallholders than for large producers, based on some of the environmental issues discussed below.

Social and Economic Impact of Pongamia Production

The by-products from oil production, especially the leftover meal (oil cakes), have a high value. They contain up to 30 percent protein and are primarily used as a feed supplement for cattle, sheep, and poultry. The oil cakes are also used as organic fertilizer and natural pesticide. Women's groups in rural areas have generated income from selling Pongamia seed oil and oil cakes (Wani and

---

Box B.2   Income Generation from Small-Scale Pongamia Oil Production

Communities in the Adilabad district of Andhra Pradesh, in India, are using Pongamia oil to fuel power generators. Smallholder-run enterprises, managed primarily by women, have been in the forefront of these efforts. These enterprises manage the entire chain, from seed collection to oil extraction, marketing, and sales of the oil and oil cake residue. The initiative, begun at one site in Adilabad in 1999 and since expanded throughout the state, has provided a source of employment and income to the rural poor, particularly poor women.

In one rural village, two power generators that had the capacity to run on Pongamia oil were installed at a cost of $6,000. The local government paid this capital cost, but the operation and maintenance costs were met by the local women's group. The generators require 2 liters of oil (equivalent to 8 kilograms of Pongamia seeds) to produce one hour of electricity. In order to meet the necessary supply of seeds, each household supplies about 1 kg of seed/day (300 kg/ year). To ensure future oil supply, 30,000 Pongamia saplings (about 75 hectares) were planted in the village over the course of three years. Using this system, the village is able to generate 10–12 KW to power 12 homes and public areas. The women's group has greatly benefited from the venture, and local incomes have increased.

Carbon income is an additional incentive of the program. In 2003 carbon emissions associated with travel to a World Bank conference in Washington, DC, were offset by purchasing reductions in CO_2 emissions in the village of Powerguda in Adilabad district. A certificate was issued in the amount of $645 to the community to offset the estimated 147 tons of the CO_2 emissions. The transaction was handled by 500PPM, a carbon trading firm. The money was used to expand a Pongamia nursery.

Source: Adapted from D'Silva 2005.

Sreedevi n.d.). Pongamia leaves are used as fertilizer, fodder, and insect repellent in stored grains (Scott and others 2008).

Impact of Pongamia Production on the Use of Land and Other Resources

Pongamia pinnata has the potential to be cultivated at a small scale on marginal land. It is less likely than other biofuel crops to compete with food crops.

Environmental Impact of Pomgamia Production

Native to tropical and subtropical environments, Pongamia can withstand a wide range of climatic conditions. However, it attracts a wide variety of pests and diseases (Daniel 1997). This raises questions of the suitability of the species for large-scale production of biofuels, as plantations are the most efficient way to produce large quantities of fuels and trees in plantations are particularly susceptible to disease. Because of these concerns, it is possible that Pongamia is better suited for small-scale community production.

A 2006 study estimates that over the course of a 25-year period, one Pongamia tree has the potential to sequester 767 kg of carbon (table B.10). The carbon sequestration ability of Pongamia was calculated for 3,600 trees planted in the Powerguda village in India. Over the course of seven years, the trees are estimated to sequester 147 MT of carbon equivalent and yield about 51,000 kg of oil, resulting in a total value for the village of about $845 (table B.11).

Impact on Water Resources

Pongamia thrives in areas with annual rainfall of 500–2,500 millimeters. It can withstand temperatures in the range of 1–38°C. Pongamia can grow on a wide variety of soil conditions, ranging from sands to clays. It can survive water logging of both freshwater and saltwater. Because it is a saline- and

Table B.10 Carbon Sequestration Potential of Pongamia within 5- and 10-Year Intervals

Pongamia age (years)	Carbon sequestered (kg)
5	17
10	72
15	331
25	347
Total	767

Source: Wani and others 2006.

Table B.11 Projected Value of Carbon Sequestration in Powerguda, India, 2003–12

Year	Oil yield (kg)	Total oil yield (kg)	C(t)	CO_2 eq (t)	Current $	Net present value (at 3 percent discount rate) ($)
						Value
2003	0	410	0.32	1.17	6.72	6.72
2004	0	494	0.39	1.41	8.09	7.85
2005	0	590	0.46	1.69	9.66	9.08
2006	0.5	1,125	0.88	3.22	18.43	16.77
2007	1.0	3,600	2.81	10.31	58.97	50.71
2008	1.5	5,400	4.21	15.46	88.45	51.89
2009	2.0	7,200	5.62	20.61	117.94	96.71
2010	2.5	9,000	7.20	26.43	151.24	119.48
2011	3.0	10,800	8.42	30.92	176.90	134.45
2012	3.5	12,600	9.83	36.07	206.39	150.66

Source: Wani and others 2006.

drought-tolerant species, *Pongamia pinnata* is well suited to plant on marginal lands (Daniel 1997).

Impact on Soil Resources

Pongamia trees are legumes. The roots help replenish soil nitrogen, and the dense root structure helps control soil erosion.

Impact on Biodiversity

Pongamia has a demonstrated capacity to spread outside its zone of cultivation. Although it is not listed as an invasive species, care should be taken regarding where it is introduced and its management (Low and Booth 2007).

NOTES

1. According to one report, 12 million forested hectares were cleared and timber sold, but the palm oil plantation was never actually planted (Colchester and others 2006).
2. Genetically modified soybean accounts for 90 percent of total production worldwide (100 percent in Uruguay, 98 percent in Argentina, 93 percent in Paraguay, 91 percent in the United States, and 64 percent in Brazil) (USDA 2009).
3. N_2O, a by-product of fertilizer application, is a greenhouse gas with an average global warming potential almost 300 times that of CO_2.

4. Growth is estimated at more than 1 million hectares each in India and the Philippines, more than 3 million hectares in Myanmar, and more than 5 million hectares in Indonesia.
5. In the 1990s, large plantations of Jatropha were developed in Central America. They were subsequently abandoned as a result of low yields and higher than expected labor costs (Jongschaap and others 2007).
6. There are large variations of production costs depending on labor costs, yields and transport distances and special treatment is required to make the leaves or meal nonpoisonous and suitable for use as animal feed.

Second-Generation Bioenergy Production

Second-generation biofuels (also referred to as "advanced" or "cellulosic" biofuels) are produced from lignocellulosic feedstocks.[1] Three principal sources of biomass are used to produce second-generation fuels: forest residues, agricultural residues, and energy crops (table C.1). Given the amount of energy available globally from these sources, there is strong potential for second-generation biofuels once the technology is refined.

Cellulosic ethanol is made by breaking down cellulose through biological conversion to sugars, which may subsequently be fermented to produce biofuels.[2] It can also be produced by thermochemical routes (figure C.1) (Royal Society 2008).[3]

Efforts are underway to develop and optimize technologies for lignocellulosic biofuels. In May 2008, the U.S. Congress passed a farm bill that provides grants of up to 30 percent of the cost of developing and building demonstration scale refineries for second-generation biofuels. The bill, which also provides loan guarantees of up to $250 million to build commercial-scale refineries, is expected to advance commercialization of these fuels. The U.S. Department of Energy has invested $385 million in six cellulosic ethanol plant projects (DOE 2008).

In 2008 the European Commission developed a directive on bioenergy that outlines a higher, mandatory target of 10 percent of transport fuels replaced by biofuels by 2020. The directive includes second-generation biofuels as a component. The Commission also issued calls-for-tender for projects targeting

Table C.1 Source of Biomass Used to Produce Second-Generation Fuels

Forest residues	Agricultural residues	Energy crops
■ Logging residues ■ Residues from forest management and land-clearing operations ■ Removal of excess biomass from forestlands ■ Fuelwood extracted from forestlands ■ Wood mill residues	■ Stover, bagasse, and other crop residues ■ Straw from grain production ■ Animal feed–processing residues	■ Perennial woody crops ■ Perennial grasses

Source: Authors.

Figure C.1 Biochemical and Thermochemical Conversion Technologies for Processing Cellulosic Biomass

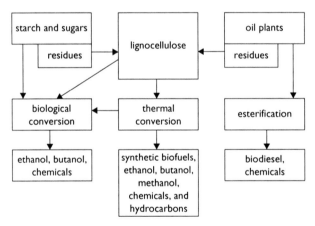

Source: Royal Society 2008.

second-generation fuels under the Seventh EU Framework Programme (OECD 2008).

Demonstration-scale processing facilities are already operational, particularly in the United States (table C.2), Europe, and Canada. Significant commercialization hurdles mean that cellulosic fuels are not expected to reach large-scale production until after 2010.

Table C.2 Second-Generation Biofuel Facilities in the United States, 2008

Company	Location	Production capacity (millions of liters per year)	Feedstock
Abengoa	Nebraska	44	Corn stover, wheat straw, milo stubble, switchgrass, and other biomass
AE Biofuels	Kansas	44	Switchgrass, grass seed, grass straw, and corn stalks
Bluefire	Montana	Small scale	
	California	68	Green waste, wood waste, and other cellulosic urban wastes (postsorted municipal solid waste)
California Ethanol + Power, LLC	California	12	
Coskata	California	208	Sugarcane; facility powered by sugarcane bagasse
	Pennsylvania	0.2	Carbon-based feedstock, including biomass, municipal solid waste, bagasse, and other agricultural waste
DuPont Danisco Cellulosic Ethanol LLC	Tennessee	0.9	Switchgrass, corn stover, corn fiber, and corn cobs
Ecofin, LLC	Kentucky	5	Corn cobs
Flambeau River Biofuels LLC	Wisconsin	23	Softwood chips, wood, and forest residues
ICM Inc.	Idaho	68	Agricultural residues, including wheat straw, barley straw, corn stover, switchgrass, and rice straw
KL Process	Wyoming	6	Soft wood, waste wood, including cardboard, and paper
Lignol Innovations/Suncor	Colorado	10	Woody biomass, agricultural residues, hardwood, and softwood
Mascoma	New York	19	Lignocellulosic biomass, including switchgrass, report sludge, and wood chips
NewPage Corp.	Michigan	151	
	Wisconsin	21	woody biomass, mill residues

(continued)

Table C.2 (Continued)

Company	Location	Production capacity (millions of liters per year)	Feedstock
New Planet Energy	Florida	30 (1st stage), 79 (2nd stage), 379 (3rd stage)	Municipal solid waste; unrecyclable report; construction and demolition debris; tree, yard, and vegetative waste; and energy crops
Pacific Ethanol	Oregon	10	Wheat straw, stover, and poplar residuals
POET	South Dakota	0.075	Corn fiber, corn cobs, and corn stalks
	Iowa	118	
Range Fuels Inc.	Georgia	76	Woodchips (mixed hardwood)
Verenium	Louisiana	5	Sugarcane bagasse, specially bred energy cane, high-fiber sugarcane
	Florida	136	
ZeaChem	Oregon	6	Poplar trees, sugar, wood chips

Source: Renewable Fuels Association 2008.

ECONOMICS OF SECOND-GENERATION BIOENERGY PRODUCTION

Capital costs for cellulosic ethanol plants have been estimated at $250–$375 million at a capacity of 50 million gallons per year (versus $67 million for a corn-based plant of similar size) (EIA 2007). By 2030 the price of cellulosic ethanol is expected to be in $0.25–$0.65/l, assuming significant technological breakthroughs are made (Royal Society 2008).

ECONOMIC IMPACT OF SECOND-GENERATION BIOENERGY PRODUCTION

Currently, the economics of second-generation fuels mean that they cannot compete with traditional fossil fuels. New incentives and government mandates are likely to drive technological innovations that could help increase competitiveness in the future. One such possible innovation is biofuel production from algae (box C.1).

Box C.1 Biofuel Production from Microalgae

Algae are oil rich: their oil content can exceed 80 percent, and 20–50 percent of their weight is dry biomass. Unlike other oil crops, microalgae grow rapidly, commonly doubling within 24 hours. These properties make them an interesting prospect for future biofuel production. Microalgae can also be processed to make methane, biodiesel, and biohydrogen. Currently, the only method of large-scale microalgae production is using raceway ponds (shallow, oval-shaped ponds) and tubular photobioreactors (clear tubes that maximize sunlight exposure), although alternatives are being researched.

Microalgae grow through photosynthesis. They require light, CO_2, water, and inorganic salts inputs and constant temperatures of 20°C–30°C. Producing 100 MT of algal biomass fixes roughly 183 MT of CO_2 (which must be provided to the system; it is not fixed from the atmosphere). One source of CO_2 inputs may be power plants, which often provide CO_2 at a minimal or no-cost to algae producers.

Producing biofuels from microalgae is more expensive than producing it from most other feedstocks. The estimated cost of producing a kilogram of microalgal biomass is $2.95 for photobioreactors and $3.80 for raceways (these estimates assume that CO_2 is available at no cost). If the annual biomass production capacity is increased to 10,000 MT, the cost of production per kilogram reduces to roughly $0.47 for photobioreactors and $0.60 for raceways. This translates to an estimated cost of $2.80 per liter for the oil recovered from the lower-cost photobioreactor biomass.

(continued)

Box C.1   (Continued)

If microalgae are used to produce biodiesel, an estimated 3 percent of the total cropping area in the United States would be sufficient to produce algal biomass that satisfies 50 percent of the United States' transport fuel needs (table). This land area is much smaller than that required by all other biofuel feedstocks.

Table   Oil Yields from Microalgae

Crop	Oil yield (liters/hectare)	Land area needed (M hectares)	Percent of U.S cropping area
Microalgae (70 percent oil by weight in biomass)	136,900	2.0	1.1
Microalgae (30 percent oil by weight in biomass)	58,700	4.5	2.5

Source: Chisti 2007.

IMPACT OF SECOND-GENERATION BIOENERGY PRODUCTION ON THE USE OF LAND AND OTHER RESOURCES

Land-use impacts from second-generation biofuels are generally considered to be less than first-generation fuels if they are produced primarily from forest and agricultural residues. If short-rotation woody crops or grasses are planted, there may be land-use implications (see chapter 2).

David Tilman of the University of Minnesota questions whether cellulosic ethanol could provide an incentive for forest clearing. His calculations show that a typical hectare of rainforest could yield about 15,000 gallons of cellulosic ethanol per hectare, generating more than $36,000 in revenue and up to $7,000 in profit. In this case, it would be more profitable to clear cut forests for fuel than to plant fuel crops like oil palm, sugarcane, or soybeans on previously cleared lands (Butler 2009).

Where biomass for second-generation fuels is produced from dedicated crops, the impact on crop markets and land use strongly depends on what type of land use is already present. Sensitive areas should be excluded from conversion to crop land or biomass production, and greenhouse gas emissions from existing carbon stocks in the soil should be minimized. These steps should be taken whether the converted land is used directly for the production of fuel-biomass or for food and feed commodities.

ENVIRONMENTAL IMPACT OF SECOND-GENERATION BIOENERGY PRODUCTION

Greenhouse gas reductions from second-generation technologies are estimated at 60–120 percent of those of traditional fuels (OECD 2008).[4] Fischer-Tropsch (FT) fuels that use crop and forest residues are likely to have the highest emissions reductions. If energy crops rather than residues are used as feedstock, the emissions reductions are lower, because the benefit of residue disposal is lost. The greenhouse gas reduction potential of cellulosic fuels may increase even more with advances in technology (Mabee 2006).

NOTES

1. Lignocellulose (plant cell walls) is found in biomass. Lignocellulose is a complex matrix made up of many different polysaccharides, phenolic polymers, and proteins.
2. Biochemical technologies for production of cellulosic ethanol involve hydrolysis of mostly the hemicellulose and cellulose fractions of the biomass into their component sugars, fermentation of the resultant sugars into ethanol, and concentration or purification of the ethanol by distillation.
3. Thermochemical conversion technologies typically involve gasification and subsequent catalytic conversion of the resultant synthesis gas to liquid fuels, such as ethanol. This process is sometimes referred to as Fischer-Tropsch (FT) or gas to-liquid (GTL) technology.
4. The improvement with respect to traditional fuels can exceed 100 percent because of CO_2 credits from the co-production of electricity.

Third-Generation Bioenergy Production

The third generation of biofuels focuses on new, specially engineered energy crops that allow for a broader variety of biomass feedstocks than the previous generations of biofuels (Biopact 2007a). CGIAR (2008) defines third-generation biofuels as those made from energy and biomass crops that have been designed so that their very structure or properties conform to the requirements of a particular bioconversion process. The bioconversion agents (bacteria, microorganisms) are bioengineered so that the bioconversion process becomes more efficient. The purpose behind developing third-generation biofuels is to greatly increase the global productivity of energy crops for biofuel production while maintaining desirable physical and chemical traits.

Much of the discussion surrounding third-generation biofuel crops is similar to that encountered with first- and second-generation crops, with the added concerns surrounding genetically modified organisms. This appendix addresses some of the major points in that debate that are relevant to biofuel feedstocks.

Research is identifying the fundamental constraints on biofuel feedstock productivity and using genomic tools to address those constraints. Several types of genetic manipulations have been identified that could help increase biomass yield or reduce the cost of converting biomass into fuels (Ragauskas and others 2006; Biopact 2007d, 2007f). They include the following:

- Manipulating photosynthesis to increase the initial capture of light energy to induce faster plant growth

- Increasing plant tolerance to adverse conditions, including acidic soils or arid conditions
- Manipulating genes involved in nitrogen metabolism, which can also increase biomass production
- Transferring genetically engineered versions of plant defense genes to crop plants[1]
- Increasing overall plant biomass by delaying or preventing energy-intensive reproductive processes
- Increasing sugar content
- Reducing or weakening plant lignin in order to more easily break down the plant material into sugars
- Extending a plant's growth phase by delaying or shortening winter dormancy
- Enhancing bacterial digestion or sugar release by altering lignin and cellulose structure
- Containing cellulase enzymes within a plant to break down the plant material into sugars that can be converted to ethanol.

Some plants undergoing genetic manipulation for the purpose of producing biofuels include eucalyptus and poplar trees, sweet sorghum, and corn. Researchers are working to sequence the genome of oil palm and cassava in order to develop crops more suitable for the biofuels industry (Biopact 2007d).

Economics of Third-Generation Biomass Production

These crops are in the very early stages and are estimated to be at least 15 years from being used for biofuel production. The economics of third-generation biofuels are far from established. If fewer inputs are needed to grow and process third-generation biofuels, the costs could conceivably be lower than for first- or second-generation fuels.

Economic Impact of Third-Generation Bioenergy Production

It may be difficult to deliver these new systems in regions such as Africa, as evidenced by the difficulties in establishing improved varieties of staple foods. Considerations such as the costs of the technology must be taken into account if the developing world is to benefit (World Bank 2008b).

Impact of Third-Generation Bioenergy on the Use of Land and Other Resources

With higher yields and easier bioconversion for third-generation fuels, less land and fewer inputs will be needed to grow, harvest, and transform biomass into fuel (Biopact 2007d). Improved productivity from genetically modified organisms may mean that biofuel cultivation could take place on marginal lands and not take prime agricultural lands from food crops (FAO 2003).

Environmental Impact of Third-Generation Bioenergy Production

Concerns have been raised that transgenic crops may pass along inserted genes to other species. Scientific evidence and experience from 10 years of commercial use do not support the development of resistance in the targeted pests or environmental harm from commercial cultivation of transgenic crops, such as gene flow to wild relatives, when proper safeguards are applied. This track record notwithstanding, environmental risks and benefits need to be evaluated case by case, comparing the potential risks of alternative technologies and taking into account the specific trait and agroecological context in which it will be used (World Bank 2008b).

NOTE

1. This technique has been used to make crops grow faster under drought and high- and low-temperature stress and to increase their ability to survive pathogen attack.

REFERENCES

Abe, H. 2005. *Summary of Biomass Power Generation in India*. Report prepared for Japan International Cooperation Agency. http://www.crest.org.

American Soybean Association. 2008. "Soy Stats." http://www.soystats.com/2008/Default-frames.htm.

APEC (Asia-Pacific Economic Cooperation). 2008. APEC Biofuels. http://www.biofuels.apec.org/activities_summary.html.

Arnold, M., G. Kohlin, R. Persson, and G. Shepherd. 2003. *Fuelwood Revisited: What Has Changed in the Last Decade?* CIFOR Occasional Paper 39, Center for International Forestry Research, Bogor, Indonesia.

ARRPA (Agriculture and Related Resources Protection Act 1976). 2004. *Declared (Noxious) Plants Listing for Western Australia*. Perth.

Ash, Mark, Janet Livezey, and Erik Dohlman. 2006. *Soybean Backgrounder*. OCS-2006-01, U.S. Department of Agriculture, Washington, DC. http://www.ers.usda.gov/publications/ocs/apr06/ocs200601/ocs200601_lowres.pdf.

Associação Nacional dos Fabricantes de Veículos (Anfavea). 2008. http://www.anfavea.com.br/tabelas.html.

Associated Press. 2008. "Farmers Say Don't Blame Ethanol for Food Prices: Industry Spokesman Calls Linking the Two 'Manufactured Hysteria.'" April 30. http://www.msnbc.msn.com/id/24393951/.

Aye, Daphne Khin Swe Swe. 2007. *Burma Bio-Fuels Update 2007*. USDA Gain Report Bm7015, U.S. Department of Agriculture, Washington, DC.

Barros, G. S. A. C. A. "Estimação das importações Brasileiras de leite, 1991 a 2003." *Revista de Economia e Sociologia Rural* 45: 237–53. São Paulo.

Batidzirai, B. 2007. "Bioethanol Technologies in Africa." Paper presented to the UNIDO/AU/Brazil First High-Level Biofuels Seminar in Africa, Addis Ababa, July 30–August 1. http://www.unido.org.

Berg, C. 2004. *World Fuel Ethanol Analysis and Outlook*. Tunbridge Wells, United Kingdom: F. O. Licht. http://www.distill.com/World-Fuel-Ethanol-A&O-2004.html.

Bergesen, C. 2008. *Power Plants around the World Database*. http://www.industcards.com.

Better Sugarcane Initiative. 2009. www.bettersugarcane.org.

Bezlova, Antoaneta. 2008. "China: High on Ethanol Despite Rising Food Prices." Inter Press Service, April 24. http://ipsnews.net/news.asp?idnews=42108.

Biodiesel Magazine. 2008. Dedini's Blend: Ethanol moves in with biodiesel. Elizabeth Ewing. http://www.biodieselmagazine.com/article.jsp?article_id=2387.

Bioenergy International. 2005. "Pellets Map 2005–06." *Bioenergy International* 17 (December). www.bioenergyinternational.com.

Biomass Task Force. 2005. *Report to Government*. York, United Kingdom. October. http://www.defra.gov.uk.

Biopact. 2007a. "Agrivida and Codon Devices to Partner on Third-Generation Biofuels." August 3, Heverlee, Belgium. http://biopact.com/2007/08/agrividia-and-codon-devices-to-partner.html.

———. 2007b. "Brazilian Government Frees Sugarcane Debt 'Slaves.'" July 4, Heverlee, Belgium. http://biopact.com/2007/07/brazilian-government-frees-sugarcane.html.

———. 2007c. "Malaysian Company Thinks It Can Produce 6.48 Billion Liters of Ethanol from Nipah." April 10, Heverlee, Belgium. http://biopact.com/2007/04/malaysian-company-thinks-it-can-produce.html.

———. 2007d. "A Quick Look at 'Fourth Generation' Biofuels." October 8, Heverlee, Belgium. http://www.biopact.com/2007/10/quick-look-at-fourth-generation.html.

———. 2007e. "Rapeseed Biodiesel Has A Weak Greenhouse Gas Balance. Study." April 23, Heverlee, Belgium. http://www.biopact.com/2007/04/rapeseed-biodiesel-has-weak-greenhouse.html.

———. 2007f. "Third-Generation Biofuels: Scientists Patent Corn Variety with Embedded Cellulase Enzymes." May 5, Heverlee, Belgium. http://biopact.com/2007/05/third-generation-biofuels-scientists.html.

———. 2008. "Quantum Group to Invest $250 Million in 4 Ethanol Plants, 100,000ha in Sumba; 60,000 Jobs for Poor Local Farmers." February 14, Heverlee, Belgium. http://biopact.com/2008/02/quantum-group-to-invest-us250-million.html.

Bios Bioenergysysteme. 2004. *Techno-Economic Evaluation of Selected Decentralised CHP Applications Based on Biomass Combustion in IEA Partner Countries*. Report Prepared for IEA Task 32. http://www.ieabcc.nl.

Biran, Adam, L. Smith, J. Lines, J. Ensink, and M. Cameron. 2007. "Smoke and Malaria: Are Interventions to Reduce Exposure to Indoor Air Pollution Likely to Increase Exposure to Mosquitoes?" *Transactions of the Royal Society of Tropical Medicine and Hygiene* 101: 1065–71. http://whqlibdoc.who.int/hq/2008/who_hse _ihe_08.01_eng.pdf.

Boddiger, David. 2007. "Boosting Biofuel Crops Could Threaten Food Security." September 15 http://www.biofuel-africa.org/IMG/pdf/Boddiger_Lancet_15-09- 07-1.pdf.

Boland, Michael. 2004. "Rapeseed." Agricultural Marketing Resource Center, Kansas State University, Manhattan, KS. http://www.agmrc.org/agmrc/commodity/ grainsoilseeds/rapeseed/.

Bonell, M., and L. A. Bruijnzeel, eds. 2005. *Forests, Water and People in the Humid Tropics: Past, Present and Future Hydrological Research for Integrated Land and Water Management*. International Hydrology Series. Cambridge: Cambridge University Press.

Bonskowski, R. 1999. *The U.S Coal Industry in the 1990s: Low Prices and Record Production.* U.S Department of Energy, Energy Information Administration, Washington, DC. http://www.eia.doe.gov/cneaf/coal/special/coalfeat.htm.

Bressan, A., and E. Contini. 2007. "Brazil: A Pioneer in Biofuels." Paper presented at the workshop "Global Biofuel Developments: Modelling the Effects on Agriculture." Washington, DC, February 27. http://www.farmfoundation.net/news/templates/widetemplate.aspx?articleid=826.

Broadhead, J. S., J. Bahdon, and A. Whiteman. 2001. *Past Trends and Future Prospects for the Utilisation of Wood for Energy.* Rome: Food and Agricultural Organization.

Buchholz, T., and T. Volk. 2007. *Designing Short-Rotation Coppice-Based Bioenergy Systems for Rural Communities in East Africa.* Biosyrca Project Final Report, U.S. Agency for International Development, Washington, DC.

Butler, Rhett. 2009. "Indonesia Confirms That Peatlands Will Be Converted for Plantations." Mongabay.com. February 19. http://news.mongabay.com/2009/0219-indonesia.html.

Canadian Renewable Fuels Association. 2008. "Canadians Support Fueling Change with Biofuels." Public Opinion Survey Report, Ottawa. http://www.greenfuels.org/files/CRFAPraxicusPollRelease043008.pdf.

Carroll, Rory. 2008. "U.K. Palm Oil Consumption Fuels Colombia Violence, Says Report." The Guardian, May 12. http://www.guardian.co.uk/world/2008/may/12/colombia.food.

CEC (Commission of the European Communities). 2006a. *An EU Strategy for Biofuels.* October 12. Brussels.

———. 2006b. *Report on the Progress Made in the Use of Biofuels and Other Renewable Fuels in the Member States of the European Union: Review of Economic and Environmental Data for the Biofuels Progress Report.* Communication from the Commission Com 2006 (845) Final, Brussels. http://eur-lex.europa.eu/LexUriServ/site/en/com/2006/com2006_0845en01.pdf.

CGIAR (Consultative Group on International Agricultural Research). 2007. "Study Warns That China and India's Planned Biofuel Boost Could Worsen Water Scarcity, Compete with Food Production." Press Release, Washington, DC.

———. 2008. *Biofuels Research in the CGIAR: A Perspective from the Science Council.* http://www.sciencecouncil.cgiar.org/publications/pdf/CGIAR%20SC%20position%20paper%20on%20Biofuels.pdf.

CHAPOSA (Charcoal Potential in Southern Africa). 2002. *Charcoal Potential in Southern Africa.* Final Report. Stockholm Environment Institute, Stockholm.

Childs Staley, Britt, Rob Bradley. 2007. *Plants at the Pump: Biofuels, Climate Change, and Sustainability.* World Resources Institute, Washington, DC. http://www.wri.org/publication/plants-at-the-pump.

China Daily. 2008. "Deeper Income Gap Calls for Reform to Solve Deeper Conflict." September 13. http://www.chinadaily.com.cn/bizchina/2008-09/13/content_7025186.htm.

Chisti, Yusuf. 2007. "Biodiesel from Microalgae." *Biotechnology Advances* 25: 294–306.

Clover, Charles. 2007. "Scrapping Set-Aside 'Threatens Farmland Birds.'" Telegraph, March 9. http://www.telegraph.co.uk/earth/main.jhtml?xml=/earth/2007/09/03/eabirds103.xml.

Colchester, Marcus, Norman Jiwan, Andiko, Martua Sirait, Asep Yunan Firdaus, A. Surambo, and Herbert Pane. 2006. *Promised Land: Palm Oil and Land Acquisition in Indonesia: Implications for Local Communities and Indigenous Peoples.* Forest Peoples Programme, Perkumpulan Sawit Watch, HuMA, and the World

Agroforestry Centre, Moreton-in-Marsh, United Kingdom. http://www.forestpeoples .org/documents/prv_sector/oil_palm/promised_land_eng.pdf.

Corley, R. H. V., and P. B. Tinker. 2003. *The Oil Palm*, 4th ed. London: Blackwell Science Ltd.

Corpuz, Perfecto G. 2009. *Philippine Bio-Fuel Industry Outlook*. USDA Gain Report 9019. http://gain.fas.usda.gov/Recent%20GAIN%20Publications/General%20Report _Manila_Philippines_6-1-2009.pdf.

Cotula, Lorenzo, Nat Dyer, and Sonja Vermeulen. 2008. *Bioenergy and Land Tenure: the Implications of Biofuels for Land Tenure and Land Policy*. International Institute for Environment and Development, London.

Crutzen, P. J., A. R. Mosier, K. A. Smith, and W. Winiwarter. 2008. "N₂O Release from Agro-Biofuel Production Negates Global Warming Reduction by Replacing Fossil Fuels." *Atmospheric Chemistry and Physics* 8: 389–95.

Currie, Jeffrey. 2007. *Food, Feed and Fuels: An Outlook on the Agriculture, Livestock and Biofuel Markets*. Goldman Sachs International, New York.

Dalgaard, R., J. Schmidt, N. Halberg, P. Christensen, M. Thrane, and W. A. Pengue. 2007. "LCA of Soybean Meal." *International Journal of Life Cycle Analysis* 13 (3): 240–54. http://dx.doi.org/10.1065/lca2007.06.342.

Dalibard, Christophe. 1999. "Overall View on the Tradition of Tapping Palm Trees and Prospects for Animal Production." Livestock Research for Rural Development 11: 1.

Daniel, Joshua N. 1997. *Winrock International, Forest, Farm, and Community Tree Network (Fact Net)*. http://www.winrock.org/fnrm/factnet/factpub/factsh/p_pinnata.html.

Del Lungo, A., J. Ball, and J. Carle. 2006. "Global Planted Forests Thematic Study: Results and Analysis." Working Paper FP/38, Food and Agricultural Organization, Rome. http://www.fao.org/forestry/site/10368/en.

Denham, Ryan, and Peter Rowe. 2005. "Jojoba." Government of Western Australia, Department of Agriculture Farmnote 85/99, Perth.

DESA (United Nations Department of Economic and Social Affairs). 2007. *Small-Scale Production and Use of Liquid Biofuels in Sub-Saharan Africa: Perspectives for Sustainable Development*. http://www.un.org/esa/sustdev/csd/csd15/documents/ csd15_bp2.pdf.

DOE (U.S. Department of Energy). 2003. *Gasification-Based Biomass Cofiring: Phase I, Final Report* National Energy Technology Laboratory, Pittsburgh. www.eere.energy.gov.

———. 2004. *Biomass Cofiring in Coal-Fired Boilers*. Federal Technology Alert DOE-EE/0288, Washington, DC. www.eere.energy.gov.

———. 2005. *Feedstock Platform Analysis 2005 OBP Bi-Annual Peer Review*. U.S. Department of Energy, Washington, DC, www.eere.energy.gov.

———. 2008. "U.S. Department of Energy Selects First Round of Small-Scale Biorefinery Projects for Up to $114 Million in Federal Funding." January 29. http://energy.gov/ news/5903.htm

———. 2009. "The Coming of Biofuels: Study Shows Reducing Gasoline Emissions Will Benefit Human Health." May 27. http://newscenter.lbl.gov/feature-stories/ 2009/05/27/biofuels-and-human-health/.

DOE–EPA (U.S. Department of Energy–Environmental Protection Agency). 2000. *Carbon Dioxide Emissions from the Generation of Electric Power in the United States*. Washington, DC. http://tonto.eia.doe.gov/ftproot/environment/co2emiss00.pdf.

Doornbosch, Richard, and Ronald Steenblik. 2007. "Biofuels: Is the Cure Worse Than the Disease?" Paper presented at the Round Table on Sustainable Development, Organisation for Economic Co-operation and Development, Paris, September 11–12. http://www.rsc.org/images/biofuels_tcm18-99586.pdf.

D'Silva, Emmanuel. 2005. *The New Oil Economy of the Rural Poor: Biofuel Plantations for Power, Water, Transport, and Carbon Credits. A Case Study from Adilabad District, Andhra Pradesh, India.* International Tropical Timber Organization, Forest Trends, Rights and Resources Insititute, Yokohama, Japan, and Washington, DC.

DSIRE (Database of State Incentives for Renewables & Efficiency). 2008. http://www.dsireusa.org.

EEA (European Environment Agency). 2004. *Energy Subsidies in the European Union: A Brief Overview.* Copenhagen. http://www.eea.eu.int.

———. 2007. *Environmentally Compatible Bio-Energy Potential from European Forests.* Copenhagen. http://www.eea.eu.int.

EIA (U.S. Energy Information Agency). 2007. *Annual Energy Outlook 2007. With Projections to 2030.* DOE/EIA-0383. Washington DC. http://tonto.eia.doe.gov/ftproot/forecasting/0383(2007).pdf.

———. 2008a. *Heating Oil and Propane Update.* http://tonto.eia.doe.gov/oog/info/hopu/hopu.asp.

———. 2008b. *Official Energy Statistics from the U.S. Government.* http://www.eia.doe.gov.

———. 2008c. *Residential Natural Gas Prices: What Consumers Should Know.* http://www.eia.doe.gov/neic/brochure/oil_gas/rngp/index.html.

El-Beltagy, Adel. 2000. "Land Degradation: A Global and Regional Problem." Paper presented at international conference "On the Threshold: The United Nations and Global Governance in the New Millennium," United Nations University, Tokyo, January 19–21.

Eneas, Godfrey. 2006. "Cassava: A Biofuel." Bahamas News Online Edition, February 8. http://www.jonesbahamas.com/?c=47anda=7415.

Enters, T. 2001. "Trash or Treasure? Logging and Mill Residues in Asia and the Pacific." RAP Publication 2001/16, Food and Agricultural Organization, Bangkok. http://www.fao.org/docrep/003/x6966e/x6966e00.htm.

EPA (Environmental Protection Agency). 2007. *Biomass Combined Heat and Power Catalog of Technologies.* Washington, DC. www.epa.gov/chp.

———. 2008. *Renewable Fuel Standard Program.* Washington, DC. http://www.epa.gov/OMS/renewablefuels.

Eurobarometer. 1997. *European Opinion and Energy Matters.* Eurobarometer 46.0, Commission of the European Communities, Brussels. http://ec.europa.eu/public_opinion/index_en.htm.

———. 2002. *Energy: Issues, Options and Technologies. Science and Society.* Eurobarometer 57.0, Commission of the European Communities, Brussels. http://ec.europa.eu/public_opinion/index_en.htm.

———. 2007. *Energy Technologies: Knowledge, Perception, Measures.* Eurobarometer 65.3, Commission of the European Communities, Brussels. http://ec.europa.eu/public_opinion/index_en.htm.

———. 2008. *Europeans' Attitudes towards Climate Change.* Eurobarometer 69.2, Commission of the European Communities, Brussels. http://ec.europa.eu/public_opinion/index_en.htm.

Fairless, Daemon. 2007. "The Little Shrub That Could—Maybe." *Nature* 449: 652–55.

FAO (Food and Agriculral Organization). 2001. "Reform of Fiscal Policies in the Context of National Forest Programmes in Africa." Forest Finance Working Paper FSFM/MT/01, Rome.

———. 2002a. *Small-Scale Palm Oil Processing in Africa.* Rome. http://www.fao.org/docrep/005/Y4355E/y4355e00.HTM.

——. 2002b. *Towards Equitable Partnerships between Corporate and Smallholder Partners: Relating Partnerships to Social, Economic and Environmental Indicators*. Workshop Proceedings. Rome. http://www.fao.org/DOCREP/005/Y4803E/Y4803E00.HTM.

——. 2003. *Weighing the GMO Arguments*. Rome. http://www.fao.org/english/newsroom/focus/2003/gmo8.htm.

——. 2004. *UBET*. Rome. http://www.fao.org/DOCREP/007/j4504E/j4504E00.HTM.

——. 2005. *Forests and Floods: Drowning in Fiction or Thriving on Facts?* RAP Publication 2005/03, Bangkok. http://www.fao.org/docrep/008/ae929e/ae929e00.htm.

——. 2007. *Food Outlook: Global Market Analysis*. No. 1: *Cassava*. Rome. http://www.fao.org/docrep/010/ah864e/ah864e06.htm.

——. 2008a. FAOSTAT (FAO's online statistical database). Rome. http://faostat.fao.org.

——. 2008b. *International Commodity Prices*. Rome. www.fao.org/es/esc/prices.

——. 2008c. *Sorghum bicolor (L.) Moench*. Grassland Species Profiles, Rome. http://www.fao.org/ag/agp/agpc/doc/gbase/data/pf000319.htm.

FAO/AGLW (Land and Water Development Division). 2002a. *Soybean*. Rome. http://193.43.36.103/ag/AGL/aglw/cropwater/soybean.stm.

——. 2002b. *Sugarcane*. Rome. http://193.43.36.103/ag/AGL/aglw/cropwater/sugarcane.stm.

Fargione, Joseph, Jason Hill, David Tilman, Stephen Polasky, and Peter Hawthorne. 2008. "Land Clearing and the Biofuel Carbon Debt." *Science* 319 (5867): 1235–38.

Flanagan, Robert, and Stephen Joseph. 2007. *Mobilising Rural Households to Store Carbon, Reduce Harmful Emissions and Improve Soil Fertility; Introduction of Third-Generation Stoves*. Bonn, Germany. http://www.unccd.int/publicinfo/poznanclimatetalks/docs/Natural%20Draft%20Stove.pdf.

FO Licht. 2008. *Ethanol and Biodiesel*. Kent. http://www.agra-net.com/portal2/.

Forest Products Laboratory. 2004. *Wood Biomass for Energy*. Techline Publication WOE-1, Madison, WI. Francis, George, Raphael Edinger, and Klaus Becker. 2005. "A Concept for Simultaneous Wasteland Reclamation, Fuel Production, and Socio-Economic Development in Degraded Areas in India: Need, Potential and Perspectives of Jatropha Plantations." *Natural Resources Forum* 29: 12–24.

Gaya, Julio, Cesar Aparicio, and Martin K. Patel. 2003. *Biodiesel from Rapeseed Oil and Used Frying Oil in European Union*. Copernicus Institute and Universiteit Utrecht, the Netherlands. http://www.chem.uu.nl/nws/www/publica/Studentenrapporten/Studentenrapporten2003/I2003-35.pdf.

GBEP (Global Bioenergy Partnership). 2005. "The Global Bioenergy Partnership White Paper." Paper prepared by the Italian Ministry for the Environment and Territory with the participation of Imperial College London, Itabia, and E4tech. http://www.globalbioenergy.org.

Genomeindia. 2008. *About Sugarcane*. http://www.genomeindia.org/sugarcane/sugarabout.html.

GEXSI. 2008. *Global Market Study on Jatropha: Main Findings*. Study prepared for the Roundtable on Sustainable Biofuels, Brussels, May 15. http://www.jatropha-platform.org/Liens/Download/Doc/GEXSI_Global_Jatropha_Study_Presentation%20RSB%20v5.pdf.

GISP (Global Invasive Species Program). 2008. *Biofuel Crops and the Use of Non-Native Species: Mitigating the Risks of Invasion*. Nairobi; Arlington, VA; and Delémont, Switzerland.

GlobeScan. 2008. *Climate Decision Maker Survey: Wave 1 Report of Findings*. Toronto. http://www.globescan.com/news_archives/climate_panel.

Government of India Planning Commission. 2003. *Report of the Committee on Development of Biofuel*. http://planningcommission.nic.in/reports/genrep/cmtt_bio.pdf.

Grassi, Giuliano. n.d. *Sweet Sorghum: One of the Best World Food-Feed-Energy Crops*. Latin America Thematic Network on Bioenergy (LAMNET), Florence. http://www.eubia.org/fileadmin/template/main/res/pdf/publications/04_Brochures_Leaflets/LAMNET%20-%20sweet%20sorghum.pdf.

Green Gold Label. *Green Gold Label*. 2009. Rotterdam. http://certification.controlunion.com/certification/default.htm.

Greenergy. 2008a. *Bioethanol: A Greenergy Perspective*. London. http://www.greenergy.com/perspectives/Bioethanol.pdf.

———. 2008b. *Jatropha: A Greenergy Perspective*. London. http://www.greenergy.com/perspectives/Jatropha.pdf.

Greenpeace. 2006. *Devorando la Amazonia*. Madrid. http://www.greenpeace.org/raw/content/espana/reports/devorando-la-amazonia.pdf.

Greiler, Yuka. 2007. *Biofuels, Opportunity or Threat to the Poor?* Swiss Agency for Development and Cooperation, Berne. http://www.deza.admin.ch/ressources/resource_en_159527.pdf.

Gunstone, Frank D. 2004. *Rapeseed and Canola Oil: Production, Processing, Properties and Uses*. Boca Raton, FL: CRC Press.

Hakkila, P. 2004. *Developing Technology For Large-Scale Production of Forest Chips*. Technology Programme Report 6/2004, National Technology Agency, Helsinki. http://akseli.tekes.fi.

Hall, R. L. 2003. *Grasses for Energy Production: Hydrological Guidelines*. DTI New and Renewable Energy Programme, U.K. Department of Trade and Industry, London.

Harman, David. 2007. "China's Rapeseed to Bio-Diesel Industry Begins to Take Off." March 30. http://www.resourceinvestor.com/pebble.asp?relid=30407.

Henning, Reinhard K. 2008. *Identification, Selection and Multiplication of High Yielding Jatropha curas L. Plants and Economic Key Points for Viable Jatropha Oil Production Costs, for the International Consultation on Pro-Poor Jatropha Development*. http://www.ifad.org/events/jatropha/agronomy/henning.pdf.

Hill, Jason, Erik Nelson, David Tilman, Stephen Polasky, and Douglas Tiffany. 2006. "Environmental, Economic, and Energetic Costs and Benefits of Biodiesel and Ethanol Biofuels." *Proceedings of the National Academy of Sciences of the United States of America* 103 (30): 11206–11210. http://www.cedarcreek.umn.edu/hilletal2006.pdf.

Hill, Jason, Stephen Polasky, Erik Nelson, David Tilman, Hong Huo, Lindsay Ludwig, James Neumann, Haochi Zheng, and Diego Bonta. 2009. "Climate Change snd Health Costs of Air Emissions from Biofuels and Gasoline." *Proceedings of the National Academy of Science* 106 (6): 2077–82. http://cbey.research.yale.edu/uploads/Environmental%20Economics%20Seminar/PNAS%202_09_polasky.pdf.

Hodes, Glenn S. 2006. *Expanding Biofuels in Africa: Opportunities for South-South Technological Cooperation*. http://www.olade.org.ec/biocombustibles/documents/pdf-17.pdf.

ICRISAT (International Crops Research Institute for the Semi-Arid Tropics). 2008. *Sweet Sorghum: A New Smart Biofuel Crop that Ensures Food Security*. Patancheru, Andhra Pradesh, India. http://www.icrisat.org/Media/2008/media6.htm.

IEA (International Energy Agency). 2004. *Biofuels for Transport: An International Perspective*. Paris. http://www.iea.org/textbase/nppdf/free/2004/biofuels2004.pdf.

———. 2006a. *Renewable Energy RD&D Priorities: Insights from IEA Technology Programmes*. Paris. http://www.iea.org.

————. 2006b. *World Energy Outlook 2006.* Paris. http://www.iea.org.

————. 2007. *Renewables Information 2007 Edition: Documentation for beyond 2020 Files.* Paris. http://wds.iea.org/wds/pdf/doc_renewables.pdf.

————. 2008a. *Database of Biomass Cofiring Initiatives.* Paris. http://www.ieabcc.nl.

————. 2008b. *IEA Statistics.* Paris. http://www.iea.org/Textbase/stats/index.asp.

IFEU (Institute for Energy and Environmental Research). 2007. *Screening Life Cycle Assessment of Jatropha Biodiesel.* Heidelberg. http://www.ifeu.de/landwirtschaft/pdf/jatropha_report_111207.pdf.

IITA (International Institute of Tropical Agriculture). 2007. *Cassava.* Ibadan, Nigeria. http://www.iita.org/cms/details/cassava_project_details.aspx?zoneid=63& articleid=267.

INPE (Instituto Nacional de Pesquisas Espaciais). 2009. *Monitoramento da floresta Amazônica Brasileira por satélite projeto (PRODES).* http://www.obt.inpe.br/prodes/index.html.

Institute of Pacific Islands Forestry. 2006. *Sorghum Bicolor (PIER Species Info.) Moench, Poaceae, Pacific Island Ecosystems at Risk (PIER) Project: Plant Threats to Pacific Ecosystems* U.S. Forest Service. http://www.hear.org/Pier/species/sorghum_bicolor .htm.

International Biochar Initiative. 2009. *White Paper: Biochar: A Soil Amendment that Combats Global Warming and Improves Agricultural Sustainability and Environmental Impacts,* Brief 5. http://www.ifpri.org/2020/focus/focus16/focus16_05.pdf.

IPCC (Intergovernmental Panel on Climate Change). 2007. *Climate Change 2007: Synthesis Report, Contribution of Working Groups I, II and III to the Fourth Assessment Report of the Intergovernmental Panel on Climate Change.* Geneva.

Ita, E. O. 1993. *Aquatic Plants and Wildlife Resources of Nigeria.* CIFA Occasional Paper 21, Food and Agriculture Organization, Rome. http://www.fao.org/docrep/005/T3660E/T3660E00.HTM.

Johnson, T. 2006. "Biomass Cofiring Experience in Utility Pulverized Coal Power Plants." Presentation to Smallwood, May 16, Richmond, VA.

Jongschaap, R. E. E., W. J. Corré, P. S. Bindraban, and W. A. Brandenburg. 2007. *Claims and Facts on* Jatropha Curcas L: *Global Jatropha Curcas Evaluation, Breeding and Propagation Programme.* Plant Research International, Report 158, Wageningen, the Netherlands. http://www.jatropha.de/news/Claims%20and%20facts%20on %20Jatropha%20curcas%20L%5B5%5D.%20Wageningen%20UR-Plant %20Research%20International-Jongschaap%20et%20al%202007.pdf.

Joshi, Laxman, Usha Kanagaratnam, and Dedi Adhuri. 2006. *Nypa Fruticans: Useful But Forgotten in Mangrove Reforestation Programs? In Resilience, Rights and Resources: Two Years of Recovery from the tsunami in Coastal Zone Aceh (Indonesia).* World Agroforestry Centre, Bogor Barat, Indonesia. http://www.worldagroforestrycentre .org/SEA/W-New/datas/Aceh30Nov06/7.%20Nypa%20fruticans-useful%20but %20forgotten%20in%20mangrove.pdf.

Kartha, S., G. Leach, and S. C. Rajan. 2005. *Advancing Bioenergy for Sustainable Development: Guideline for Policymakers and Investors.* ESMAP Report 300/05, World Bank, Washington, DC. www.esmap.org.

Katers, J. F., and J. Kaurich. 2007. "Net Energy Study." Presentation at the annual conference of the Pellet Fuels Institute, July 19–21, Pinehusrt, NC.

Khokhotva, O. 2004. "'Optimal' Use of Biomass for Energy in Europe: Consideration Based upon the Value of Biomass for CO_2 Emission Reduction." MSc diss.,

International Institute for Industrial Environmental Economics, Lund University, Sweden. www.biomatnet.org/publications/2118rep.pdf.

Kline, Keith L., Gbadebo A. Oladosu, Amy K. Wolfe, Robert D. Perlack, Virginia H. Dale, and Matthew McMahon. 2008. *Biofuel Feedstock Assessment for Selected Countries*. Report ORNL/TM-2007/224, Oak Ridge National Laboratory, Oak Ridge, TN. http://www.osti.gov/bridge/servlets/purl/924080-y8ATDg/924080.PDF.

Koh, Lian Pin, and David S Wilcove. 2007. "Cashing in Palm Oil for Conservation" *Nature* 448 (30): 993–94.

Koivisto, Jason. n.d. *Glycine max L*. Food and Agriculture Organization, Rome. http://www.fao.org/ag/agP/agpc/doc/Gbase/data/Pf000543.htm.

Kojima, Masami, and Todd Johnson. 2005. *Potential for Biofuels for Transport in Developing Countries*. World Bank, Energy Sector Management Assistance Program (ESMAP), Washington, DC. http://www.esmap.org/filez/pubs/31205Biofuelsfor Web.pdf.

Kojima, Masami, Donald Mitchell, and William Ward. 2007. *Considering Trade Policies for Liquid Biofuels*. World Bank, Energy Sector Management Assistance Program (ESMAP), Washington, DC. http://siteresources.worldbank.org/INTOGMC/ Resources/Considering_trade_policies_for_liquid_biofuels.pdf.

Koopmans, A., and J. Koppejan. 2007. "Agricultural and Forest Residues: Generation, Utilization and Availability." Paper presented at the Regional Consultation on Modern Applications of Biomass Energy, January 6–10, Kuala Lumpur. http://www.rwedp.org.

Kszos, L. A., S. B. McLaughlin, and M. Walsh. 2001. "Bioenergy from Switchgrass: Reducing Production Costs by Improving Yield and Optimizing Crop Management." Oak Ridge National Laboratory, Oak Ridge, TN. http://www.ornl.gov/~webworks/ cppr/y2001/pres/114121.pdf.

Kumar, A., P. C. Flynn, and S. Sokhansanj. 2006. "British Columbia's Beetle Infested Pine: Biomass Feedstocks for Producing Power." Presentation at the Bioenergy Conference and Exhibition, Prince George, British Columbia, Canada, May 31–June 1.

Kumar, A., and S. Sokhansanj. 2007. "Switchgrass (*panicum vigratum, l.*) Delivery to a Biorefinery Using Integrated Biomass Supply Analysis and Logistics (IBSAL) Model." *Bioresource Technology* 98 (5): 1033–44.

Lal, Rattan. 2009. *Agriculture and Climate Change: An Agenda for Negotiation in Copenhagen for Food, Agriculture, and the Environment, The Potential for Soil Carbon Sequestration*. International Food Policy Research Institute, Focus 16, Brief 5, Washington, DC. http://www.ifpri.org/2020/focus/focus16/Focus16_05.pdf.

Landais, Emmanuelle. 2007. "Plant Offers Eco-Friendly Energy Option." Gulf News online, February 3. http://archive.gulfnews.com/articles/07/02/03/10101394.html.

Lane, Jim. 2008. "Myanmar Announces Jatropha Biodiesel JV with Japan Development Institute." *Biofuels Digest*, October 28. http://www.biofuelsdigest.com/blog2/2008/ 10/28/myanmar-announces-jatropha-biodiesel-jv-with-japan-development-institute/.

Latner, Kevin, Caleb O'Kray, and Junyang Jiang. 2006. *Bio-Fuels, Peoples Republic of China: An Alternative Future for Agriculture*. USDA GAIN Report CH6049, U.S., Department of Agriculture, Washington, DC. http://www.fas.usda.gov/gain-files/200608/146208611.pdf.

Layzell, D. B., J. Stephen, and S. M. Wood. 2006. *Exploring the Potential for Biomass Power in Ontario*. BIOCAP Canada Foundation, Kingston, Ontario, Canada.

Lebedys, A. 2004. "Trends and Current Status of the Contribution of the Forestry Sector to National Economies." Forest Finance Working Paper FSFM/ACC/07, Food and Agricultural Organization, Rome. http://www.fao.org/forestry/site/34127/en.

Liu, D. 2005. Chinese Development Status of Bioethanol and Biodiesel." Paper presented at the International High-Level Forum on Bioeconomy, September 13–15, Beijing.

LMC International. 2008. "Implications of biofuel production for crop production and land use." Produced for World Bank, London.

Loeffler, D., D. E. Calltin, and R. P. Silverstein. 2006. "Estimating Volumes and Costs of Forest Biomass in Western Montana Using Forest Inventory and Geospatial Data." *Forest Products Journal* 56 (6): 31–37.

Lord, Simon, and Jason Clay. n.d. *Environmental Impacts of Oil Palm: Practical Considerations in Defining Sustainability for Impacts on the Air, Land and Water.* http://www.rspo.org/resource_centre/Environmental%20impact%20of%20oil%20 palm%20(Simon%20Lord).pdf.

Low, Tim, and Carol Booth. 2007. *The Weedy Truth about Biofuels.* Invasive Species Council, Carlton, Victoria, Australia. http://www.invasives.org.au/downloads/isc _biofuels_revised_mar08.pdf.

Luger, E. 2002. *Energy Crop Species in Europe.* BLT, Wieselburg, Austria. http://www .blt.bmlf.gv.at/vero/artikel/artik013/Energy_crop_species+.pdf.

Mabee, Warren. 2006. *Economic, Environmental and Social Benefits of 2nd-Generation Biofuels in Canada.* BIOCAP. Vancouver. http://www.biocap.ca/rif/report/ Mabee_W.pdf.

Malimbwi, R. E., E. Zahabu, and B. Mchome. 2007. *Situation Analysis of Dar es Salaam Charcoal Sector.* Consultancy report submitted to the World Wildlife FederationTanzania Program Office, Dar es Salaam.

Mann, M. K., and P. L. Spath. 2001. "A Life Cycle Assessment of Biomass Cofiring in a Coal-Fired Power Plant." *Clean Production Processes* 3: 81–91.

Martines-Filho, Joao, Heloisa L. Burnquist, and Carlos E. F. Vian. 2006. "Bioenergy and the Rise of Sugarcane-Based Ethanol in Brazil." *CHOICES* 21 (2): 92–96. http://www.choicesmagazine.org/2006-2/tilling/2006-2-10.pdf.

Matthews, Emily, Richard Payne, Mark Rohweder, and Siobhan Murray. 2000. *Pilot Analysis of Global Ecosystems: Forest Ecosystems.* World Resources Institute, Washington, DC. http://pdf.wri.org/page_forests_008_woodfuels.pdf.

McKeever, D. B. 2004. "Inventories of Woody Residues and Solid Wood Waste in the United States, 2002." Paper presented at the 9th International Conference on Inorganic-Bonded Composite Materials, Vancouver, Canada, October 10–13. http:// www.treesearch.fs.fed.us/pubs/9135.

Mongabay.com. 2008. "Next Gen Biofuels Could Decimate Rainforests." May 27. http://news.mongabay.com/2008/0527-tilman.html.

Moraes, M.A.F.D. 2007. "Indicadores do mercado de trabalho do sistema agroindustrial da cana-de-açúcar do Brasil no período 1992–2005." *Estudos Econômicos* 37 (4). http://www.scielo.br/scielo.php?script=sci_issuetoc&pid=0101-416120070004& lng=en&nrm=iso.

MPOB (Malaysian Palm Oil Board). 2009. *Malaysian Palm Oil Statistics 2008.* Economics and Industry Development Division, Kuala Lumpur. http://econ.mpob.gov.my/ economy/EID_web.htm.

National Biodiesel Board. 2000. *Reports Database.* Jefferson City, MO. http://www .biodiesel.org/.

Nichols, D. L., S. E. Patterson, and E. Uloth. 2006. *Wood and Coal Cofiring in Interior Alaska: Utilizing Woody Biomass from Wildland Defensible-Space Fire Treatments and Other Sources.* USDA Forest Service Pacific Northwest Research Station Research Note PNW-RN-55, U.S. Department of Agriculture. Portland, OR.

Nguyen, Thu Lan Thi Shabbir, H. Gheewala, and Savitri Garivait. 2007. "Energy Balance and GHG–Abatement Cost of Cassava Utilization for Fuel Ethanol in Thailand." *Energy Policy* 35 (9): 4585–96. http://www.sciencedirect.com/science?_ob=ArticleURL& _udi=B6V2W-4NRMDC3-1&_user=1916569&_coverDate=09%2F30%2F2007& _rdoc=1&_fmt=full&_orig=search&_cdi=5713&_sort=d&_docanchor=&view=c&_a cct=C000055300&_version=1&_urlVersion=0&_userid=1916569&md5=4e1abdec6b 99ebe775c40b0fdcaedfc5#secx7.

Nilsson, S. 2007. "Biofuels: From Oil to Alcohol Addiction?" Paper presented at the EURO-FORENET Conference, Brussels, November 20. http://www.euroforenet.eu/wp -content/uploads/File/EUROFORENET_useofwoodforbiofuel.pps.

Nisbet, T. 2005. "Water Use by Trees." Information Note FCIN065, Forestry Commission, Edinburgh. http://www.forestry.gov.uk.

OECD (Organisation for Economic Co-operation and Development). 2008. *Biofuel Support Policies: An Economic Assessment.* Paris. http://www.oecd.org.

O'Hair, Stephen K. 1995. "Cassava, New Crop FactSHEET." Purdue University Center for New Crops and Plant Products, Lafayette, IN. http://www.hort.purdue.edu/ newcrop/CropFactSheets/cassava.html.

OPEC (Organization of Petroleum Exporting Countries). *Monthly Oil Market Report.* 2009 http://www.opec.org/home/

Pahariya, N. C., and Chandan Mukherjee. 2007. *Commodity Revenue Management: India's Rapeseed/Mustard Oil Sector.* International Institute for Sustainable Development (IISD), Winnepeg, Manitoba, Canada. http://www.iisd.org/pdf/2007/trade_price_case _rapeseed.pdf.

Pavilion Technologies. 2007. *Knowledge, Perceptions and Usage of Biofuels in America.* Austin, TX. www.pavtech.com/ethanolsurvey.

Peksa-Blanchard, M., P. Dolzan, A. Grassi, J. Heinimö, M. Junginger, T. Ranta, and A. Walter. 2007. "Global Wood Pellets Markets and Industry: Policy Drivers, Market Status and Raw Material Potential." Paper prepared for IEA Bioenergy Task 40. http://www.bioenergytrade.org.

Perry, M., and F. Rosillo-Calle. 2006. "Co-firing Report: United Kingdom." Paper prepared for IEA Bioenergy Task 40, London. http://www.bioenergytrade.org.

Peskett, Leo, Rachel Slater, Chris Stevens, and Annie Dufey. 2007. "Biofuels, Agriculture and Poverty Reduction." *Natural Resource Perspectives* 107, Overseas Development Institute, London. http://www.odi.org.uk/Publications/nrp/ NRP107.pdf.

Pimentel, David, and Tad W. Patzek. 2005. "Ethanol Production Using Corn, Switchgrass, and Wood; Biodiesel Production Using Soybean and Sunflower." *Natural Resources Research* 14 (1). http://petroleum.berkeley.edu/papers/Biofuels/ NRRethanol.2005.pdf.

PPRP (Power Plant Research Program). 2006. *The Potential for Biomass Cofiring in Maryland.* Maryland Power Plant Research Program, Maryland Department of Natural Resources, Annapolis, MD. http://esm.versar.com/PPRP/bibliography/PPES_06 _02/PPES_06_02.pdf.

Preechajarn, S., P. Prasertsri, and M. Kunasirirat. 2007. *Thailand Bio-Fuels Annual 2007.* USDA GAIN (Global Agriculture Information Network) Report TH7070, U.S. Department of Agriculture, Washington, DC.

PREMIA. 2006. *Impact Assessment of Measures towards the Introduction of Biofuels in the European Union*. PREMIA Report TREN/04/FP6EN/S07.31083/503081, Brussels. http://www.premia-eu.org.

Prueksakorn, Kritana, and S. H. Gheewala. 2008. "Full Chain Energy Analysis of Biodiesel from *Jatropha curcas L*. in Thailand." *Environmental Science and Technology* 42 (9): 3388–93.

Public Agenda. 2008. "Food, Fuel and the Public." New York. www.publicagenda.com.

Ragauskas, Arthur J., Charlotte K. Williams, Brian H. Davison, George Britovsek, John Cairney, Charles A. Eckert, William J. Frederick, Jr., Jason P. Hallett, David J. Leak, Charles L. Liotta, Jonathan R. Mielenz, Richard Murphy, Richard Templer, and Timothy Tschaplinski. 2006. "The Path forward for Biofuels and Biomaterials." *Science* 311 (5760): 484–89.

Rajagopal, Deepak. 2007. "Rethinking Current Strategies for Biofuel Production in India." Paper presented at the International Water Management Institute Conference, Hyderabad, India January 29–30. http://www.lk.iwmi.org/EWMA/files/papers/rajagopal_biofuels_final_Mar02.pdf.

Rajagopal, Deepak, and David Zilberman. 2007. "Review of Environmental, Economic and Policy Aspects of Biofuels." World Bank Policy Research Working Paper, Washington, DC. http://www-wds.worldbank.org/external/default/WDSContentServer/WDSP/IB/2007/09/04/000158349_20070904162607/Rendered/PDF/wps4341.pdf.

Raswant, Vineet, Nancy Hart, and Monica Romano. 2008. *Biofuel Expansion: Challenges, Risks and Opportunities for Rural Poor People: How the Poor Can Benefit from this Emerging Opportunity*. International Fund for Agricultural Development, Rome. http://www.ifad.org/events/gc/31/roundtable/biofuels.pdf.

Raynes, Emma. 2008. "Pai, Estou Te Esperando/Father, I Am Waiting for You." Lewis Hine Fellow Program. http://cds.aas.duke.edu/hine/raynes.html.

Reddy, Belum V. S., A. Ashok Kumar, and S. Ramesh. 2007. "Sweet Sorghum: A Water Saving Bio-Energy Crop." Paper presented at International Water Management Institute Conference, Hyderabad, India, January 29–30. http://www.icrisat.org/Biopower/BVS ReddyetalSweetSorghumWatersavingJan2007.pdf.

REN21. 2008. *Renewables 2007: Global Status Report*. REN21 Secretariat, Paris. http://www.ren21.net.

Repórter Brasil. 2008. "Brazil of Biofuels: Impacts of Crops on Land, Environment and Society." http://www.reporterbrasil.org.br/documentos/brazil_of_biofuels_v1.pdf.

Renewable Fuels Association. 2008. *Annual Industry Outlook. 2008*. Washington, DC http://www.ethanolrfa.org/

Rismantojo, Erlangga. 2008. "Biodiesel Plant: Jatropha Curcas Feedstock in Sumbawa Case Study." Paper presented at the TBLI (Triple Bottom Line Investing) conference, Bangkok, May 29–30.

Rosen, Stacey, and Shahla Shapouri. 2008. "Rising Food Prices Intensify Food Insecurity in Developing Countries." *Amber Waves* 6 (1). Economic Research Service, U.S. Department of Agriculture, Washington, DC. http://www.ers.usda.gov/AmberWaves/February08/PDF/RisingFood.pdf.

Rosenthal, Elisabeth. 2009. "Third-World Stove Soot Is Target in Climate Fight." *New York Times*, April 15. http://www.nytimes.com/2009/04/16/science/earth/16degrees.html.

Rossi, Andrea, and Yianna Lambrou. 2008. *Gender and Equity Issues in Liquid Biofuels Production: Minimizing the Risks to Maximize the Opportunities*. Rome: Food and Agriculture Organization. ftp://ftp.fao.org/docrep/fao/010/ai503e/ai503e00.pdf.

Roundtable on Sustainable Biofuels. 2009. http://cgse.epfl.ch/page65660.html.

Roundtable on Sustainable Palm Oil. 2009. http://www.rspo.org.

Roundtable on Sustainable Soy. 2009. http://www.responsiblesoy.org.

Royal Society. 2008. *Sustainable Biofuels: Prospects and Challenges*. Policy Document. London. http://royalsociety.org/displaypagedoc.asp?id=28914

Rutz, Dominik, and Rainer Janssen. 2008. *Biofuel Technology Handbook*. WIP Renewable Energies, Munich. http://www.compete-bioafrica.net/publications/publ/Biofuel _Technology_Handbook_version2_D5.pdf.

Sample, Ian. 2003. "Jojoba Oil Could Fuel Cars and Trucks." New Scientist, March 6. http://www.newscientist.com/article/dn3464-jojoba-oil-could-fuel-cars-and-trucks.html.

Schroers, J. O. 2006. *Zur Entwicklung der Landnutzung auf Grenzstandorten in Abhängikeit Agrarmarktpolitischer, Agrarstrukturpolitischer und Produktions-Technologischer*. Rahmenbedingungen, University of Giessen, Germany. http://geb.uni-giessen.de/geb/ volltexte/2007/4511/.

Scion. 2007. *Bioenergy Options for New Zealand: A Situation Analysis of Biomass Resources and Conversion Technologies*. Rotorua, NZ. www.scionresearch.com.

Scott, Paul T., Lisette Pregelj, Ning Chen, Johanna S. Hadler, Michael A. Djordjevic, and Peter M. Gresshoff. 2008. "*Pongamia pinnata*: An Untapped Resource for the Biofuels Industry of the Future." *BioEnergy Research* 1 (1): 2–11.

Selim, Mohamed Younes El-Saghir. n.d. "New Fuel Derived from Jojoba Oil Could Fuel Cars, Trucks and Buses." http://www.scienceyear.com/sciteach/hotspots/pdf/hotspots _emirates_jojoba_02.pdf.

Shapouri, Hosein, J. Duffield, and M. Wang. 2009. *The Energy Balance of Corn Ethanol: An Update*. USDA GAIN Report 813, U.S. Department of Agriculture, Washington, DC.

Simino, Stella. n.d. *Future Perspective of the Soya Agribusiness: Biodiesel, The New Market*. http://www.lasojamata.org/files/soy_republic/Chapt05FuturesPerspectivesSoy Agribusiness.pdf.

Sokhansanj, S., and J. Fenton. 2006. "Cost Benefit of Biomass Supply and Pre-Processing." BIOCAP Research Integration Program Synthesis Paper, BIOCAP Canada Foundation, Ottawa, Canada. http://www.biocap.ca.

Sovero, Matti. 1993. "Rapeseed, a New Oilseed Crop for the United States." In *New Crops*, ed. J. Janick and J. E. Simon, 302–307. New York: Wiley. http://www.hort.purdue .edu/newcrop/proceedings1993/V2-302.html.

Soyatech. 2007. *Quarterly Oilseeds Outlook*. Economist Intelligence Unit, November 14. http://www.soyatech.com/news_story.php?id=5586.

Spath, P. L., and M. K. Mann. 2004. *Biomass Power and Conventional Fossil Systems with and without CO_2 Sequestration*: Comparing the Energy Balance, Greenhouse Gas Emissions and Economics. Report NREL/TP-510-32575, National Renewable Energy Laboratory, Golden, CO. http://www.osti.gov/bridge.

Sundermeier, Alan, R. Reeder, and R. Lal. 2005. "Soil Carbon Sequestration: Fundamentals." Extension Factsheet, Ohio State University, Columbus, OH. http://ohioline .osu.edu/aex-fact/pdf/0510.pdf.

Swaan, J. 2006. "North American Wood Pellet Industry Update." Presentation to Bioenergy Days, Lidkoping, Sweden, August 24. www.bioenergydays.com.

Star. 2007. "Pioneer Bio Industries Corp., Malaysian Company Says Bio-Fuel from Nipah Can Help Halt Global Warming." April 10. http://biz.thestar.com.my/news/ story.asp?file=/2007/4/10/business/20070410184839&sec=business.

Time. 2009. "Biofuel Gone Bad: Burma's Atrophying Jatropha." March 13. http://www .time.com/time/world/article/0,8599,1885050,00.html.

UN (United Nations). 1987. *Energy Statistics: Definitions, Units of Measure and Conversion Factors.* New York.

————. 2000. "On the Threshold: The United Nations and Global Governance in the New Millennium." Tokyo, January 20–21. http://www.unu.edu/millennium/ environment.html.

Undersander, D. J., E. A. Oelke, A. R. Kaminski, J. D. Doll, D. H. Putnam, S. M. Combs, and C. V. Hanson. 1990. *Jojoba.* University of Wisconsin Cooperative Extension Service, University of Minnesota Extension Service, and the Center for Alternative Plant and Animal Products. http://www.hort.purdue.edu/newcrop/ afcm/jojoba.html.

UNICA. 2008. *Dados e Cotações: Estatísticas.* http://www.unica.com.br/dadosCotacao/ estatistica/.

UNIDO (United Nations Industrial Development Organization). n.d. *Cleaner Production in a Paper Mill: The Case of Raval in India.* Vienna. http://www.un.org/esa/dsd/dsd _aofw_mg/mg_worktradunio_specday/casestud4.shtml.

Uryu, Y., and others. 2008. *Deforestation, Forest Degradation, Biodiversity Loss and CO_2 Emissions in Riau, Sumatra, Indonesia.* WWF Indonesia Technical Report, World Wildlife Fund, Jakarta. http://assets.panda.org/downloads/riau_co2_report__wwf _id_27feb08_en_lr_.pdf

USDA (U.S. Department of Agriculture). 2008a. *Counter-Cyclical Payment Rates and Average Market Prices.* Washington, DC. http://www.fsa.usda.gov/FSA/webapp?area =home&subject=ecpa&topic=foa-cc.

————. 2008b. *USDA Foreign Agricultural Service (FAS) Biofuels Reports.* Washington, DC. http://www.fas.usda.gov/cmp/biofuels/biofuels.asp.

————. 2009. National Agricultural Statistics Service, Washington, DC. http://www .nass.usda.gov/Data_and_Statistics/.

Van Dam, A., M. Junginger, A. Faaij, I. Jürgens, G. Best, and U. Fritsche. 2006. *Overview of Recent Developments in Sustainable Biomass Certification.* Paper written within the frame of IEA Bioenergy Task 40. http://www.fairbiotrade.org.

Vermeulen, Sonja, and Nathalie Goad. 2006. *Towards Better Practice in Smallholder Palm Oil Production.* International Institute for Environment and Development, London. http://www.rspo.org/PDF/Projects/STF/final%20IIED%20report%20on%20small holder%20palm%20oil.pdf.

Von Braun, Joachim, and R. K. Pachauri. 2006. *The Promises and Challenges of Biofuels for the Poor in Developing Countries.* International Food Policy Research Institute, Washington, DC. http://www.ifpri.org/pubs/books/ar2005/ar05e.pdf.

Wang, Q., K. Otsubo, and T. Ichinose. 2002. "Estimation of Potential and Convertible Arable Land in China Determined by Natural Conditions." *Journal of Global Environment Engineering* 8: 67–78.

Wani, Suhas P., M. Osman, Emmanuel D'Silva, and T. K. Sreedevi. 2006. "Improved Livelihoods and Environmental Protection through Biodiesel Plantations in Asia." *Asian Biotechnology and Development Review* 8 (2): 11–29. http://www.icrisat.org/ Biopower/WanietalBiodieselPlantationAsia.pdf.

Wani, Suhas P., and T. K. Sreedevi. n.d. *Pongamia's Journey from Forest to Micro-enterprise for Improving Livelihoods.* International Crops Research Institute for the Semi-Arid Tropics (ICRISAT), Patancheru, Andhra Pradesh, India. http://www.icrisat.org/ Biopower/Wani_Sreedevi_Pongamiajourney.pdf.

WEC (World Energy Council). 2004. *Comparison of Energy Systems Using Life Cycle Assessment*. Special Report, London. http://www.worldenergy.org/documents/lca2.pdf.

Wegner, S. 2007. "Realities in Cellulose Ethanol from Wood." Paper presented to the Biomass Energy: Biorefineries Seminar, Resources for the Future, Washington, DC, April 4.

Whiteman, A. 2001. "An Appraisal of the Licensing and Forest Revenue System in Zambia." Forest Finance Working Paper FSFM/MISC/04, Food and Agricultural Organization, Rome. ftp://ftp.fao.org/docrep/fao/003/X6824E/X6824E00.pdf.

WHO (World Health Organization). 2007. *Indoor Air Pollution: National Burden of Disease Estimates*. WHO/SDE/PHE/07.01 rev, Geneva.

Wiegmann, Kirsten, K. J. Hennenberg, and U. R. Fritsche. 2008. *Degraded Land and Sustainable Bioenergy Feedstock Production Issue Paper*. Joint International Workshop on High Nature Value Criteria and Potential for Sustainable Use of Degraded Lands, Paris. http://www.uneptie.org/ENERGY/activities/mapping/pdf/degraded.pdf.

Woods, J., R. Tipper, G. Brown, R. Diaz-Chavez, J. Lovell, and P. de Groot. 2006. *Evaluating the Sustainability of Co-Firing in the UK*. Report URN 06/1960, Thema Technology, London. www.berr.gov.uk/files/file34448.pdf.

World Bank. 2008a. *Rising Food Prices: Policy Options and World Bank Response*. Washington, DC. http://siteresources.worldbank.org/NEWS/Resources/risingfoodprices _backgroundnote_apr08.pdf.

———. 2008b. *World Development Report: Agriculture for Development*. Washington, DC: World Bank. http://go.worldbank.org/ZJIAOSUFU0.

———. 2009. *Environmental Crisis or Sustainable Development Opportunity? Transforming the Charcoal Sector in Tanzania*. Environmental and Natural Resources Unit for the Africa Region, Washington, DC.

WRI (World Resources Institute). 2008. Project POTICO: Palm Oil, Timber's Carbon Offsets in Indonesia, Washington, DC. http://www.wri.org/project/potico#indonesia .forests.

Wright, P. 1999. "U.S. Coal-Fired Power Plant Employment Trends." *Coal Age* 104 (8): 47–48.

WWF (World Wildlife Fund). 2005. *Agriculture and Environment: Commodities*. http://www.panda.org/about_wwf/what_we_do/policy/agriculture_environment/ commodities/sorghum/environmental_impacts/habitat_conversion/index.cfm.

———. 2008. *Position Paper on Bioenergy*. http://assets.panda.org/downloads/wwf _position_paper_bioenergy_update_june_2008_final_2_.pdf

———. 2009. Monitoramento mostra resultados positivos da moratória da soja. http://www.wwf.org.br/informacoes/?19363/Monitoramento-mostra-resultados-positivos-da-Moratria-da-Soja.

———. n.d. *Sugar and the Environment: Encouraging Better Management Practices in Sugar Production*. http://www.bettersugarcane.org/assetsgeneral/PrintableSugar Brochure.pdf.

Yokoyama, Miki. 2007. *The Top 5 Biofuel Crops*. Allianz Knowledge, September 26. http://knowledge.allianz.com/nopi_downloads/downloads/biofuels%20crops.pdf.

Zhang, Y., S. Habibi, and H. L. Maclean. 2007. "Environmental and Economic Evaluation of Bioenergy in Ontario, Canada." *Journal of the Air and Waste Management Association* (August). http://www.entrepreneur.com/tradejournals/article/168103336.html.

INDEX

Boxes, figures, notes, and tables are indicated with b, f, n, and t following the page number.

ethanol production and
consumption, 91
corn production, 163, 163*t*
soybean production, 186, 186*t*, 189
sugarcane production, 161
Asia. *See* East Asia and Pacific; Europe
and Central Asia; South Asia
Australia
biodiesel production and
consumption, 94*f*, 95*t*, 96*f*
consumption targets, 34*t*
rapeseed production, 190
subsidies, 38, 38*t*
ethanol production and
consumption, 91*f*, 92, 92*t*, 93*f*
consumption targets, 30*t*
renewable energy targets, 27*t*
TPES components, 45–47*f*

B
Bangladesh, palm oil consumption in,
178, 180*f*
Belgium, electricity production with
biomass pellets in, 77
Better Sugarcane Initiative, 24
biochar production, 5, 62–63*b*
biodiesel, 93–96
biodiversity and, 132
from cellulose, 90
defined, 11
in East Asia and Pacific, 128
from edible oils, 90
issues and impacts related to, 114–17*t*
in Latin America and Caribbean, 137
long-term trend, 94–95, 94*f*, 95*t*
from nonedible oils, 90
outlook for, 14, 14*f*, 95–96, 96*f*
policies and targets for, 5, 33,
34–36*t*, 37
subsidies, 38, 38*t*
water resources and, 119
biodimethylether, 11
biodiversity impact
biofuels, 120
cassava production, 173
corn production, 167
Jatropha production, 197
jojoba production, 199

Nypa palm production, 175
palm oil production, 132, 184
Pongamia production, 202
rapeseed production, 193
solid biomass production, 64–65
soybean production, 189
sugarcane production, 162–63
sweet sorghum production, 170
bioenergy
alcohol fuel production, 157–75
consumption outlook, 13–17, 15–16*f*
oilseed crops production, 177–203
second-generation production,
205–11
solid biomass production, 41–87
targets, policies, and instruments,
25–38
third-generation production, 213–15
TPES contribution of, 12–13
types, 8–11
Bio Energy Development Corp., 101*b*
bioengineering, 213–15
bioETBE, 11
bioethanol. *See* ethanol
biofuel carbon debt, 118
biogas, 10, 12, 14, 14*f*
biogasoline, 11
biomass pellets energy systems
economic impact, 81
economic viability, 77–81
environmental impact, 82
greenhouse gas emissions, 61
heat and power production, 5,
76–85, 78*t*, 79–81*f*, 128
land and other resources impact, 82
biomass plantations, 43
biomethanol, 11
bioMTBE, 11
black carbon, 61
black liquor, 5, 19, 19*b*
blending mandates, 26, 33, 38, 39*n*8, 95
Bonskowski, R., 53
Brazil
biodiesel production and
consumption, 33, 93, 95
Jatropha production, 193
soybean production, 186, 186*t*,
188, 188*f*

public opinion on bioenergy
development, 21–23*b*
renewable energy targets, 16, 28*t*
second-generation biofuels and,
205–6
solid biomass imports, 60
Strategy for Biofuels, 19
TPES components, 12, 45–47*f*

F

FAO. *See* Food and Agriculture
Organization
FAOSTAT database, 12
feedstocks
See also specific crops
biodiesel production, 33,
37, 96–97
ethanol consumption policies and,
26, 33
liquid biofuels incentives and,
37–38, 37*t*
water resources used by, 119
fertilizer, 103, 118, 119, 166
Fischer-Tropsch, defined, 11
flex-fuel vehicles, 91–92, 107,
160, 160*f*, 175*n*4
FO Licht, 12
Food and Agriculture Organization
(FAO), 8, 42–43, 54*b*, 86*n*2
food security, 99–100, 124, 130
forestry and forests
as biomass source, 3, 8, 44, 56–58*t*,
59–60
employment, 52, 52*t*
plantations, 53–54
processing waste, 48
second-generation biofuels and,
205, 206*t*
soil resources and, 62*b*
thinnings and, 86*n*5, 150
traditional use of solid biomass
and, 67
Forest Service (U.S.), 170
fossil fuels
See also specific fuels
biofuels production and, 103
energy ratio, 118, 118*f*
TPES and, 10

France
biodiesel production and
consumption, 94, 191
ethanol production and
consumption, 92
fuelwood
as affordable energy option, 42, 86*n*9
as biomass source, 65, 67
defined, 86*n*2
environmental impact, 135, 139
opportunity cost of gathering, 67
plantations, 20, 67

G

gasification technology, 19*b*, 73
gender concerns
land use conflicts and, 101
liquid biofuels impact on, 103
solid biomass impact, 53
traditional use of solid biomass
and, 68
geothermal energy, 10
German Federal Environmental
Agency, 191
Germany
biodiesel production and
consumption, 94, 190, 191
ethanol production and
consumption, 92
Ghana, Jatropha production in, 193
GHG. *See* greenhouse gases
Global Bioenergy Partnership, 25
Global Invasive Species Program,
184, 197
Global Subsidies Initiative, 38
grasses for bioenergy production,
53–54, 64
Green Gold Label, 24
greenhouse gases (GHG)
biochar production and, 62–63*b*
biofuels impact, 20
cassava ethanol production
and, 172
co-firing and, 87*n*14
corn ethanol production and,
165–66, 166*t*
Jatropha biodiesel production
and, 196

traditional uses for solid biomass
    energy, 65–70
  consumption outlook for, 13
  economic viability, 65–67
  environmental impact, 68–70
  health impact, 68
  land and other resources
    impact, 68
transpiration, 63
transport
  biomass pellets, 82
  charcoal production and, 66*b*
  solid biomass costs for, 47, 48,
    49–50*t*, 51*f*, 69

U
Ukraine, rapeseed production and
    consumption in, 190
UNCTAD BioFuels Initiative, 25
UN Energy, 25
United Arab Emirates University, 198
United Kingdom (UK)
  biodiesel production and
    consumption, 94
  Renewable Transport Fuel
    Obligation (RTFO), 39*n*6
  water resources used by energy
    crops, 63
United Nations Convention to Combat
    Desertification, 20
United Nations Environment
    Programme (UNEP), 55*b*
United Nations Industrial Development
    Organization (UNIDO), 19*b*
United States
  biodiesel production and
    consumption, 93, 94, 95
  consumption targets, 33
  jojoba production, 197
  rapeseed production, 190
  soybean production, 186–87*t*,
    186–88
  subsidies, 38, 38*t*
  biofuel carbon debt and, 118
  biofuels data, 12
  biomass pellet energy
    production, 78*t*, 79–80,
    80–81*f*

ethanol production and
    consumption, 90, 91, 92,
    93, 98, 100, 164*f*, 164*t*
  corn production, 163, 163*t*, 164*f*
  public opinion on bioenergy
    development, 23*b*
  Renewable Fuel Standard, 92
  second-generation biofuel
    production, 207–8*t*
USDA Foreign Agricultural Service, 12

V
value chain of charcoal production, 66*b*
vegetable oil waste biodiesel
    production, 93, 95
Venezuela, ethanol consumption
    policies in, 33
virtual water, 189

W
waste
  biodiesel production from waste
    vegetable oils, 93, 95
  bioenergy production from, 59, 60
  industrial, 10, 19–20, 19*b*
  municipal, 10, 39*n*3
  postconsumer, 48
waste treatment, environmental impact
    of, 20
water resources impact of bioenergy
    production
  biofuels, 119, 132, 145
  cassava ethanol, 173
  corn ethanol, 166
  Jatropha biodiesel, 196–97
  jojoba biodiesel, 199
  Nypa palm ethanol, 174–75
  palm oil biodiesel, 184
  Pongamia biodiesel, 201–2
  rapeseed biodiesel, 193
  solid biomass, 63
  soybean biodiesel, 189
  sugarcane ethanol, 162
  sweet sorghum ethanol, 169–70
wind power, 10, 26
women
  See also gender concerns
  land use conflicts and, 101, 103

LaVergne, TN USA
19 February 2010
173701LV00007B/35/P